Praise for
RETHINKING WORK

"Generational, technological, and cultural discontinuities are reimagining work and unbundling workplaces. Rishad Tobaccowala insightfully brings together these varying and dramatic shifts underway. He challenges leaders to rethink how they attract, coach and develop, and retain talent in a hyperfragmented world, recognizing that it is in the empathy and humanity of leadership that future advantage lies"

—LAXMAN NARASIMHAN,
former CEO, Starbucks

"Rishad provides invaluable advice to leaders by sharing insights from successful contemporary leaders while also providing a framework on how the future will evolve. This is a great book for those who will lead today, tomorrow, and the decade after that."

—DAVID W. KENNY,
executive chairman, Nielsen

"In *Rethinking Work*, Rishad masterfully unpacks the converging forces—technological, generational, attitudinal, cultural, and societal—that are reshaping the workplace as we know it. Gone are the days when we traded loyalty for security with a single entity. Today's workers, led by Gen Z, demand mission, meaning, and mentorship from their workplaces. With clarity and insight, Rishad guides readers through these profound shifts, explaining not only the changes in the work itself but also how we, as leaders, workers, and a society, must adapt. This is the essential road map for navigating the postpandemic world of work."

—HEATHER E. MCGOWAN,
keynote speaker, future of work strategist, and coauthor of
The Empathy Advantage and *The Adaptation Advantage*

"Insightful and timely, this book is a must-read! Rishad brilliantly captures the dramatic shifts happening in the workplace and offers practical strategies to adapt. Whether you're a seasoned leader or just starting out, it empowers you to embrace new opportunities with confidence."

—SANJAY KHOSLA,
senior fellow and adjunct professor, Kellogg School of
Management, Northwestern University, and
former president, Kraft International

"*Rethinking Work* achieves something truly remarkable: It brings together five complex forces that are reshaping our world and offers a compelling vision for how these forces will upend work as we know it. As a lifelong learner, I found the book's mix of data and storytelling to be enlightening, sobering, and optimistic. As a leader, I found Tobaccowala's recommendations on reimaging the workplace to be transformational. This is that rare book that simultaneously helps you look at the world, your work, and your life in new ways."

—SETH GREEN,
dean, Graham School, University of Chicago

"Rishad Tobaccowala continuously teaches us that the future does not fit into the containers of the past, and *Rethinking Work* is no exception. This book is a visionary guide to the seismic shifts reshaping our work lives and an invitation to rethink, retrain, and reimagine what we can become as individuals and organizations. It's a must-read for leaders and individuals preparing for the future."

—NIRIT COHEN,
founder of WorkFutures and intel veteran

"Several different trends seem to be 'changing everything' for leaders all at once. Tobaccowala parses each of them in a way that will help you stay oriented. Throughout, he reminds us that only one thing is certain: We must center our humanity as we navigate these changes. "

—KIM SCOTT,
author of *Radical Candor* and *Radical Respect*

"In an era where work is analyzed, predicted, and debated like never before, Rishad Tobaccowala's book offers a profound rethinking of its essence. By exploring work across its many dimensions—the current and the enduring, the public and the personal, the technical and the emotional—Rishad challenges us to engage our creativity and envision new ideas for the future. This book masterfully adjusts what we observe today into what we imagine the future can contain. It's what Rishad does best and what anyone thinking about work needs most."

—EMMANUEL ANDRE,
chief talent officer, Publicis Groupe

"For anyone thinking, 'When will work norms return to what we remember from before the pandemic?' the answer is . . . 'Never.' It is time to fully understand the magnitude of change in the way companies and their workforces now engage with each other and how this will continue to evolve. Renowned futurist Rishad Tobaccowala has always been several steps ahead of major change waves, helping companies to fully comprehend the underlying forces of these shifts so they can move to gain advantage and avoid irrelevancy. In his book *Rethinking Work*, Rishad uses data to illustrate profound changes employers are facing, and he covers technology that enables remote working, collaboration, and new forms of creativity where, of course, AI is playing a big role. Importantly, the book dives deep into the mindset of workers, particularly newer entrants to the workforce. Competition to hire and retain this next generation of workers will intensify, and Rishad prescribes approaches that will keep them motivated to perform. Consider *Rethinking Work* as a handbook for rethinking organizational structure, adapting new working and hiring policies, and creating platforms and environments that enable teams to do their best work."

—SARAH FAY,
chair of Ziff Davis and former CEO of Aegis Media America

RETHINKING
WORK

SEISMIC CHANGES IN THE WHERE, WHEN, *and* WHY

RISHAD TOBACCOWALA

HarperCollins
Leadership

An Imprint of HarperCollins

Published by HarperCollins Leadership, an imprint of HarperCollins Focus LLC.

Any internet addresses, phone numbers, or company or product information
printed in this book are offered as a resource and are not intended in any way
to be or to imply an endorsement by HarperCollins Leadership, nor does
HarperCollins Leadership vouch for the existence, content, or services of these
sites, phone numbers, companies, or products beyond the life of this book.

ISBN 978-1-4002-4931-2 (eBook)
ISBN 978-1-4002-4930-5 (HC)

Library of Congress Cataloging-in-Publication Data
Library of Congress Cataloging-in-Publication data has been submitted.

Printed in the United States of America

24 25 26 27 28 LBC 5 4 3 2 1

CONTENTS

SECTION III
PREPARING FOR THE FUTURE OF WORK

INTRODUCTION

In every field and in every size company, a sea change is occurring—a change so monumental that it is making us reinvent the traditional ideas of where work is done, when work is done, how work is done, and what work itself is.

Five interlocking forces are sculpting the future of work:

- **FORCE ONE—Generational Shifts:** For the first time, four and possibly five generations will work in the same firms. The youngest employees in their twenties are Gen Zers, and they are about to become the largest component of the workforce. The eldest employees are baby boomers, the youngest of whom are turning sixty, and they have dominated the workplace in numbers, income, and impact until now. In between are millennials and Gen X. The mindsets, expectations, and worldviews of each group are significantly different. In addition to the rise of Gen Z, we are seeing a rapid aging of the workforce and declining population growth.

- **FORCE TWO—Technology:** We are entering an AI-infused age when the cost of knowledge may soon be zero. More than half of the workforce in high-income countries are knowledge workers. Imagine the implications when this new AI reality becomes prevalent. Every job will be changed. How many will be lost and what new careers will be forged?

- **FORCE THREE—Marketplaces:** Today hundreds of marketplaces such as Upwork allow talent to be procured from anywhere. Etsy and Shopify allow individuals to access customers from everywhere. App stores and cloud services from Apple, Amazon, Google, Microsoft, and OpenAI allow small and medium firms to access billion-dollar tech.

- **FORCE FOUR—New Ways of Working:** Demographics, technology, and marketplaces are now enabling vastly different ways of working, which is giving rise to a world of side hustles and side gigs.

- **FORCE FIVE—The Long-Term Impact of COVID:** COVID is just one of the five factors creating seismic change at work, and its biggest impact may not be on where people work but on the emotional rewiring it caused when, during the pandemic's nearly three years, people reconsidered the role of work in their lives.

For these reasons, a few years from now work may differ from today as much as today differs from 2019 and as 2019 differed from the age before low-cost telecommunication, computers, mobile phones, and the internet.

We have a choice. We can either be reactive and struggle to adjust to transformational events on the fly, or we can be proactive and control the narrative—reinventing work to align with the evolving environment.

As a futurist who has had a highly successful career because I've anticipated and capitalized on emerging trends, I advocate the latter. Unfortunately, many organizations are still mired in traditional practices and structures. They attempt to preserve the status quo, tweaking it in order to keep up with changes but retaining the foundational elements of work—the boss-employee relationship; the supervised, centralized structure; the emphasis on financial motivation; the one-size-fits-all work environment; and the culture of loyalty, seniority, and consensus.

It's a bad strategy, especially after two-plus years of COVID and its impact on how we work.

Our minds and behaviors are like champagne corks—they've swelled and no longer can fit back in the bottle.

Consider a few statistics:

By 2027, 86.5 million people, or half the workforce, will be freelancers.

In 2022, more than one-third of US workers and two-thirds of those under age thirty juggled different "gigs" (rather than work full time at one job). The "fractionalized" employee (my term) is becoming a reality.

According to research conducted by the McKinsey consulting firm, 80 percent of people who worked at home during COVID liked it, and 41 percent asserted they were more productive than they were working from the office. *Fifty-nine percent of respondents (in a study conducted by Owl Labs) said they would be more likely to choose an employer that offered remote work over companies that didn't.*

But the need to rethink work goes beyond even these statistics about remote work and the shift from full-time to part-time and gig jobs. For instance, people used to work primarily for income and achievement. While these factors are still important, we're seeing a growing number of people choosing jobs based on meaning (the work is fulfilling, satisfying them on a deeper level), community (connection with like-minded people), and social purpose. Millennials and Gen Zers, especially, are searching for work experiences that fit their personal beliefs and styles—they want the freedom to work where, when, and how they want.

A true holacracy (a bossless office) may never become widespread, but we're going to see a trend toward less supervision and more independence—a trend that will have an enormous impact on everything from hiring to culture to performance reviews.

To rethink work can be a scary thought, especially for those with a vested interest in the current system. But it's also an absolutely necessary thought. Schools, banks, law firms, start-ups, medical offices—every sector will be affected by the current or soon-to-be-emerging trends and events that I'll describe.

We can either bury our heads in the sand and hope the emerging changes will go away—a really bad idea—or we can prepare for and capitalize on all the opportunities they spawn. This means a major rethinking of work, and I hope to open people's minds to all the possibilities.

This book will enlighten and empower its readers to thrive in a world where the who, what, why, where, when, and how of work will be transformed.

WHO WILL PEOPLE WORK FOR? Until recently, most people worked for someone else for a relatively long period of time—a large corporation, the government, an educational institution, and so on. But communication technology advances, new business models and marketplaces, and changing generational mindsets are transferring power to the individual. This transfer gives people work options, and they're exercising them in all sorts of ways. For instance, a growing number of individuals are choosing to work for themselves. Zoom, Slack, and other platforms facilitate work processes; Etsy, Shopify, and Substack help users leverage their capabilities and scale themselves and their ideas to growing markets. Others are opting for greater control over whom they work for. Digital natives have lived through 9/11, the Great Recession, and

COVID, and their attitudes have changed—they believe much more in themselves than in organizations. As a result, people are rejecting the old model of working for one organization for a decade or longer. Instead, they're choosing to be gig workers, to create start-ups, to become fractionalized employees, to dedicate themselves to and work for a cause. To mix and match employers. Just as employees have numerous options, so too do organizations. This book will help leaders capture talent by structuring jobs in ways that appeal to this new work sensibility.

WHAT WILL ORGANIZATIONS LOOK LIKE? Like nothing in the past. We will no longer have a single organizational model or design but instead have a wide range of operating styles, structures, and sizes. In the past, organizational models were like classical music, with a conductor, orchestra, and well-rehearsed score. In the future, they will be like jazz, involving different players who take the music in surprising, unpredictable directions. Companies will be fluid, forming and reforming themselves to fit the market and emerging needs. They'll mix full-time and part-time workers, in-office and remote employees, teams and individual performers; they'll shift alliances continuously, collaborating with a range of suppliers, consultants, and others as need dictates.

WHY WILL PEOPLE WORK? People have always worked for a variety of reasons—income, identity, community, social purpose, and personal meaning. As noted earlier, COVID and shifting social norms are causing more people to choose jobs and careers based on factors other than income. Empowering technologies also make it easier for people to pursue meaningful work. But another trend has a profound effect on why. In the past, one full-time job rarely satisfied all our reasons for working. The law firm partner was well paid but found little personal satisfaction in his job. Or the social worker found satisfaction in helping others, but she was micromanaged, hampering her personal work style. Today, however, we're seeing a shift to people satisfying all or most of their whys by having more than one job—two-thirds of those under age thirty are combining different gigs. A mix of roles—side hustles, volunteer positions, and so on—is much better able to satisfy all our work requirements than a single job can.

WHERE WILL PEOPLE WORK? In the metaverse. At home. In morphing offices that will bear little resemblance to traditional places of business. In planes. And perhaps in the not-so-distant future, in self-driving cars. According to a Stanford University study, "Compared to 2019 levels, employees' average distance from their home to their employer has risen 2.7 times: The mean distance to work rose from ten miles in 2019 to twenty-seven miles at the end of 2023. The share of workers living more than fifty miles from their employer rose more than five-fold." COVID certainly has powered this trend, but so too has our entering the Third Age of the Internet—AI, 5G, the metaverse, blockchain, cryptocurrency, and other developments are reshaping industries and companies. US companies have formed alliances with organizations in India, China, Brazil, Russia, Vietnam, and elsewhere; people work virtually and sometimes physically far from home, and they will do even more of this in the future. It's not just that people are working remotely. It's that they are working on teams with members from seven different countries, and that their customers and suppliers are located on different continents. In the future, being a global company isn't just a description of office locations but of a mindset—we are becoming workers of the world. To answer this "where" question, I'll offer advice about how to maximize flexible workspaces, creating policies and cultures that cater to locational agility.

WHEN WILL PEOPLE WORK? Whenever. The nine-to-five day has long since passed. Until recently, work was confined to certain days and hours because of rigid structures—we all needed to work together in the same place for efficiency, for people to be managed properly. Now we require temporal flexibility for many reasons. Most obviously, if we're doing business with people on the other side of the world, the time zones are different. Less obviously, efficiency is less important than innovation, disruption, and agility. These qualities are less likely to emerge if we confine our work to rigid schedules. Great ideas surface in the middle of the night, when we're exercising, when we become inspired by a piece of music at the symphony. We need to feel empowered to call, text, or email our colleagues to obtain their feedback and ideas at this moment of inspiration. This doesn't mean that we become 24/7 workaholics. Instead, our work hours become fluid, dictated by work projects, time frames, and our own preferences—we might need to take time off to recharge in the middle of the traditional workday, and we might need to meet virtually with colleagues at midnight.

HOW WILL LEADERSHIP CHANGE? We are witnessing the decline of the manager and the rise of a new type of leader. In the past, the managerial role was essential to efficient organizational operation—they managed by walking around and checking in on their people. In an increasingly distributed world where people often work virtually, you can't manage by walking around. Younger generations, especially, hate being monitored. While employees used to rely on managers for news and expertise, they can now use YouTube, Khan Academy, Open AI, and other online tools to learn what they need to know. Managers, therefore, are becoming anachronisms, while a new type of leader is becoming crucial for organizational success. This type of leader displays three traits: a growth mindset (growing people and businesses, macro-imagining possibilities rather than micromanaging employees); improvisation skills (the agility to pivot on a dime); and a thirst for learning (in a world of rapid change, continuous learning is the only way to survive).

THIS BOOK IS divided into three sections. The first section examines why we need to rethink work—the factors that are causing traditional structures and styles to be ineffective. The second section analyzes the ways in which work needs to be rethought. The third section addresses what we can do about it—the steps that organizations can take to change themselves so they'll be prepared for the Great Rethinking.

This book is for everybody who works, whether you are a long-time senior leader or a brand-new employee, whether you work in a large company or for yourself, and whether you work in a developed or developing market.

Work is central to our lives and as it gets redefined, nothing is as important as being informed and provided with tools to thrive in the coming transformation.

THE FORCES DRIVING
THE GREAT RETHINKING

CHAPTER 1

SEISMIC SOCIETAL SHIFTS

We tend to think of workplace changes in terms of technology. How various platforms may turn physical office spaces into anachronisms. How algorithms may replace human decision-making.

Societal shifts can affect work just as profoundly. Consider five trends:

1. The rise of the individual

2. Aging and shrinking populations

3. Multiple generations with different life experiences and mindsets in the same workplace

4. The freelance revolution

5. Disengagement

These changes are already altering our perspective on everything from hiring to compensation to leadership. In some instances, the impact is obvious: we create open workspaces that help attract young talent.

Many times, though, we're unaware of all the ramifications.

How are these societal shifts affecting our teams, our hiring practices, our retention policies? How might they play out in the future?

We need to be aware of these issues. And we need to know what to do about them.

To that end, let's begin with how COVID has shifted the balance of power away from the organization and toward the individual.

The Rise of the Individual

Changes that were underway though largely unseen for years became visible and impactful during COVID. The virus affected the way people worked and caused them to question how they would work, why they would work, whom they would work for, where they would work, and what work meant to them.

This changed consciousness has empowered individuals and disempowered organizations. Consider:

- People can work productively away from the office.

- The traditional notion of a boss is an anachronism.

- Some people work best late at night or early in the morning or on weekends.

- Others prefer to be and are more effective as "fractional-ized" employees, juggling different part-time gigs rather than full-time ones.

The entire workforce now understands that companies could allow individuals to work in a spectrum of ways without losing competitiveness or productivity. It is like we all woke from a dream and saw the light. There is no unseeing. Nonetheless, some managers wish to go back to the way work was pre-COVID, leading to a rift between these traditionalists and the rethinkers.

The rethinking argument is particularly strong when you view it based on how individuals have been empowered by recent technological, demographic, and cultural shifts. Specifically, individuals now have:

- *become more informed* due to a plethora of new platforms (for example, Glassdoor or Reddit) that have decreased the organizational ability to keep information secret or hard to get;

- *had their minds expanded* by working in different ways over the past three years and, like champagne corks, have swelled and no longer can fit back into containers of the past;

- *discovered new tools and platforms* that allow them to find work globally and deliver solutions using top-notch technology at accessible cost, reducing the need to work for companies; and

- *taken charge of their careers* and are much less willing to trust their future to corporations and managers after the Great Recession and COVID. They now want to control their own destinies. They are less interested in working for others and more interested in working for themselves.

This is very much a mindset shift. People think about their jobs and careers differently than in the past. Too often, the upholders of the status quo castigate this mindset, but many times, it's because they misunderstand it. To foster a better understanding of what an individual-centric mindset translates to, here are four principles that shape it:

- People are not leaving work but leaving work as it is done today.

- They're not quitting work but walking away from bosses and organizations that do not suit them.

- They are not saying work does not matter but that work is not all that matters.

- They do not compartmentalize their beliefs and their job but look for alignment; they value their work highly and believe it should reflect their values (not merely be something one does).

Aging and Shrinking Populations

As of this writing, many companies are struggling to fill positions. Based on the data, this situation is only going to get worse. It's a matter of supply and demand, and the supply is dwindling. The population in most of the world outside Africa and, to some extent, India, has started to decline. The year 2021 was the first time since 1937 that the US population grew by fewer than one million people, the lowest numeric growth since at least 1900, when the Census Bureau began annual population estimates. Just as significant, the population is aging.

The organizational reflex is to focus on the *next big thing*, on the *new and emerging*, and especially on the *young*. Understandably, perhaps, they're most concerned about attracting the best and brightest Gen Zers and millennials and keeping them happy. As a result, they are myopic about what will come and miss the value of those who have come before.

They may not realize that we are entering the Age of the Seasoned.

It's estimated that *25 percent* of the European and US populations will be over age sixty by 2050 and will control 70 to 75 percent of the wealth. Even before then, people who are fifty-five and older will represent a significant percentage of the population and control a great deal of knowledge and wisdom. They will be seasoned by years of work, which will make them extraordinarily valuable to organizations desperate for workers with experience—the people who used to be referred to as "old salts" and "village elders," as individuals who "know the ropes."

The fight against sexism and racism may well extend to ageism, producing compelling reasons for organizations to increase the number of older workers they hire.

Perhaps more importantly, the flexible work schedules and technological tools popularized during COVID are tailor-made for seasoned workers. In the past, they might have retired. Today and especially in the coming years, they can be crucial members of organizations, providing insights based on hard-won experiences.

Consider, too, that even organizations skeptical of seasoned workers may be forced to hire them out of necessity. The workforce is shrinking. Retirement-age people are working longer out of financial necessity. Anti-immigration sentiments are restricting the flow of people to Western countries.

Hiring older employees may be the only way to fill certain positions.

Given this environment, here are three issues that every organization should contemplate:

ISSUE ONE—Polarizing divisions

Will the tensions between seasoned employees and younger generations be exacerbated by the former group staying on the job longer than the latter groups think they should?

Will the disparate wealth/salaries of the groups be another driver of polarization?

Young people with socialist leanings may wonder if they will ever do as well as the older generations, with many ladders of advancement and wealth creation in short supply. Organizations need to consider how they might ameliorate the tensions between seasoned and unseasoned, especially when they're asked to work together on teams.

ISSUE TWO—Accommodating seasoned employees

Too often, workspaces these days are being designed for younger workers. The open work areas, the relatively high noise level (music, games, lack of quiet zones) and the overreliance on digital communication may alienate seasoned employees. HR and talent management need to ensure that they can take advantage and leverage older talent. This might mean introducing and adapting workplace products and designing services with seasoned employees in mind—standing desks for people with bad backs, small offices for people who work better with a degree of privacy.

ISSUE THREE—Career planning for older as well as younger employees

These days, careers last a long time—five decades in some cases. Someone who is fifty-five or sixty may not be looking for a promotion but a graceful exit strategy over the next five years. Another individual may want one last hurrah (a position of responsibility and impact) before exiting. Companies that provide seasoned employees with coaching and options are more likely to attract and keep them. There's also the issue of acculturating seasoned employees to new realities so they can flourish. As firms increasingly leverage distributed and unbundled work to find new ways to design teams, most people are going to work across generations and not just across time zones. What emotional and intellectual skills and what expertise and craft will they need in order to flourish, and how will they reinvent themselves in an increasingly plug-and-play world?

Generation Gaps

Most companies have employees who span four generations:

- Baby boomer (born 1949–1964)

- Generation X (born 1965–1980)

- Millennial (born 1981–1996)

- Generation Z (born 1997–2012)

The two younger generations grew up in a world quite different from the older two, especially in terms of economics and media. Not only are these differences creating tensions in the workplace, but they are giving rise to expectations about jobs and careers that veer from the norm. Grasping the differences will enable organizations to create policies that manage the generational conflicts and meet career and job expectations.

The younger generations' upbringing in a world of digital media not only was fragmented but also gave them voice. Graduating from college with significant debt and dealing with difficult economic times, they have less trust in government and organizations than previous generations; they also question capitalism and are often strong supporters of unions.

Less positive about the future than baby boomers and Gen Xers, they strive for more than work-life balance; they want to work for companies aligned with their purpose and values and not just for a paycheck. Diverse and open to fluid identities and concerned about climate change, they have perspectives on social and environmental issues that often differ from their parents.

Those parents, many of whom are baby boomers, grew up in a capitalist economy that lifted all boats and made life better. For them, work represented the external validations of money and power—purpose and meaning were typically not a significant concern. During their careers, women often didn't have positions of power and Caucasians dominated leadership positions.

All these generational traits have produced the opposite work effect of what one might expect based solely on age: older generations are wanting or needing to work past traditional retirement ages because of declining safety nets and pensions or for reasons of identity and community; younger generations are quitting quietly or noisily because traditional workplaces are antithetical to their beliefs and preferences.

What does all this mean for organizations? The two biggest generations, baby boomers and millennials, are starkly different in their attitudes and values. Let's focus on just these two generations and the issues that leaders must assess:

- **Authority.** Millennials question authority and want a voice while baby boomers are more likely to go along with management policies and practices and accept less participation in decision-making.

- **Success.** Baby boomers consider themselves successful based on their earnings and their place on the corporate ladder. Millennials judge their achievements based on the balance between work and family, money and personal growth, and external validation leavened with internal satisfaction.

- **Worldview.** Baby boomers often possess a parochial perspective, more comfortable in homogeneous groups in familiar surroundings. Millennials grew up in a more diverse cultural milieu and a low-cost travel environment, producing a broader perspective that is not only more global but more empathetic toward those who are different from them in terms of gender, race, and religion.

Gen Zers are more extreme versions of millennials, being more anxious, digitally savvy, driven to speak up about purpose and to question working for a given organization. Both these younger generational groups are the future, and they're going to be driving a lot of organizational change. Some older organizational leaders may not like their attitudes and behaviors, but they ignore them at their peril.

Employers may especially dislike their propensity to change jobs. A Microsoft 2022 Work Trend Index predicted that 43 percent of employees are somewhat or extremely likely to consider changing jobs in the coming year, and that 52 percent of Gen Z and millennial respondents may change jobs. This same index suggested that many of these younger employees are looking beyond their day jobs for rewarding work: 70 percent of Gen Z and 67 percent of millennials said they were considering earning additional income via a side project or business in the next year.

These shifts toward side gigs and increased job mobility create challenges for business leaders. How do they retain their best and brightest people in this environment? How do they engage current employees who are increasingly finding outside pursuits that are more satisfying than their "regular" jobs?

The culture reflects these shifts, most notably in Beyoncé's song about the Great Resignation, "Break My Soul," with the lyrics:

I just quit my job
I'm gonna find new drive

I'm lookin' for motivation
I'm lookin' for a new foundation, yeah
And I'm on that new vibration
I'm buildin' my own foundation, yeah

Rex Woodbury, principal at a venture capital firm, offers a perceptive interpretation of Beyonce's lyrics:

The song is effectively about saying no to the nine-to-five grind, instead forging your own path. It captures a general sentiment in the zeitgeist: exhaustion with hustle culture, with working for a corporation ("the man"), with salaried and hourly work. Last year, more than 47 million Americans voluntarily left their jobs—an all-time record.

What's interesting is how young people entering the workforce are trying their hand at new paths. Many are earning income as content creators, or starting small businesses, or launching start-ups. This is facilitated by a new set of companies.

Pietra, for instance, lets anyone launch a product line—a skin-care line, a candle line, a streetwear line. Pietra abstracts away complexity, handling sourcing, fulfillment, e-commerce. Rather than needing the wealth and connections of Kylie Jenner (Kylie Cosmetics), Gwyneth Paltrow (Goop), or George Clooney (Casamigos) to launch a brand, anyone can do it.

Free at Last

The freelance revolution in recent years is another societal shift that organizations need to address, especially as it picks up steam in the coming years. Today, nearly 70 million Americans earn income as freelancers; by 2028, that will swell to 90 million. In 2026, America will become a majority-freelance economy, according to Statista.

This trend obviously poses recruitment and retention problems for large companies with many positions to fill. It's even more instructive, though, to consider what's motivating people to freelance. A May 2021 survey of a thousand US adults showed that 39 percent would consider quitting if their employers weren't flexible about remote work. Among millennials and Gen Zers, that figure was 49 percent.

Clearly, they're searching for workplaces where people are granted more freedom and independence than is traditionally allowed. They've seen what has happened to their parents and even their grandparents who adhered to restrictive rules and conditions, only to be fired when economic conditions worsened. They don't want to rent themselves to corporations. They believe that management doesn't have their best interests at heart. They want the freedom to work when and how they want. They also want the satisfaction and equity that comes with doing their own thing.

Organizations are fooling themselves if they believe that tweaks to policies—that is, providing the option of working from home one day a week—is sufficient to satisfy most employees' need for greater independence. This is especially true for Gen Z employees, though with the taste of independence that COVID provided, it's an attitudinal shift that affects all generations to some extent.

Sam Parker, a British journalist and content strategist, wrote about this issue in the *Guardian*, noting that given Gen Z's experiences (housing crisis, personal debt, and so on), we should "realise how ridiculous it is to expect them to tackle the challenges we left behind by working tirelessly and without complaint for one corporation or another, hoping it'll all be OK. They're far too shrewd, too determined, too hopeful for that."

Broken Engagements

People work harder, smarter, and more innovatively when they care about what they do. Unfortunately, many people are now just going through the motions. Every year there is a new theme, from "quiet quitting" to the "lying flat" movement, but regardless of what it is called the phenomenon is less about laziness and ennui and more about disengagement at work, as well as a desire to escape the stress of heavy workloads and managers who still run their groups in a pre-COVID manner.

Disengagement has a number of causes, and an ADP (Automatic Data Processing) study identifies stress as a primary one. Nearly seven in ten workers surveyed said they experience stress at work at least weekly, up from 62 percent prepandemic. One in seven said they feel stressed at work every day. Key stressors include the length of the workday and concerns over job security.

A Gallup study found that workers who reported declines in engagement cited a lack of clarity about expectations from managers, not feeling connected to a company's mission or purpose, little to no recognition for hard work, and receiving scant career development as key reasons for their disengagement.

The Gallup study also noted that disengagement was a particular problem among Gen Z and younger millennials, as the following data indicates:

- The percentage of engaged employees under the age of thirty-five dropped by six percentage points from 2019 to 2022. And during the same time frame, the percentage of actively disengaged employees increased by six points.

- Younger workers have dropped ten or more points in the percentage who strongly agree that someone cares about them, someone encourages their development, and they have opportunities to learn and grow.

- Fully remote and hybrid young workers dropped twelve points in strong agreement that someone encourages their development.

- Disturbingly, less than four in ten young remote or hybrid employees clearly know what is expected of them at work.

Quiet quitting is understandable but self-defeating. It prevents the figurative quitters from finding work that they're passionate about and that engages them fully. Just as alarming, their attitude may eventually cause their companies to quit on them.

A lack of engagement is not just an American phenomenon. In China, the route to success used to be hard work, marriage, and children. Many people there viewed the country's authoritarianism as a fair trade-off for being lifted out of poverty. But with employees working longer hours and housing prices rising faster than incomes, young Chinese especially fear that they will be the first generation that doesn't do better than the previous generation.

These young Chinese even have a name: the lying flat generation.

To "lie flat" means to forgo marriage, not have children, stay unemployed, and eschew material wants such as a house or a car. Leon Ding, for instance, is a twenty-two-year-old who has been lying flat for three months and thinks of his act as "silent resistance"; he dropped out of his last year of university because he didn't like the computer science major his parents had chosen for him.

The epidemic of disengagement, then, seems to be spreading globally, at least among younger workers. To counteract the spread and treat this condition, organizations need to help their people find meaningful work.

Responding to Societal Shifts

The various societal shifts described here aren't going away. That's why organizations need to reimagine their workplaces to remain agile and productive. Here are three suggestions for that reimagining:

Enhance flexibility.
The modern company will need to make work more flexible in three different ways:

1. Where one works

2. When one works

3. How much one works

Modern technology and COVID-related effects have made distributed work far more common than before. Work had already been unbundled and distributed due to offshoring, but flexibility will be key to remain competitive in an environment of declining workers and new generations looking for a work-life balance.

For the same reasons, working hours will need to fit into people's lives versus their working hours fitting into a company's needs.

Finally, to retain older workers and to attract younger workers, companies will need to offer the option of becoming a fractionalized employee.

Focus on diversity.
This isn't diversity for diversity's sake but for competitive advantage. To attract and keep younger workers, consider generational issues:

- Gen Z and millennials expect diversity in the workforce.

- Gen Z and millennials are far more diverse than baby boomers and Gen X due to a combination of more women in the workplace and the growth of immigration.

Diverse workplaces are likely to be more innovative and resonate with their customer bases.

Be sensitive to purpose and sustainability.
The two younger generations, both as potential employees and purchasers, care deeply about a company's policy on sustainability, diversity, and equity.

If there is one word that should drive the workplace structures, policies, programs, and cultures of tomorrow, it is *open*. More specifically, here are five ways they should strive to be open:

1. *Open to different ways of working:* not just the flexibility to work from a distance or in the office but providing people with several different ways to be categorized, from part-time to full-time work, each with its own trade-offs.

2. *Open to different lifestyles and viewpoints:* being receptive to diversity in talent and diversity in opinion.

3. *Open about their policies on sustainability, diversity, and wellness:* incorporating these factors in all their recruiting and promotional materials.

4. *Open about key decision-making and compensation:* making their pay scales and benefits transparent for all levels. Firms will need to be transparent about compensation, just as public companies have to publish the

compensation of their most senior members and the government needs to show salary ranges for all positions.

5. *Open scorecards:* publishing and benchmarking key policies from gender mix, sustainability, and other variables, including tracking over years.

CHAPTER 2

COMMUTING TO
THE MULTIVERSE

It shouldn't surprise anyone that technological advances are changing the nature of work. What might surprise a lot of people, however, is the range of these changes. Even more surprising: the emerging and future impact of tech on how, where, and when we work. People tend to focus on the way in which technology enables employees to work remotely, and as significant as that shift is, it merely scratches the surface of the ongoing metamorphosis.

Consider that as little as five or ten years ago, the title of this chapter might have seemed like science fiction. We have come so far so fast that it's difficult to keep up with all the technological innovations and how they're affecting the workplace. To stay current, we need to understand the tech evolution as it relates to work—the subject of this chapter.

Let's start by looking at a company that has changed in response to and in anticipation of technological advances.

Operating Live, Synchronous, and Asynchronous

Having worked for many years at Publicis Groupe, I can tell you that the company I joined many years ago bears little resemblance to the one that exists today. While the impetus for the changes are varied, technology has driven many of them. This is especially true when it comes to the three different ways employees now "gather":

Live

To counteract the effects of remote work–facilitating technologies, companies like Publicis have come up with ways to bring their people together. The current policy for most countries requests that employees be physically present in the office three days a week. Ideally, their presence is coordinated so they all are in the same space on these three days, providing opportunities for personal interaction. Publicis makes exceptions for individuals on a case-by-case basis, so this is not a draconian attendance policy.

Live events are also integrated into Publicis's work routines. Individual markets and teams gather in person at celebratory, client, and training events, either scheduled or designed for industry events such as South by Southwest (SXSW), Consumer Electronics Show, and Cannes Film Festival. Teams gather with one another and clients to hear speakers or participate in training events.

Synchronous

Using the Marcel platform, a proprietary AI technology, Publicis brings together all hundred thousand employees online simultaneously two or three times a year for important events—management announcements as well as outside speakers such as Michelle Obama and Elon Musk.

They also have a wide range of training sessions where people Zoom in from all over the world and participate in live workshops, including training sessions on future technologies such as Web3 and AI creation.

Less formally, the company also offers virtual coffee breaks where employees in offices all over the world can sign up to participate in Zoom sessions where they drink coffee and discuss whatever subjects interest them.

Asynchronous

An array of videos, interactive courses, recorded talks, and much more are accessible to individuals in different markets driven by AI and regulatory/competitive constraints. The company makes personalized recommendations of courses and learning to advance people's careers. New technologies make it possible for Publicis employees to work on projects anywhere in the world.

This is just one example of many. Just about every major organization has been affected in dramatic ways by technology, and this effect is going to broaden and deepen in the future. Tech's impact is evolutionary—the strongest technologies survive and then assume higher-level forms. Though we can't predict the future, we can be sure that it will have its roots in innovations taking place today. For this reason, it's valuable to look at technological evolution in a historical context, seeing how we got from point A to point B and looking ahead toward point C.

The Relationship Between Technology and Work

The advent of steam engines and railroads, electricity, and the modern assembly line were the three key advances that redefined work as we moved from the Agricultural Age to the Industrial Age. The modern factory and office and theories of management were optimized for a world defined by centralized work locations near these huge engines of mass production that in turn were clustered around raw material or easily accessed means of transport.

People and opportunities moved from rural locations (agricultural jobs and craft-based industries) to cities (industrial jobs built around mass production). The advent and expansion of personal computers in the 1980s, the creation of the World Wide Web in the 1990s, and the rise of mobile phones in the first decade of the 2000s thrust us into the Information Age by 2010. More than 80 percent of all jobs are now in the service sector, according to the Bureau of Economic Analysis.

Even as jobs moved from manufacturing to services beginning in the '70s and accounted for four out of five jobs in the '00s, the centralized and clustered model of work built for the manufacturing aged dominated.

This ended March 2020, when the entire world began a three-year experiment with alternative modes of working. The results from the experiment proved that most companies had been using an outmoded model of work. Technology had eliminated many of the reasons that people needed to cluster together in centralized places for a large portion of their work lives.

In this new paradigm, productivity did not decline—it increased. The cost of doing business declined as companies could hire from anywhere and eliminate many costs of housing and moving people.

Work satisfaction increased as people could do their jobs from anywhere and find more balance between work and family.

For this reason, most office buildings are only 60 percent occupied on the busiest day of the week, and it is becoming clear that there is no going back.

Broadband penetration, powerful and cheap mobile and computing devices, and cloud computing have ushered in a new world of work. Business-to-business and business-to-consumer software removed not only the friction of distance but the friction of mechanical movement of work.

We have arrived at the dawn of the Third Connected Age of Technology.

The First Connected Age began in 1993, featuring computers, rudimentary online service, and the advent of the World Wide Web. Search and e-commerce began in this age, as did Amazon and eBay.

In 2007 we entered the Second Connected Age, turbocharging the workplace not just because broadband speeds increased and costs were lowered but because smartphones and social media were now truly mobile, connected to almost everybody from everywhere all the time. The cloud came into being, and millions of new businesses were born because of the ability to advertise on search and social and to ship using e-commerce while accessing world-class technology. Every business invested heavily in technology and reinvented its processes and workflow. Companies like Dropbox and Zoom flourished, connecting people and workflow quickly and inexpensively.

Because of COVID, every company was rewired around connected workers working with connected workflow. In two years, decades of computing technology produced a quantum jump of how work was done.

We learned there was a better way to work.

And we would not and could not unsee it.

Which brings us to the Third Connected Age.

Four Redefining Technologies

In this third age, four new technologies will redefine work:

1. The power of AI.

2. The new ways of connecting leveraging AR (augmented reality) and VR (virtual reality), which is known as the metaverse or spatial computing.

3. The much faster connection of 5G.

4. New trust connections on Web3 driven by blockchain. Blockchain is a public cryptographically signed ledger that cannot be fiddled with and therefore can be trusted.

AI: While artificial intelligence dates back to 1956, it's having a major impact on society and work only in the last decade. Increasing access to massive amounts of data, more powerful computers, and breakthroughs in software has made AI more affordable, easier to use, and more broadly applicable. AI capabilities are doubling faster than Moore's law with exponential growth in every area, because of GPTX, Sora, Microsoft Copilot, Runway, Claude from Anthropic, Gemini from Google, Llama from Meta, and many more.

METAVERSE: The metaverse is an umbrella term, applicable to 3D worlds where the real is augmented by the virtual as in augmented reality. Examples include the heads-up display in an automobile or the real inserted into a virtual 3D world of a Roblox or Meta's Horizon world. The metaverse is most apparent in the gaming industry and is the gateway to the next generation of virtual reality.

5G: This technology enhances connectivity in two ways. It is much faster (up to a hundred times at the extreme) than average speeds; and it reduces latency (the time it takes between sending and receiving information) by up to two hundred times. This will mean that devices can be smaller and much more powerful since the computing power will be in the cloud and advanced AI capabilities and multimedia will be available anywhere. Remote surgery will also become a possibility as will self-driving cars.

WEB3: It combines a technology called blockchain with an open web ideology that builds upon the reading and open ethos of Web1 and the publishing and economics of Web2 to create an open but monetizable world of Web3. Chris Dixon of the venture capital firm Andreessen Horowitz describes these as the Read (Web1), Write (Web2), and Own (Web3) eras.

TOGETHER, THEY HAVE the potential to reinvent business in four ways:

1. Creating new ways of interacting that are different than in person or on video, using avatars, spatial computing, and other technologies that blur the differences between in person and remote.

2. Enabling ways of enabling monetization of work due to blockchain wallets and ensuring that the items or the supply chain are trusted.

3. Transforming every knowledge worker's job as AI makes knowledge increasingly free and available to everybody, compelling companies to redesign themselves and redesign jobs.

4. Enhancing capabilities of all professions, from doctors— who now will have AI assistants to help diagnose and identify issues and 5G to enable remote surgery—to lawyers—who will need to spend very little time preparing briefs, doing prior case work, or checking for loopholes in NDAs (nondisclosure agreements), which will all be done and summarized by AI, in turn enabling them to spend more time on new case law that AI will create, due to copyright and other issues, and to quality check AI results.

How These Advances Will Evolve Work

Most people understand the basic ways that technology has changed our work lives, from making remote work feasible to giving birth to a wide range of tech start-ups to enabling online sales. But this is just the start. In the Third Connected Age, advances and innovations will come fast and furiously. To be prepared for them, let's look at some of the ways they will affect work.

Acceleration

Tighter deadlines. Faster decisions. Greater urgency to implement strategies. As new technology collapses distance and time, it also increases the speed of business. We need to acclimate to working faster.

The steam engine, telegraph, telephone, airplane, fax, email, and the internet all reduced the time it took to span distances, making the world smaller and the pace of business both faster and continuous. When one part of the world is asleep, work is handed off and continues seamlessly in another part of the world. No gap exists between the sending and the receiving, creating expectations for immediate or almost immediate response.

AI, 5G, the metaverse, and Web3 all further collapse time and distance.

5G can make delivery over the web five hundred times faster and reduce latency to near zero.

AI allows hardware and software to parse through billions of decisions a second, spewing out a range of answers and options in almost real time.

The metaverse brings holographic and increasingly realistic avatars "to life" and creates the illusion that they are in the same room. The immersive environments in Apple's new Vision Pro make you feel like you are in the environment, whether it be a hippo reserve, Alicia Keys's studio, or walking on a tightrope across a Nordic fjord.

Web3's decentralizing and web-opening capacities increase the number of creators and makers as well as the number of places and organizations, such as decentralized autonomous organizations.

The metronome of business, already ticking at a fast pace, will accelerate exponentially.

Complexity

We have to learn not just to work faster but to acquire new competencies and develop better integration skills. To understand the complex challenge this poses, let's look at how these demands might translate in one particular field.

You're in the travel business, responsible for booking space for conventions. In the "old days," you mailed photographs of the location and descriptions to potential customers. You discussed these issues on the phone with them and scheduled site visits.

Today, you use the internet to email materials and Zoom for conversations; you also may conduct limited video 3D tours.

Tomorrow, the video you send will be rich and deep due to 5G. You'll conduct virtual walk-throughs in 3D, providing customers with experiences that are the equivalent to being there. You and your customers can use AI and other software to change the design and look of the space, experiencing every room, restaurant, and site without being there physically. Because of Web3, your network of suppliers (tour guides, entertainers, and so on) can plug and play their wares and accept cross-border payments much faster and easier globally using blockchain technology.

These new technologies will not only eliminate the need for physical travel and the lengthy and often cumbersome process of making convention reservations, but they will also be accessible from anywhere, all the time. Concurrently, they create a more complex work environment.

The technological innovations mean that organizations must develop new skills. Every world-class provider will learn to leverage

AI, the metaverse, and Web3, removing friction in discovery, customization, and billing.

They'll also have to engage in benchmarking of competitors, ensuring that customers who "sample" these experiences online will feel the experiences are world-class. Just like in the old days, when one had to make sure one had a website that was easy to navigate and looked professional, companies will need to ensure that their virtual worlds and immersive environments are easy to navigate and feel realistic and aligned with their brand. Modern technology will allow a lot of companies and small businesses to compete with established players.

Finally, they'll need to integrate experience and teams. As businesses span the real and the virtual, the analog and the digital, human and digital assistants, they must find ways to integrate these different worlds with the right balance to create a unified experience.

Reconfigured work environments

Here are some of the common complaints of people who work in unbundled and distributed environments: the number of meetings in a world of Zoom has increased, the time to recover between frequent back-to-back meetings has decreased, and the former guardrails of a nine-to-five working day have all but vanished.

This environment is likely to become more intense and require adaptation. Meta Horizon Worlds, while still in development, allows people to feel that they're actually in the same room as people who are physically distant. Instead of having a Zoom conversation, it will be *Star Trek* like, where people are virtually beamed to different locations.

In addition to the pace picking up, the visual and verbal artist will now need the following skills:

- Learning the new tools

- Determining how best to use them: many AI tools require prompting skills. Very much like how search results differ based on what you search for, the creative results will be very sensitive to how the queries and commands are worded.

- Reinventing our careers: just as word processors and email reduced the need for assistants and Photoshop eliminated the need for darkrooms and touch-up artists, the speed and capabilities of these technologies will require fewer people than before but may create the need for new careers.

More dispersed

Invariably, the dispersion-of-work trend will continue and gain strength. That's because we'll have the power of mainframe computers and advanced software easily accessible from anywhere. The costs of accessing the technology will decline, and it will be easier for people to acquire the skills necessary to use this technology—the power will shift from the organization to the individual. Chips and software will infiltrate every nook and cranny of organizations, every task in every function. All of us will need to learn how to work more effectively with machines.

The Challenge of Technology

In my previous book, *Restoring the Soul of Business: Staying Human in the Age of Data*, I examined the organizational challenge of managing digital and analog, machine and human. In recent years, this challenge has become even more significant. As AI, the metaverse, 5G, and Web3 change where and how we work, businesses must find the right balance between technology and people. Technology's charms are seductive, and companies need to resist the impulse to fall completely under its spell. Maintaining the human element in the face of increasingly wondrous technology, then, is the challenge.

Technology has always been a double-edged sword; it can be a positive and a negative.

Overall, technology allows for greater options and wealth creation. While there are drawbacks to electricity, modern pharmaceuticals, the automobile, and modern computers, few people would like to return to the days of typewriters and horse-drawn carriages.

With technological advances accelerating, many companies grapple with both the upsides and downsides. Studies of ten thousand office workers conducted last year by Future Forum, a research group backed by Slack, suggest that women and people of color were more likely than their White male colleagues to see working remotely as beneficial. And globally, 50 percent of working mothers who participated in the studies reported wanting to work remotely most or all of the time, compared with 43 percent of fathers.

Adapting to these technology-driven, varied mindsets isn't easy, but astute organizations are attempting to evolve along with their people.

Quilt.AI (full disclosure: I'm on their board) uses AI to interpret and convert data into insights about people. It has workers in Singapore (the home office), India, and across the US. As its employees began to work across three countries, and COVID rules in Singapore made gathering difficult, Quilt gave up its leases and allowed everyone to work from home, retaining a small hub in Singapore.

Management found that while the quality of product and client relationships continued to remain at a high level, the company culture was weakening. Because the cofounders all believed this was a key metric, they assessed why it was going south and identified three reasons:

1. It was harder to train and onboard people remotely.

2. Team dynamics were weakening, especially as many new employees had not met established employees or other employees in person.

3. Innovation and improvements to the product were slower due to a decline in idea creation.

The company decided to counter these dynamics by having company-wide, in-person meetings in different parts of the world (Dubai, Singapore) every few months. These meetings lasted almost a week and involved training, outside speakers, fun entertainment and events, and lots of time for people to rest, relax, and get to know one another.

This strategy maximized the benefits of hiring diverse people in low-cost or high-talent markets, offering employees flexibility in the ways they work but also maximizing culture, creativity, and productivity.

Today the culture metrics are at an all-time high, product innovation is outstripping engineering ability to productize, and retention metrics have soared.

Learn from the Past About the Future

For nearly three decades my career has been deeply intertwined with technology, allowing me to observe its changes at Publicis Groupe and its clients.

The communications business has always changed as technology shifted. The company was first a print-based business and then a print and broadcast business, with radio initially and then television dominating it. In the early '90s with the advent of the internet, a team of us began some of the first digital marketing and digital media companies, and in the past three decades, the entire business of marketing, media, and communications has restructured itself around the internet. Wave after wave of technology, from search to e-commerce to social to mobile to now AI and Web3, have shifted every aspect of all businesses.

Having observed all of this firsthand, I've come to three conclusions that apply to all organizations experiencing this technological evolution.

1. Technology does not care about anybody's business model or way of working.

Nearly fifteen years ago, I spoke to leaders at a major newspaper conference, imploring them to rethink their business in the light of search and mobile technology. I warned them that every aspect of their business model, from local monopolies and distribution routes to auto, classified, and other advertising, would disappear unless they embraced the internet, stopped thinking about their paper publication as central, embraced multimedia with continuous publishing, and attracted new talent. Essentially, I was suggesting that they rethink every aspect of their organization.

Most papers did not adapt, and the newspaper industry is a shell of its former self.

Just as technology rendered many newspapers obsolete, it's having the same effect on a wide range of industries and functions today. Business models cannot be sacrosanct. "Adapt or die" is a good adage for an age of rapidly advancing technology.

2. Technology can be used as an accelerant, but its real power is often the capacity to reinvent.

Companies may invest deeply in technology to automate and upgrade their way of working, but they still fail.

This is because they often do not change their way of doing business.

Procter & Gamble invested deeply in technology to automate its manufacturing plants and be a leader in digital marketing. They leveraged search and mobile and video to reach people as their habits changed.

But what technology really enabled was not just better ways to communicate but new ways to do business, giving rise to a range of competitors.

For instance, social media leveraged YouTube video's cost effectiveness and ease of distribution. The advent of e-commerce made it possible to sell without Walmart or Walgreens, and companies like Harry's and Dollar Shave Club were born and ate into Gillette's market share, despite Gillette having a superior product, brand, distribution, and spending. The new media allowed for direct distribution, subscription services, word of mouth, and sampling, and customers recognized that the new blades were good enough but much cheaper and much more convenient.

3. It is not the technology—it is the talent.

As technology is widely distributed it helps individuals as much as it does institutions, and *every advance in technology places a premium on superior ability.*

Remind yourself that the typewriter did not write *A Farewell to Arms*; Hemingway did. If I had a word processor and ChatGPT and Hemingway has a pen, he still would write better. Of course, if Hemingway also had ChatGPT, he would be that much better than me. Hemingway with a Substack would have scaled amazingly better than most.

As talented individuals do with TikTok.

Today, streaming and the internet make the popular courses on justice at Harvard and on happiness at Yale available to everybody for free. It's not the technology that makes these courses great, but the talent of professors Michael Sandel and Laurie Santos, respectively.

Finding the Right Balance

Let me conclude this chapter by returning to my earlier theme of striking a balance between working digitally and interacting personally. The remote-versus-in-person debate continues to rage, and given the amazing technological tools that have emerged, it's tempting to concede: "Okay, as much as we might miss the fun and energy of people being in the same room, that's the old paradigm, and it's time to move onto the new, more efficient paradigm that technology has made possible."

This concession is a mistake.

We know that in-person interactions produce three crucial benefits: *learning, relationship building, and problem-solving/creative idea generation.*

LEARNING: Some types of learning take place by watching others in action or being mentored by bosses in an apprentice/guild-like model. This is probably true for many industries and particularly for people early in their career or new to a company.

RELATIONSHIP/NETWORK BUILDING: While relationships can be built online (for example, with dating apps), in-person meetings can help deepen and strengthen relationships. Organizations should seek a combination of the physical and the virtual to facilitate relationship building.

PROBLEM-SOLVING/CREATIVE IDEA GENERATION: If innovation is about fresh, insightful connections, then the give-and-take between people can provide opportunities for this linkage. Whether it be the unexpected interaction between two colleagues or the in-person back-and-forth of brainstorming, these are benefits that result from being together.

AT THE SAME time, it's also a mistake to go too far in the other direction—to subordinate digital options and opportunities to in-person interactions. This is especially true as of this writing since many companies are implementing return-to-office policies. According to a recent Slack study:

> Work-related stress and anxiety has hit the highest levels since our surveying began in the summer of 2020:
>
> More than a third of knowledge workers (34%) have reverted to working from the office five days a week, the greatest share since Future Forum began surveying in June 2020.
>
> With this shift, scores have dropped to near-record lows across all eight employee experience measures that we survey. Work-related stress and anxiety is at its worst since our surveying began, dropping 28% compared with last quarter, while work-life balance dropped 17% quarter over quarter.

Given these problems, businesses would be wise to take a cue from a company like L'Oréal, which even before COVID recognized that they needed to find a way maximize technology's benefits while also offsetting its drawbacks. As a result of this recognition, L'Oréal made a series of changes in offices from Copenhagen to Paris.

In November 2017, L'Oréal opened new offices at Levallois-Perret on the outskirts of Paris. Named Seine 62, the campus is the latest in a series to have been opened in the Paris region, Copenhagen, and Manhattan. Reflecting the new ways of working among its employees, the group is moving to office spaces that are specially designed to be agile and collaborative, and ensure interaction across teams.

Equipping the offices with the latest technology for working together, the company created links not only between the group's different operating units within the campus but also with people outside, as a way of encouraging a collaborative way of working in general. "With our videoconference service, you can talk to someone in Shanghai as if they were standing in front of you," said Jean-Michel Duffieux, property project director in charge of facilities at one of L'Oréal's new buildouts in Rio De Janeiro.

In addition, L'Oréal's Nordics tower in Copenhagen has been specifically designed to enable employees to arrange their own personal timetable. An individual space with a view over the canal is provided for people who want to work alone and to find inspiration, while other areas have been created for group projects. For those who want to shut themselves away to concentrate, a special "focus" space has been created. The building also features numerous meeting rooms and places to talk informally.

The various initiatives have helped to raise employee satisfaction levels at L'Oréal in Copenhagen from 64 percent to 71 percent.

I don't think it's a stretch to project that other companies will be searching for ways to improve their technologies while addressing individual employee concerns. No doubt, organizations will go about this challenging task in different ways. There's also little doubt that some may tilt too far in the technology direction and neglect their people's wishes.

Technology has always come with a price. It allows us to work with greater speed, effectiveness, and flexibility but also can have a dehumanizing effect. The best companies will learn how to maximize all of technology's benefits and minimize its human costs.

CHAPTER 3

THE NEW MARKETPLACES

Throughout history, marketplaces have evolved. Starting with the open-air marketplaces of Greece, Babylon, and other ancient lands to the shopping malls of more recent times, we've always looked for ways to improve the marketplace experience. Sellers have continuously changed how, where, what, and when they sell. They've made it easier to buy with credit cards. They've bypassed retailers with direct-to-consumer methods. They've made it possible to purchases at kiosks, pop-ups, and other variations of the retail norm. They've decreased the time from purchase to delivery. They've offered a greater variety of goods and services. They've cut customer costs.

These changes accelerated with the introduction of the internet and the emergence of new technologies, some of which we discussed in the previous chapter.

Already these changes have enabled smaller companies to thrive and compete in an ecosystem of larger companies. The marketplaces allow both whales and plankton to coexist, feeding off and thriving with one another.

Now and in the coming years, however, marketplace innovation isn't just accelerating but taking quantum leaps. The changes that are taking place will change the world of work in ways both obvious and nuanced. We need to understand these new and emerging marketplaces and how they will affect everything from careers to the competitive landscape.

Marketplace Types

Technology has enabled employers and employees, individuals and businesses, buyers and sellers to engage with one another in friction-reducing ways, eliminating the distance between themselves and the marketplace, reducing the need for sophisticated skills or minimal capital to set up a store, and making it easier to develop content, find an audience, operate globally, and accept a payment.

This has been enabled by digitized marketplaces that live in the cloud and can be accessed through any internet-connected device.

Most people are aware of and have used at least some of these marketplaces, including Shopify, Uber, and Airbnb. Organizations, however, should be aware that these marketplaces vary from each other and can be categorized in three different ways:

1. **Marketplaces that connect.** These linkages run the gamut, from buyers to sellers such as Amazon; from renters to space owners like Airbnb; and from employers to talent like Upwork.

2. **Marketplaces that empower.** Shopify is a well-known example of a marketplace that permits anyone to set up a store cost effectively. These marketplaces provide scale-based solutions that previously would require a large amount of capital.

3. **Marketplaces that enable.** Put simply, these marketplaces facilitate a range of services for individuals and organizations that were difficult if not impossible to create before technological advances. SafetyWing, for example, provides global medical insurance for self-employed digital nomads as well as companies that need to cover employees in different markets. Similarly, Deel makes it possible for companies to hire people in 150 different countries, and the Deel technology handles all legal compliance, benefits, and payroll relevant to each country.

These marketplaces provide tremendous advantages when entrepreneurs and companies are small and growing. They offer greater access to technology benefits and dramatically reduce the need for significant resources and capital dramatically. They also have been responsible for the proliferation of side hustles. They offer flexibility that didn't exist previously—people with day jobs can also create and sell products and services using their mobile devices through Shopify and Etsy, and they can find side jobs through Upwork and Fiverr. In addition, these new marketplaces provide transparency, opening up a world of valuable information to new businesses—everything from lists of prospective customers to salaries to data on underserved markets.

As we'll see, even the largest organizations can benefit from these new marketplace advantages. Right now, however, individuals and small businesses are the ones who are most likely to capitalize on them.

A Small Revolution

A *Wall Street Journal* article, relying on labor data and an analysis from Jefferies, an investment banking and capital markets firm, determined that small companies were responsible for all of the net job growth since the start of the pandemic and accounted for four out of five job openings. According to the US government's Job Openings and Labor Turnover Survey, companies with fewer than 250 employees hired 3.67 million more people than have been laid off or who quit since February 2020. Larger companies, on the other hand, have eliminated a net 800,000 jobs during this same time frame.

Perhaps the most significant development is that many younger employees dream of starting a small business. For many Gen Zers and millennials, creating an app and launching a start-up has replaced working for a Fortune 100 company as a career goal. Though this dream hasn't been realized for a lot of younger workers—millennials own just 7 percent of small businesses, while Gen Zers own only 1 percent—this all will change. The average age for starting a business is around thirty-five, so inevitably, these percentages will increase.

Per a Prosper Insights & Analytics survey, more than 10 percent of Gen Zers polled said they plan on starting or developing their own businesses in the next six months. Perhaps even more significant, numerous surveys and studies demonstrate that this generation rejects or at least resists traditional work structures. They desire balance and fulfillment from their jobs, and they want to be passionate about what they do. Entrepreneurship provides the best path to achieve these objectives.

The new marketplaces dovetail with Gen Z's consciousness. They provide less risky ways to launch a business than in the past. Distributed work and enabling technologies allow people to stay in current jobs while testing a new business concept. They may decide to quit their day jobs and devote all their time to this business, or they may continue these jobs and pursue this business as a side gig. The new marketplaces give them options they never had before.

It's not just Gen Z and millennials who are taking advantage of the small revolution. In a world where many populations are aging and numerically declining, the new marketplaces provide wonderful opportunities for baby boomers who still want to work—or who need to work for financial reasons. The combination of facilitating technologies and emerging business opportunities provides older workers with the chance to work beyond traditional retirement age. It also offers them the chance to translate talents and experience into dynamic small businesses, with a relatively minor financial investment.

Big Changes in How People Work

As new marketplaces continue to emerge and multiply, they are having a profound effect on the nature of work, shattering traditional notions of how we define a job. Perhaps the two most significant changes involve the explosion of self-employed and gig workers and the increasingly global nature of work.

According to the Pew Research Center, 16 percent of Americans have earned money from a gig platform. The relatively high percentage of people doing gig work is obviously made possible by new marketplaces like ride-sharing and delivery apps, and these gigs are most appealing to younger workers. Less obviously, and perhaps more significantly, the rise in gig work is setting a precedent and a pattern. Instead of being an anomaly, gig work is becoming an accepted part of the work landscape, and it's bound to encompass more skilled tasks in the future.

Shopify, Airbnb, Uber, and other marketplaces are also fueling the self-employment trend—the Bureau of Labor Statistics shows that 16.9 million US citizens were self-employed in October 2022. *Bloomberg* reports that more Americans are self-employed than at any time since 2008. While a number of factors are driving this trend, the dissatisfaction with traditional jobs and the desire for greater freedom and control are primary factors. And of course, the new marketplaces make it possible for individuals to find self-employment alternatives to traditional jobs.

The Future of Work Is Global

The new marketplaces also possess a global component, one that is different from the way we defined global business in the past. Years ago, we talked about multinationals establishing markets in places like China and South America and opening offices in various international locations. But global isn't just about extending the brand or creating satellite foreign offices. The new marketplaces are inherently global because the internet doesn't recognize boundaries. Consider the following data:

At the end of 2021, of LinkedIn's 875 million members and 58 million registered businesses, more than 75 percent were from outside the US.

China's TikTok is the most popular app in the US, but it's also popular in Indonesia (100 million users), Brazil (75 million), and Russia (50 million).

Amazon has more than 2 million sellers, of which 40 percent are based in China.

It's not just that customers come from every corner of the world. It's also that the new marketplaces make it possible for sellers to operate anywhere. Shopify generates half its business outside of the US by enabling individuals in any country to sell in any other country that has the necessary resources (to handle translation, currency transfers, and so on).

Employees, too, can come from anywhere. IBM has more employees from India than from the US. The people who keep the new marketplaces up and running don't always need to work at headquarters, given that the very notion of headquarters may become antiquated in the future.

More and more, that future will be one where bits, not atoms, are the critical components; data and content can be moved around the world easily.

Thanks to the new marketplaces, an emerging global mindset exists in the US and other countries. I know this from personal experience. When I came to Chicago from India more than forty years ago, I struggled to adjust to two things. The cold. And the bland food.

Fortunately, I was able to adjust to the latter when I discovered Tabasco sauce—I added it to everything. Now, Chicago and all US cities have discovered spicy food. Global travel, food TV shows, immigration, and other factors have changed people's food shopping habits and what they order at restaurants. The same global mindset has spread to other sectors.

The US-centric or European-centric perspective is being replaced by a multipolar, global view that combines Western, Indian, Chinese, Latin, and African influences. When companies limit their views to their own countries, they also limit their opportunities because those can come from anywhere.

From Start-up to Megacorp

Never have so many small companies grown so big so fast. The new marketplaces are accelerating growth, turning businesses no one has heard of into household names, sometimes in a matter of months. As a result, people find themselves working for an informal operation where everyone knows everyone else one day, and the next they're one of thousands of employees following rules and policies.

Businesses are growing and scaling with unprecedented speed because of a number of factors, including a massive infusion of money from venture capital and private equity. The new marketplaces, however, are fostering fast scaling because they possess the following four capabilities:

1. **Faster (than hardware) software.** As software platforms, these marketplaces can iterate quickly. After they reach scale in the world of bits, they extend to the world of atoms. A good example: Amazon's extension to real-world stores and its warehouses and delivery system.

2. **Network effects.** All good things flow from widespread usage, a hallmark of successful new marketplaces. More users make the platform more attractive. Increased usage generates better data, lower cost, and greater choice (Amazon) or connection (Facebook).

3. **Mobile turbocharged.** Given that seven billion smartphones exist, the services of new marketplaces are available to nearly everyone in the world, all day and night.

4. **Plug and play.** Companies in this space use their ability to plug and play into each other and existing ecosystems, relying on common software or application protocol interfaces (such as app stores) to build on top of what has already been created.

These capabilities are available to everyone through cloud-based marketplaces that enable and empower small companies to scale themselves rapidly. As Web3 technologies allow for more ownership, 5G allows for faster and more accessible cloud-based computing and storage, and AI provides magical superpowers to almost everyone, we are likely to see growth and scaling accelerate. Specifically, we can expect the following developments:

- *More companies will be formed.* Marketplaces and modern technology are making it much easier to start a company.

- *Companies will scale even faster.* AI reduces the cost of development, 5G enables better and more cost-effective computing, and more marketplaces offer plug-and-play solutions.

- *Individuals will create side gigs that become companies.* New, more cost-effective technologies combined with unbundled and flexible work will enable people to start companies.

Big Benefits

While I've emphasized how the new marketplaces are a boon for entrepreneurs and small businesses, they also provide advantages for savvy large organizations. They can be leveraged to help them find and hire talent, sell products and services, and build their businesses. Microsoft, Procter & Gamble, Nike, and many other major corporations are using Upwork to find freelance and part-time talent. They're also partnering with Deel to move talent cost-effectively around the globe. And they're establishing relationships with TikTok influencers, capitalizing on new forms of content creation and media delivery.

Previously, I noted how Publicis is using the Marcel platform to plug and play into other platforms. They've also created what is essentially a new marketplace internally. Instead of looking outside for talent or freelancers, they first make projects and gigs available to Publicis employees who possess relevant skills and are eligible for these types of gigs. This internal marketplace also saved more than two thousand jobs during COVID, allowing Publicis companies in countries with excess talent to provide that talent to Publicis companies in other countries that were short of talent. In a way, this marketplace operated like an internal Upwork.

Procter & Gamble created a new marketplace for ideas called Connect + Develop. They identified needs in targeted categories and then anyone—individuals or companies—could apply to be considered as an innovation partner. This marketplace allowed P&G to reach out quickly, cut costs of development, and expand its innovation team to potentially everyone in the world.

Leveraging the New Marketplaces

At a grassroots level, tech-savvy, entrepreneurial individuals have done a great job taking advantage of the new marketplaces. They've developed the knowledge and skills necessary to set up global businesses from their basements and obtain highly rewarding side jobs and gig work. Organizations, both large and small, can learn a lot from their pioneering efforts. It's the larger companies, however, that have the most to gain when they leverage the new marketplaces. Many companies remain mired in old marketplace thinking, and they need to transition to a new marketplace consciousness.

Here are five steps they should take:

1. **Prioritize the new scale over the old scale.** For decades, companies leveraged scale of production, distribution, resources, and marketing to create a competitive edge. This old scale, however, provides less of a competitive edge today than the scale of ideas, data, networks, and talent.

2. **Learn new skills and combine them with old ones.** This is the "roots-and-wings" approach. At least some of the old skills and knowledge will still be valuable in the new paradigm, including a company's brands, the defining stories, and the relationships. But it's also critical to be

46

aware of the way new marketplaces function and the capabilities necessary to maximize them. Microsoft has done an excellent job in this regard, maintaining its roots by refocusing on productivity software and business. But it's also soared with its wings, moving business to the cloud and embracing Linux and writing software for competing marketplaces and companies like Meta Quest and Apple.

3. **Manage hybrid cultures.** Most fast-growing companies are combining full-time, part-time, and contracted employees, shuffling various labor marketplaces. Mastering this mix is crucial to maintaining product quality and company cultures.

4. **Address talent burnout.** In the accelerated world of new marketplaces, this is a real risk that must be monitored and managed. Customer expectations for faster speeds combined with a fast-growing company (with the accompanying avalanche of stimuli and data) create an environment where people are highly stressed. If this stress isn't managed, burnout happens.

5. **Create fractionalized employees.** I've saved the best for last. Imagine combining the continuity and loyalty of long-term employees with the cost-management flexibility of freelancers. Further imagine doing so in a way that both grows employees and retains them long term. This is the fractionalized employee, the perfect fit for a new marketplace world where work flexibility is key. This fractionalized employee should receive work/time options: 100 percent, 75 percent, or 50 percent of their time (the lowest percentage should be the minimum needed for

health and other benefits), and they can vary the percentage based on life events (health concerns, birth of a child, and so on).

With the implementation of a fractionalized employee policy, people no longer have to choose between staying or going or being torn by trying to do two things at one time. If they wish to try out a different type of noncompetitive job (starting a gaming company, working for the social good, or writing a book), employers should accommodate them because retaining half or three-quarters of a talented person is better than retaining zero. And there will be cost savings from reduced compensation as well as eliminating the cost of severance, rehiring, and training (plus the hidden cost of the morale-depleting loss of a good employee).

Just as important, fractionalized employee policies will probably attract a lot of talent who may want to work 50 to 75 percent of their time, and it will allow companies to retain talent, grow talent, and mix and match talent in ways that are truly win-win.

CHAPTER 4

GIG WORK, SIDE HUSTLES, AND PASSION PROJECTS

In Japan, the term *shūshin koyō* means permanent employment, and until relatively recently, it was standard practice. Companies offered the security of lifetime jobs in exchange for employee loyalty and hard work. In the US and other countries, a similar "bargain" existed in the twentieth century and into the early twenty-first century. Large, blue-chip employers such as General Electric, Procter & Gamble, Johnson & Johnson, IBM, and others offered their own version of *shūshin koyō*.

This concept is still attractive to many baby boomers and even some Gen Xers who are CEOs or are in other leadership positions at large organizations. As someone who was a long-term employee at Publicis, I get it. There's great value in having long-term employees who are loyal and skilled, and who understand the culture. And there's great value for employees, who receive tremendous benefits and possess job security.

No doubt, some corporate leaders still cling to this model and resist change. They want their people to devote all their time and energy to one job and one company. But things are changing, and they're changing fast. Most people starting their careers today won't work at the same company for thirty years. Just as significant, many of these individuals will reject the idea of having one job—they'll integrate a second and even a third part-time pursuit into the mix.

This is going to happen even if some organizational leaders don't like it. The challenge will be to adapt the organization to these changing employee preferences.

Defining and Describing the New Work Modes

The gig economy has grown in the last twenty years, and it has grown exponentially during COVID. It has produced two types of gigs: side hustles and side gigs.

The former usually begins as a passion project. A marketing executive writes a play. Someone in HR creates handicrafts. An IT person develops a video game. An accountant in the financial department begins making furniture.

They pursue these interests outside of work hours and don't make any money from them initially. Eventually, though, opportunities present themselves, or they develop greater expertise that raises the quality of their work, or they need to find a way to monetize their passion project.

Whatever the reason, they find a way to generate some income from what was formerly a hobby. It becomes a side hustle, their own small business that they run (or something they do as a contractor) in addition to their main job.

A side gig differs from a side hustle in two ways. First, it's done primarily for income. Second, it involves working for someone else (Uber, TaskRabbit, and so on) rather than for oneself.

Variations exist. Some people have gigs only and no main job. Others may have two side hustles, or a side hustle and a side gig in addition to a main job. This is quite different from the past, when most people had full-time or part-time jobs as employees, or they did freelance work or were self-employed.

Why the Gig Economy Is Booming

People have always pursued passion projects, worked part-time jobs, and turned hobbies into income. What's different now is that in our post-COVID world of distributed and unbundled work, side hustles and side gigs are facilitated. Just as important, many people—especially the younger generations—are not willing to settle for the types of jobs and working paradigms their parents embraced.

More specifically, here are three factors that are driving the gig economy:

1. **New types of jobs/ways of working.** Mobile phones and the internet have atomized work, breaking down some full-time jobs into smaller gigs. For instance, instead of having to obtain a medallion to drive a taxi in major cities, people can now work for Uber part time. Or sites like Upwork and Fiverr create a digital pathway to freelance work. Or Etsy, an online marketplace, helps users monetize a passion for creating arts and crafts. Or Shopify gives individuals the tools to set up their own virtual store.

2. **More freedom and flexibility.** A growing number of people are working away from the office (full time or part time). This provides the freedom to pursue other jobs and the flexibility to juggle side hustles. People who work from home also save significant amounts of time—no

long commute to the office, no lunches, and no drinks after work. It's natural to take advantage of this freedom and flexibility to generate more income or spend more time doing what you love.

3. **Financial pressure.** Inflation, increased costs of everything from childcare to groceries, loss of income because of COVID, a volatile economy, layoffs, and other factors have motivated workers in various fields to find additional sources of income.

LendingTree, an online lending marketplace, released results from a December 2022 survey that reinforces the notion that people are more motivated now than in the past to pursue side hustles and side gigs. For instance, they found that more than half the folks who have second jobs wouldn't be able to pay their bills without this additional income. They also found that between 68 percent and 78 percent (the percentages varied based on the size of company worked for) of survey respondents said that layoffs have made freelance work more attractive than in years past.

A November 2022 LendingTree survey also found that 44 percent of Americans have a side hustle, up from 13 percent in 2020, and that an astonishing 62 percent of Gen Zers have a side hustle.

Not a Passing Fancy but a Growing Trend

There is no going back. We're not going to return to a pre-COVID nine-to-five office routine. While some pundits may predict a return to normal as COVID fears fade, the reality is that a new normal has emerged and isn't going away. Here's why:

The aphrodisiac of flexibility

After tasting the freedom of working where and when they wanted, many employees have no desire to revert to a more restrictive work environment. Mothers and other caretakers of small children in particular have benefitted, being able to find a better balance between work and parenting. Some hated the headaches of commuting and prefer working from home, while others enjoy doing their tasks without being locked into a rigid office structure where they're continuously supervised. No doubt, some employees miss the camaraderie of being in communal workspaces, but this need for human connection can be met via alternative work environments and coming into the office occasionally.

The work ethic of older folks

Many baby boomers still want to work, but they don't want to work full time. Some are in difficult financial straits and drive for a ride-sharing service or take similar jobs because they need the money, but a lot of older folks have other motivations. They work for identity, community, and personal growth. Their desire to keep working—whether starting a small business or doing gig work—is filling employee ranks at places like Uber and creating online companies in many different fields.

Tech innovations

As I've discussed previously, tech innovations connect people to powerful resources for little or no cost (AI), let them be "present" in many places (5G/AR/VR), and find ways to monetize their work (Web3). Many of the gigs we've discussed wouldn't exist without these technologies. What's particularly instructive is how quickly people adopt them and adapt to them.

Next generations' entrepreneurial mindsets
Millennials and Gen Zers are more interested in working for themselves than for companies. They seek control, security, and self-expression.

Given these driving forces, the question is: Will organizations learn how to remake themselves in order to capitalize on the changing work attitudes and behaviors?

Benefits: Talent, Reputation, and Costs

If organizations answer the previous question negatively—if they stubbornly refuse to alter their policies and practices—they will not only lose older talent but also fail to attract and keep younger talent whose skills are crucial to organizational success. They'll also fail to realize the benefits of a flexible workforce—the cost management advantages and agility that accrues to organizations able to accommodate the changing requirements of their workforce. Organizations face many challenges, from creating a sense of belonging for workers who aren't always present to offering health care and other benefits to people who may not work full time. But the most immediate challenge is creating policies that allow their people to work on other projects. In the past, such a concept was heretical. Today, it's a win-win for organizations and employees.

First, such a policy attracts and retains talent. Think of it as a perk that will both bring in top people to the organization and provide an incentive for them to stay.

Second, allowing people to pursue side hustles and gigs fosters skill and reputation development. Employees broaden their knowledge and competencies, and at the same time, they may become well-known because of their second or third jobs and be viewed as "stars," attracting other talent to the company and enhancing its reputation.

Third, which might be the most overlooked benefit, is one related to costs. When you allow employees to work on other projects, start businesses, and work part time for others, you are essentially giving them a raise that doesn't come out of your pocket. Without these side gigs and hustles, at least some of the most talented employees would either demand raises or leave the company for higher-paying jobs elsewhere.

Given these three benefits, organizational leaders may recognize the value of policy change but wonder how to implement it. Fortunately, three industries provide good models that others can learn from: entertainment/Hollywood, journalism, and academia.

When you stop and think about how Hollywood businesses are structured, you realize that they're an unusual mix of gig work, long-term deals, side hustles, and other alternative approaches. Many Hollywood employees are gig workers, since the unit of work is inherently a gig—a television show, a movie, and so on. To produce this unit of work, a company or companies gather people with the right combination of skills, and then everyone disbands once the production is complete, coming together again at some point in the future for the next gig.

To ensure fluidity and minimize friction, employees—actors, writers, set designers, sound technicians, and so forth—belong to a guild or union that negotiates compensation. In addition, many of these workers are employees of film studios, editing houses, and music firms, who are allowed to accept side gigs and participate in passion projects. Even well-paid producers and directors who have first-look development deals with certain studios are allowed to moonlight for others.

This is true for many television stars. Michael Strahan is primarily an employee of Disney, working on ABC's *Good Morning America*, but he also is a cohost of *Fox NFL Sunday*. Anderson Cooper is an employee of CNN who also occasionally hosts on

CBS's *60 Minutes* and has side hustles such as writing books and producing a recent podcast series on loss, called *All There Is*.

Hollywood may not provide a model that is exactly transferrable to other industries, but the agility and open-mindedness they demonstrate should provide CEOs of all types of companies with ideas for transitioning to the gig economy environment.

In journalism, newspapers and magazines employ a variety of people—from full-time employees to freelancers to syndicated columnists—and they also permit side hustles. The *New York Times*, for instance, allows their top talent to combine their main jobs with side gigs and hustles outside the *Times*. Maggie Haberman is the *Times*'s White House correspondent but also appears as a commentator on CNN and took time off to work on her book about Donald Trump. Ezra Klein was lured to the *New York Times* from *Vox* to be an op-ed writer but was allowed to launch and host *The Ezra Klein Show* podcast.

Other publications encourage their reporters and editors to appear on radio and talk shows, create blogs, teach in local journalism programs, and freelance for other (noncompetitive) media outlets. Newspaper and magazine executives know that most of their people aren't particularly well compensated and letting them find other ways to make money will help increase their tenure at their publications. This policy has the added benefit of raising the profile of their publications—it's free public relations when their employees appear on shows or give talks and the names of their magazines and newspapers are mentioned.

Universities also provide their people with options to pursue side hustles and gigs. Tenured professors are allowed and often encouraged to do research, write books and articles, and speak at conferences, and they are given sabbaticals for this purpose. Professors in certain disciplines—business, computer science, engineering, medicine—often moonlight as consultants, and their income from consulting may be higher than their university salaries. Certain professors also can start their own companies, using university research facilities as a base. In some instances, professors join institutes either associated with the university or independent from it to pursue a particular field of study, often with financial benefits for the professor and the university.

Admittedly, universities, journalistic publications, and the entertainment industry can provide these various job options because the work is easily compartmentalized. This enables time commitments, compensation, and benefits to be allocated without too many conflicts or too much complexity. Hollywood projects are a defined movie, show, or other event. Journalistic pursuits involve writing or speaking on a particular subject. In universities, classes and publications can be compartmentalized (though it's a little more difficult when it comes to professors starting companies or launching research projects in conjunction with outside groups; how much compensation the university receives can be a matter of some debate).

Companies where the work isn't easily compartmentalized, however, have also made strides in offering alternatives to the traditional nine-to-five, one-job structure. Even though they may not give their employees opportunities for side jobs and hustles, they've changed their policies in ways that dovetail with the gig economy. Specifically, here are three common innovations:

1. **Flexible and hybrid work.** They've reduced the amount of time people have to be in the office to two or three days. Though they might not have an official policy about side hustles and passion projects, they provide de facto opportunities for employees to focus on other activities during work hours. Just by saving them commuting time two or three days a week, they open up the schedule for other pursuits.

2. **Four-day workweek.** This experiment is gaining popularity in a number of industries, and it usually involves no work on Friday. In essence, this becomes the day for employees to do their own thing—sometimes to make more money, sometimes to work at a hobby or other interest that they love.

3. **Job sharing.** This option has been around for a while but has become more popular after COVID. Essentially, two people share the same job and split the salary. It's a great option for employees who have side gigs that compensate them well or are committed to pursuing work about which they're passionate. And it's a great option for a company, in that two talented people can provide more knowledge and skills than one, resulting in greater productivity.

In my career, I've always encouraged side hustles because of the benefits I noted earlier: attracting/retaining talent, enhancing the company's reputation, and reducing costs. Two decades ago, I saw these benefits firsthand when my Starcom IP cofounder, Tim Harris, announced that he was leaving to start his own gaming company; gaming was his passion.

After discussions with Tim and my management, we worked with Tim to design two parallel jobs that would allow him to focus on his gaming but do so in a way that was a win-win for him and Starcom.

We recognized that games marketing was going to be something that companies would need. For this reason, we had Tim spend half his time starting a new unit of Starcom IP called Play, focused on gaming. The other half of his time would be devoted to the launch of his new company. Because he was both creating a gaming company and helping clients enter the gaming world, he would be more credible and connected to this world than anyone else in our company.

We reduced his compensation by half but retained his health benefits so he didn't have to worry about a lack of insurance for his family. Our arrangement with him also allowed him to receive some income while investing in a business. Starcom saved half of his salary, giving us the money to hire another gaming-focused employee. Tim could train this person, who would be available full time for our clients.

Play was a major success, helping clients like General Motors navigate the world of gaming, and we retained Tim for three more years before he switched full time to his entrepreneurial endeavors, which he continues to work on today.

Our willingness to be flexible with Tim gave us a model for use with other talented employees. We used it to attract world-class talent and then use variations of the model to launch units built around the passions of some of our key talent: Reverb, a unit focused on social media long before Twitter (now X) or Facebook, and Digits, a group that specialized in mobile before the iPhone.

Innovators in the Gig Space

It's not solely the businesses that can compartmentalize easily that are accommodating employees who want to pursue passion projects or side gigs. A number of companies in different industries have been exceptionally creative in designing policies and programs that meet their people's needs.

Rebel Business School is a company that offers free courses in entrepreneurship (they use a sponsorship model as their funding source). They permit employees to have a side hustle that isn't competitive with their core business, and they write this permission into employee contracts. The company believes a business benefit exists when side hustles are allowed. They value the entrepreneurial experience of employees who start their own businesses and find that these employees can apply this learning to their work at Rebel Business School.

As CEO Simon Paine put it in an interview with CNBC, "If the majority of the team have got their own experience of starting and failing, starting and succeeding . . . when they have conversations with the participants of our course, they're coming from a place of experience, and therefore, they've got more credibility."

This same CNBC story also focused on Tribal Worldwide London, a digital agency that encourages side hustles. Tom Roberts, their CEO, explained that employees are encouraged to have their own businesses, whether that means running a shop on Etsy or launching a coffee subscription brand. He, too, asserted that their company's clients value people who have side hustles because such people have personal experience with the business problems facing clients.

I'm on the board of a company called Nimble, which has engineered side hustles into its DNA. Providing talent to advertising agencies in order to augment these agencies' internal teams, Nimble employs full-time employees who are contracted out to one or more agencies. These people manage their hours and gain valuable experience while also having the benefits and stability of being full-time employees.

Perhaps it's easier for smaller, relatively young companies than older, larger corporations to create these gig-friendly policies. But the latter can and should learn from the former. This is the way of the future, and it will not only help them attract and retain the best and the brightest, but it will provide their people with invaluable business lessons that they can put to use for their employers.

A Matter of Trust

Can you trust people to work as hard for your company as for projects about which they're passionate or ones that may become financially lucrative businesses?

It's a reasonable question. But another question should be asked with it: What is the alternative?

If you distrust your people, you're going to bear the consequences of that distrust. Nonetheless, an entire industry has arisen based on distrust of employees who work off-site and a new type of software that monitors employees, called "tattleware." Time Doctor, for instance, captures videos of employees' screens while they work and can use the webcam to take pictures of employees every few minutes. Hubstaff tracks mouse movements and keyboard strokes and monitors web page visits. TSheets, a phone download, monitors employees' movements (locations) during work hours.

While this software is no doubt effective in preventing employees from spending time on nonwork matters, it also casts a Big Brother shadow over the enterprise.

In an interview with NPR, a woman monitored by tattleware said the following in reference to a short break for a phone conversation with a colleague, "I just feel like crap. I feel like I'm not trusted. I feel ashamed of myself. . . . My coworkers were really, really upset. But everyone was too afraid to say anything."

Organizations need to recognize that the cost savings realized through intrusive monitoring of workers isn't worth the price they ultimately pay. Perhaps more importantly, they need to address the underlying organizational attitudes that are counterproductive in the gig-economy era:

- a breakdown in trust between employer and employee

- a belief that employees belong to employers during working hours

- a measurement mismatch where companies believe they are buying hours while employees believe they are delivering outcomes

Failing to trust employees to do their main jobs well because they have side hustles and gigs is counterproductive. It betrays a twentieth-century management paranoia about workers—if you give them an inch, they'll take a mile.

The best twenty-first-century companies trust that their people will be sufficiently professional and adult to balance their commitments. They rely on communication and flexibility to ensure that the company and the employee thrive in the current environment. Side gigs or hustles may demand a greater time commitment from an employee than expected. Savvy organizations recognize this might happen, and to prevent it from being a deal-breaker, they request that employees inform management when they get enmeshed in their second jobs and work out a plan to ensure that their main work gets done effectively.

For organizations that remain skeptical about trusting their people in this environment, let me suggest that side hustles, especially, increase employee commitment to their main jobs for three reasons:

1. **Appreciation:** People are grateful to organizations for providing them with a steady income and insurance benefits as well as the chance to work at something that they love. This appreciation fosters loyalty and commitment, two qualities in short supply today.

2. **Control:** By being able to do two jobs, employees feel empowered; they believe they have some say over their future path. A sense of control is crucial during volatile, stressful periods.

3. **Pressure release:** The side hustle provides a release, especially during pressure-packed periods—layoffs, tight deadlines, a lot of travel. Rather than feeling like slaves to the demands of the organization, they value the time off from the grind—and the option of using that time off to work at something that provides a welcome change from the quotidian.

Establishing New Rules for a New Era

Every organization needs to find its own way when establishing procedures, protocols, and policies for side hustles and gigs. One size doesn't fit all, and the fast-growing start-up with many young employees may implement a different set of rules than a hundred-year-old corporation with lots of older employees.

Still, organizations should follow certain steps that will facilitate the transition to a gig-friendly culture. Here are four steps that should prove effective for both employees and employers:

1. **Discussion of mutual benefits:** Employer and employee should specify the benefits from employees' side hustles and passion projects—the benefits for both parties. When both groups understand what's in it for them, they'll be more motivated to make the new system function effectively.

2. **Expectations of deliverables:** What are the employee deliverables, outcomes, and standards? An employee should

have clarity on expectations. What work needs to be delivered (for example, products created, clients visited, and so on), what outcomes will be measured and are expected (for example, revenue generated), and what standards must be met (for example, 99 percent reliability, client satisfaction scores)? These outcomes, as long as they are met, is all that is required rather than input-driven expectations such as number of hours worked. If the work gets done, clients are happy, and a standard is maintained, then the employee is trusted to handle everything else.

3. **Code of conduct/messaging**: Establish what can and cannot be done in the side hustle, as well as what can and cannot be said to side-hustle clients/customers and vendors. By establishing codes of conduct, employees can avoid both disclosing proprietary information and conflicts, such as competing with their employer for an account.

4. **Monthly or quarterly check-ins:** Measure whether everything is working for both employees and employers. Regular discussions about whether both parties are benefitting—if employees are thriving working for the company and for themselves and if they're providing the agreed-upon deliverables—are essential. Keeping track of these issues enables course corrections to be made before things go too far off course.

CHAPTER 5

THE COVID CATALYST

If you ask people how the pandemic changed the job market, most will respond that it facilitated remote work. While this is obviously true, the ramifications of the COVID era are more far-reaching and complex than a growing number of employees working off-site. COVID not only accelerated trends that had developed before the pandemic but provided the spark for new trends. It changed not only how we worked but forced us to reexamine long-held assumptions about why we work. And it provided evidence that a new way of working was not only possible but productive and profitable.

There is no going back. Just as COVID gave us new tools to fight infectious disease, it also showed us a better way to work.

The Five Ways COVID Changed Work

Before the pandemic, the work paradigm was already evolving. Flattened organizational structures, open offices, flexible working hours, and other innovations were reshaping the workplace.

COVID, however, not only accelerated and embedded these and other changes but gave birth to new concepts, including the following five most significant areas of change:

WHERE WE WORK. This is the most obvious transformation. What may not be obvious, however, is that this change is permanent. Few white-collars jobs that can be done remotely will return to full-time office status. Yes, some companies have demanded their employees return to the office at least part of the time. But we're never going to see the old paradigm restored. Consider that only 50 percent of office buildings in San Francisco are occupied, and that New York City office rents have declined by 15 to 30 percent because of unused capacity. Before COVID, business leaders were skeptical about remote work. COVID, though, was the ultimate litmus test. It offered irrefutable proof that people could work as or more effectively outside the office.

HOW WE WORK. COVID taught everyone to Zoom. It created a comfort level with virtual meetings that had not existed previously. It helped people discover the value of project management from Salesforce and Asana. People adopted and adapted to technology out of necessity, and once they did, few wanted to return to less efficient and effective ways of doing and communicating about work.

WHEN WE WORK. The pandemic made nine-to-five an anachronism. It turned some weekends into workdays and weekdays into nonwork time. It created the realization that different people work best at different times—some are highly productive in the middle of the night while others are most creative at dawn. Liberated from the tyranny of the standard workweek, people can adjust their schedules to their natural work rhythms. A recent Stanford University study used geolocation data near US golf courses and found that 278 percent more people were playing golf on Wednesday at 4:00 p.m. in August 2022 than in August 2019. No doubt, more people are going to health clubs in the middle of the day, attending afternoon movies, and watching their kids play sports. They're also working at other times when they used to be relaxing. Instead of our life fitting around work, work is increasingly fitting around our lives.

HOW WE MANAGE AND ARE MANAGED. During the pandemic, work became unbundled and distributed. As a result, managers had to reinvent themselves and develop new skills. Pre-COVID, a great deal of their time was spent managing by walking around the office. Without the physical presence of employees, managers have been forced to rethink how they train and mentor people as well as how they inculcate corporate culture. Employees, too, need to make adjustments if they want to be managed differently. Sarah Hofstetter, president of Profitero, a board member of Campbell Soup Company, and someone I admire greatly, has this to say on the subject: "If employees want less management, more autonomy, and more flexibility, employers need to have the confidence that the employee is able to work independently, has the resilience for self-motivation, and the intellect to know when to ask for support."

Another issue, of course, is whether as much management is needed today as pre-COVID. The flattening of organizations, which began a number of years ago and picked up steam during the pandemic, is likely to continue.

And then there's "de-bossification." This means a decline in managers, controllers, monitors, evaluators, and paper pushers. COVID gave a lot of employees a taste of life without an omnipresent boss, and now many people want to make this their regular diet. Companies like Meta have been assessing why they have so many layers of managers and whether these layers add sufficient value to offset the way they slow down processes and add costs. As organizations flatten, at least some of these managerial positions will be eliminated.

WHY WE WORK. COVID jarred us into thinking differently or at least more deeply about the meaning of work. Until COVID, many of us didn't think a lot about why we work. We were the victims of inertia—we fell into routines and followed them unthinkingly until something made us examine them. That something was COVID.

- It forced us to work differently as we were pushed out of our familiar office environments.

- The death and serious illnesses of millions of people underlined the fragility of life and the importance of time, causing us to think about what was really important in our lives—both personally and professionally.

- It created new work habits, expectations, and behaviors, alternatives dictated both by necessity and preference.

People started questioning why they worked and what they liked and didn't like about their jobs; they asked themselves the following:

- Do I enjoy the work I'm doing?

- Do I respect my manager, and do I believe their role is critical?

- Do I need or want to return to my pre-COVID work routine?

- Do I have to stay in my current location to keep my job?

- Do I need a full-time job or, given the new flexibility of work, might a combination of jobs be more satisfying and meaningful?

Three COVID-Changed Companies

Crises affect both people and organizations in various ways. Going through them—whether a personal difficulty or an organizational one—often causes a change in attitude and behavior. After you enter a crucible, you exit a different person. Businesses made significant changes during the pandemic, altering a wide variety of policies and procedures. At the time, many leaders viewed these changes as temporary. Post-COVID, however, they recognized that at least some of the changes implemented during this period were beneficial and needed to be kept or even broadened in scope.

Let's look at three companies that emerged from COVID with dramatically different policies and processes.

In January 2021, leadership of the location geotechnology company TomTom created an innovative hybrid work structure in which employees decided whether they wanted to work in the office or at home. As their chief HR officer, Arne-Christian van der Tang said, "complete flexibility" is the most important feature of this work model. "Our employees know what's best for themselves," he said.

Although the company always had offices around the globe, employees can now live abroad for up to three months a year. "We've learned that our work location is less important than we thought it was," said van der Tang. "So, we're preparing for a post-COVID world where we can combine the best of both worlds—a world where choice and flexibility are key."

Capital One, a financial services business with forty thousand employees, learned a similar lesson to TomTom over the last few years, and they responded with a series of programs designed to make the company responsive to the employee, rather than vice versa. Based on employee surveys, they discovered "that associates want more individual flexibility and personal choice about where, when, and how they work," said former executive vice president Meghan Welch. "This feedback helped inform our recent decision that Capital One will be a hybrid work company going forward."

The company recognized that the pandemic caused employees to rethink their lives, and as a result Capital One also rethought their approach to what they offer employees. They determined that employees' physical, emotional, and financial well-being are closely intertwined, and the quality of each affects the other. For that reason, Capital One began offering everything from on-campus health-care centers—including access to affordable mental health care for associates and their families—to dedicated days that encourage focus on personal and professional development.

Plenty of companies went remote during the worst of the pandemic and have now defaulted to either a hybrid arrangement or brought everyone back full time. The file-storage service Dropbox, which owns DocSend and HelloSign, wanted to be more intentional. After announcing it was going "virtual first" in October 2020, Dropbox rethought its offices as "Dropbox Studios"— gathering places meant for cross-team collaboration and team building rather than everyday work. The company has also designated a four-hour window during which all employees have to be available in person or online so that they can connect and collaborate. Outside these "core collaboration hours" during the workday, the employees have flexibility on how and when they get their work done. In the quarter after instituting the change, Dropbox delivered a solid financial performance, with double-digit revenue growth compared with a year earlier, doubling its profitability.

Positive Results

Not every company has followed the lead of Dropbox, Capital One, and TomTom. A significant number of organizations have attempted to restore the status quo after the pandemic. Understandably, they find the emerging work paradigm unfamiliar and more than a little scary. Perhaps it would be less scary if they understood that COVID-catalyzed changes have improved the workplace in a variety of ways.

Perhaps the most positive outcome has been increased productivity. Contrary to many experts' expectations in COVID's early days, people are often more productive when working remotely. In The Conference Board's three-year tracking study, they determined that as company leaders and managers wrap their minds around the need for hybrid working environments and create responsive processes and structures, they began to believe their people become more productive: In April 2020, just when people began to work from home, 35 percent believed there had been a moderate to substantial drop in productivity. Two years later that number had dropped to 9 percent. Similarly, in April 2020, only 23 percent of organizations believed their talent was more productive, which soared to 57 percent by March 2022.

A recent University of Birmingham study of 597 managers has shed light on how managers' attitudes toward the hybrid work model have changed as a result of the pandemic, revealing an increasingly positive outlook toward remote and flexible working.

The study found that 52 percent of managers agreed that working from home improves concentration, 60 percent said it improves productivity, and 63 percent stated it increases motivation. This is a significant shift in attitude, as there has long been a perception that working from home can be a distraction, leading to only a lack of productivity and motivation.

The study also determined that more than seven in ten managers (73 percent) felt that giving employees flexibility over their working hours increased productivity, while 60 percent said the same for working from home. This suggests that managers are starting to recognize that giving employees more control over when and where they work can lead to better performance.

That same Conference Board three-year study also showed increased flexibility in hiring because of the pandemic and that this flexibility benefits both organizations and their employees. Before the pandemic, 46 percent of surveyed HR leaders indicated that their organizations were not willing to hire virtual employees, and 8 percent were willing in the US or globally. Now 49 percent are willing to hire 100 percent virtually, a sixfold increase. The flexibility not only makes it easier to attract talent but helps organizations acquire more diverse talent, since they're recruiting from a much larger pool.

While COVID wasn't solely responsible for company cultures becoming kinder and gentler, the toll that the pandemic took caused many leaders to take a step back and think about what's important—in work and in life. As a result, cultures have become more open—leaders are more receptive to listening to their people, to supporting the need for work-life balance, and to creating more diverse workplaces.

Time magazine interviewed representatives of three very different companies in three very different industries—JBS Foods, the world's largest global poultry producer; LinkedIn; and Jones Soda—to learn how their cultures had evolved.

JBS CEO Tim Schellpeper (who has now retired) talked about how they greatly increased the number of listening sessions with team members, attempting to engage with employees and give them more opportunities to succeed.

LinkedIn added a key question to its quarterly employee survey: *How are you?* The responses prompted the company to roll out several new employee-focused initiatives.

Jones Soda organized online Friday afternoon happy hours during COVID, where the majority of employees showed up for a semblance of their pre-COVID get-togethers at a nearby craft beer restaurant, helping people maintain and strengthen relationships with each other.

These three examples may seem like small things, but they reflect a sincere and growing desire on the part of management to treat people like people—with kindness and respect.

COVID has also prepared us for the workplace of the future. To accommodate employees during the pandemic, companies initiated programs designed to facilitate gig work and side hustles, flexible hours, and other untraditional work policies. They also introduced and improved various technologies such as augmented/virtual reality and AI. Though the goal may not have been to prepare people for the office of the future, these innovations had that effect. My first book, *Restoring the Soul of Business*, was written just before COVID hit, and I had a chapter on how to manage distributed cultures in a world of screens because it was so obvious that we were not leveraging the software and infrastructure available in 2019 but working as if it were 2009. COVID accelerated every company's technological capabilities and advanced its work policies, aligning organizations and individuals with future trends.

Changing Our Minds

As this book's title suggests, we need to rethink work, and COVID triggered this rethinking process. In a recent Oracle AI@Work study, 88 percent of respondents said the meaning of success has changed for them and that they're now prioritizing things like work-life balance, mental health, and flexibility. In a *BBC Worklife* article, Alison Omens, chief strategy officer of JUST Capital, notes, "Our data over the years has always shown that the thing people care about most is how companies treat their employees." During the pandemic, "the intensity has increased in terms of that expectation; people are expecting more from companies. The early days of the pandemic reminded us that people are not machines," says Omens. "If you're worried about your kids, about your health, financial insecurity, and covering your bills, and all the things that come with being human, you're less likely to be productive. And we were *all* worried about those things."

How has COVID changed our minds? Here are five ways:

1. Life is short, and there is more to life than work.

A pandemic causes you to think about your own mortality and making the most of the time you have. For this reason, many people—especially younger people—are unwilling to sacrifice everything for their careers. The parent with the newborn child doesn't want to be traveling two weeks every month. The person with the high-stress job doesn't want to sacrifice her physical and mental health to meet difficult deadlines and satisfy a demanding boss.

According to a recent *Harvard Business Review* article, 76 percent of the workers polled believe that employees will be more likely to prioritize lifestyle (family and personal interests) over proximity to work and will pursue jobs in locations where they can focus on both—even if it means taking a pay cut.

2. Work is now just a part of life and not one's identity.

In an article on CNBC's Make It website, therapist Shoaib Memon said that his patients talked less about work during the pandemic than previously; they no longer spent therapy sessions unpacking workplace trauma and instead focused on topics outside of work, such as being new parents or starting a hobby.

It's not that work has ceased to be important. It's that they've recognized that as important as work might be, it's not the only thing. People reprioritized during COVID. While some people still define themselves by their profession—doctors, lawyers, and so on—fewer do than previously. And obviously, many millennials and Gen Zers are more excited to work for a no-name start-up than for IBM or General Motors. In addition, many individuals find their work identity through side hustles and passion projects rather than through a single employer.

3. Hybrid work gives one control over life and has changed the balance of power, which will not be given back.

The Pew Research Center website has an article titled "COVID-19 Pandemic Continues to Reshape Work in America." A 2022 Pew study showed that among employed adults working from home part of the time (and who rarely or never worked from home pre-COVID), 64 percent say working from home has made it easier to balance work and their personal life.

This may not be a revelation, but it's revelatory to experience this shift. As I've emphasized, the power has shifted from employer to employee, and this shift facilitates the pursuit of personal and professional interests in meaningful ways. Once people have led a life that is in balance, they don't want to return to the stress of an imbalanced one.

4. People are rejecting overwork and burnout.

After two exhausting years, Sahaj Kohli, a Washington, DC-based therapist-in-training and founder of Brown Girl Therapy, says burned-out workers are having to break down the mentality that "if you're not tired at the end of the day, you're not working hard enough." Instead of working to the point of burnout, Kohli says that because of COVID and remote work, her patients have seen that they can enjoy a slower pace of living.

This doesn't mean that people will become slackers or just do the minimum necessary. It does mean that they'll find ways to get work done effectively in less time and recognize that if they're mentally and physically exhausted, their work is going to suffer. The Puritan work ethic will be replaced by a more focused one that's aligned with the current age. Working smarter, not harder, is the new mantra.

5. People no longer put up with toxic cultures.
The Great Resignation, according to the MIT Sloan School of Management, is driven by people who were fleeing from a toxic culture and poor management rather than for the usual reasons—better pay, or a more prestigious position or company.

According to the MIT Sloan analysis, toxic culture results from poor diversity efforts, a lack of inclusion, employees feeling disrespected, and unethical conduct. These issues have always been problems for organizations, but COVID lowered people's tolerance for toxicity. Life is short. You can be struck down by an illness or hit by a truck tomorrow. Therefore, why put up with an environment that makes you miserable?

Not an Isolated Event

"COVID was an anomaly."

"What happened during the pandemic stays in the pandemic."

"We shouldn't take the changes that took place over the last few years too seriously. Everything always reverts to the mean."

It's understandable why people believe these statements. Most of us prefer the familiar to the unknown, the tried-and-true to the untested.

If we take the lessons of COVID to heart, though, we understand that restoring the status quo makes no sense. As I'm fond of saying, our minds are like champagne corks: they swell and don't fit back in the bottle.

This doesn't mean that everything will be different in the future. In fact, a March 2023 headline in the *Wall Street Journal* proclaimed, "Work-From-Home Era Ends for Millions of Americans." In the retail sector, in particular, more people are working on-site. In nonretail companies, some of the workers have returned to offices, at least part of the time.

To think that this is a start of a "return to normal," however, fails to recognize that there is a new normal. The changes that picked up steam during COVID are permanent, especially the following shifts:

- **Much more remote-only work.** Many companies will offer more fully remote jobs than they did before the pandemic. Currently, the number of these jobs are three times more than the prepandemic level.

- **Hybrid becomes the norm.** Relatively few companies are insisting that all their employees return to five-day, nine-to-five schedules. For many organizations, two to three days in the office has become the norm.

- **Greater use of technology to enable distributed work.** A McKinsey study determined that COVID accelerated the rollout of technology by seven to ten years. For instance, one year into COVID, many companies had digitally enabled 80 percent of customer interactions.

Despite these shifts, some business leaders continue to insist that people must return full time to the office to preserve culture, to maintain product and service quality, to maximize team effectiveness, and to facilitate hiring and training processes. When people insist on this old paradigm, I cite three advantages of the new work protocols:

1. **Larger pools of talent.** Having implemented at least some unbundled and distributed work during the pandemic has enlarged companies' talent pools. Not only have they been able to hire from any market, but they've been able to access out-of-office talent that was previously unavailable—moms and dads looking after children, people unable to commute because of distance or other reasons, individuals who want to work only part time. After enlarging their talent pool during COVID, no company wants to shrink it post-COVID.

2. **Reduced costs.** The savings that were realized during the pandemic stem from a number of sources, including the indirect one of hiring from a larger talent pool. During the COVID era, organizations saved money through reduced travel and entertainment expenses, selling off real estate (unused or underused because of COVID restrictions or employee layoffs), reduced staff, and other decreased overhead costs, as a greater percentage of the workforce was contracted or part time. For many companies, it was startling to realize that their businesses could still run well with a smaller budget. Suddenly, what once was seen as necessary spending seemed to be overspending.

3. **Future flexibility.** During COVID, we entered the Third Connected Age of Technology. With the start of remote work, organizations were driven to implement new technologies and teach their people to use them. Without virtual meeting apps like Zoom and Microsoft Teams,

organizations would have struggled to bring their employees together to discuss and decide on key issues. Instead of having people work with 2008 technology (which companies were doing in 2019), organizations capitalized on tech innovations during COVID and prepared their workforces for the future. The tools developed over the last few years give organizations great flexibility in terms of hiring, integrating full- and part-time and remote workers, partnering with diverse groups, and so on.

Some command-and-control leaders, of course, are convinced that we will follow the lead of businesses in places like China and some European countries, where employees are spending more time in their offices than they are in the US. While many factors mitigate against a return to the office for all employees—and a return to other pre-COVID practices—the major one is this:

Unbundled and distributed work is here to stay because it enables significant competitive advantage to companies that embrace them.

Think of it this way: Imagine you're a company starting today and were asked to choose between door A and door B.

DOOR A: You are limited to accessing talent who can afford to live near your headquarters or must work full time. This talent works only for you and relies on you for their entire income. This system creates loyalty, but the employees are less likely to challenge the status quo.

This door gives you greater control over your people and a return to a simpler way to manage and organize.

DOOR B: You can access talent from anywhere in the world, and they can work for you half, three-quarters, or full time, providing you with variability in employee cost and giving them the flexibility to fit their work into their life versus fitting their life into work.

At the same time, this ability increases complexity and requires enhanced management styles. You also gain cost management flexibility.

BUSINESSES THAT MUST attract white-collar and knowledge workers and ask people to return to the office for three or four or five days a week—versus coming together for a couple of days a week or for specific training, creative endeavors, or relationship-building events—are in effect choosing door A; they will probably find themselves at a significant competitive disadvantage to companies that choose door B and plot a course through the initial messiness and complexity that comes with this door.

The New Way Forward

How do organizations adapt to all the changes that COVID has brought about? I've studied a number of companies that have prospered by choosing door B, and they share four key traits:

1. **Sensitivity to employee concerns.** During the pandemic, power shifted to employees. Many of them became willing to exercise this power, voicing their opinions on

everything from diversity policies to environmental concerns. Companies would be wise to be responsive to these voiced opinions. At the very least, they need to listen constantly to the chatter—whether online or in person—and respond to what they hear. Some organizations, for instance, have implemented wellness programs in response to employee health concerns. Others have heard their people talk about the need to support communities aligned with their passion projects (environment, diversity, and so on). Management consultant and book author Mario Moussa articulated this responsive listening approach well: "Employers and employees need to reimagine the workplace together, versus employers just imposing the policies they've always had."

2. **Willingness to adjust and adapt.** During the pandemic, many rigid rules and policies were ignored or modified. Organizations can no longer impose inflexible policies and programs on their people. The businesses that are balancing the best of unbundled work with the best of in-person interaction demonstrate admirable agility. Rather than take an either-or approach, they are attempting to obtain the best of both worlds.

3. **Trust.** During the COVID years, the best companies trusted that their people would be diligent and productive, even when they were out of the office and not being supervised—and the companies that attempted to use software to monitor their employees' every waking, working moment found that their distrust was alienating and counterproductive. Going forward, organizations must trust that their employees know how to balance remote and in-person work to deliver the best results. They must have sufficient faith that if they provide access and

resources, individuals and teams will figure out the best courses of action.

4. **Redesigned infrastructure.** The old infrastructures were rendered null and void by COVID—everything from traditional offices to outmoded technologies. Organizations that are thriving now and will thrive in the future are rethinking and rebuilding physical facilities, technologies, HR policies, and other areas to support an evolving range of behaviors and in anticipation of a new generation of technologies, such as AI.

SECTION II

WHAT WORK WILL BECOME

CHAPTER 6

FRACTIONALIZED EMPLOYEES

Perhaps you're skeptical about this chapter title's prediction. Understandably, it's difficult to imagine a time when many organizations have these hybrid employees—people who work 50 or 75 percent of the time but are provided with the benefits of full-time staff. As of this writing, at least, this employee type remains an exception rather than the rule in many companies.

I feel confident, though, that this prediction will come to pass. Part of my confidence is because of various trends and changing attitudes, which I'll detail. Part of it, though, is based on my own experience.

In June 2019, I stopped working full time at Publicis Groupe after a thirty-seven-year career. For the next year, I worked only 50 percent of the time but remained an employee of the company receiving half my previous compensation but with full health insurance and many other long-term benefits.

I used the other half of my time to write my first book.

As a freelance or as a contract employee I would not have retained employment nor the full-time employee benefits I continued to enjoy.

You may also recall the story I told in chapter 4 about Tim Harris, a highly valued employee from earlier in my career. Tim decided he wanted to start a gaming company, and to avoid losing him, I created a plan where he could pursue his passion project while retaining employment with our Starcom IP; he would work half of the time but receive full benefits like other employees (the health-care benefits were especially important, since Tim had small children at the time). The arrangement worked out great for both Tim and Starcom IP.

Admittedly, Tim's story and my own represent a small sample size for a big prediction. Therefore, we need to look at the many other compelling factors that shape my perspective. First, let's define clearly what a fractionalized employee is and might become.

A Natural Evolution

On the surface, the definition of a fractionalized employee is simple—someone who chooses to work 50 or 75 percent of the time and receives full employment benefits. The choice is made at the start of the year or when a life event occurs (health issues, birth of child, and so on). We need to look beneath the surface, however, to understand what this new employee type signifies and why it's so well suited to the current environment.

Consider how the traditional work model forces people to make impossible decisions: between staying at a company they love or leaving to pursue a passion project; between returning to work a few weeks or months after having a child or quitting the job and staying home.

Clearly, a hybrid employment policy benefits individuals who are caught on the horns of this dilemma.

Though I'll delineate the employer benefits of the fractionalized model later in this chapter, for now recognize that it helps organizations attract and retain talent, reduce costs, and motivate people to concentrate on the tasks at hand.

Despite these benefits, many companies have shied away from implementing fractionalized policies, with the exception of businesses in Europe and Australia. In the latter, up to a quarter of part-time employees receive full benefits (primarily funded and driven by high taxes and social safety nets).

Nonetheless, some early adopters have recognized the value of the fractionalized employee concept. The retail industry, including companies such as Starbucks, Costco, Chipotle, and REI, offer insurance, stock, 401(k)s, and educational stipends to anyone who works more than twenty to thirty hours weekly. Nonretailers have been slow to recognize the value of this policy, in part because they didn't feel the trade-offs were worth it—the cost, the administrative difficulty, and fear of turnover and lack of dedication to the job.

In the post-COVID environment, however, fractionalized employment aligns with many employee mindsets and helps win the war for talent (which is in increasingly short supply).

Shock to the System

In the last few years, people have started to rethink long-held assumptions about work. As I've noted, more people are working less than full time (as freelancers or part-time contractors) as they try to achieve work-life balance or focus on side hustles and gigs. AI is beginning to boost productivity and eliminate much rote and process work, enabling companies to reduce employee hours and enabling employees to earn higher salaries for fewer hours of work. The parallel with Ford Motor Company's innovation in 1914 is instructive. When Ford automated their assembly lines, they doubled worker pay to five dollars per day and created an eight-hour workday. Ford shifted everyone's perspective on work, just as AI is doing now.

Combine the work-life balance issue and the desire for side hustles and gigs with AI and an aging workforce, and you can see how a significant shock is being delivered to the system—a shock that is felt by entry-level workers as well as senior executives.

The fractionalized employee concept can help everyone weather this shock, but only if three criteria are met:

1. **Mutual benefit:** Fractionalized employment will make sense only when both the employer and the employee can benefit from such an arrangement. People don't want a system that imposes half-time work on them when they want to work full time. Companies don't want a system where they are creating part-time jobs for tasks that require full-time staff.

2. **Type of job:** Some jobs can be done half time and others cannot. For instance, demanding clients and customers will not accept an account person who is available only 50 percent of the time. Similarly, an executive with many full-time direct reports cannot be a good supervisor if she is unavailable two or three days a week.

3. **Sustained need for expertise and/or seniority:** Given that a fractionalized employee costs more than a freelance or contract employee, the hire has to be worth the additional expense. This usually translates into a fractionalized hire who possesses a certain type of expertise—the type that is needed for an extended period or is differentiated because of the individual's reputation or legacy with

88

the company. In the examples that opened this chapter, my thirty-seven-year history with Publicis, and Tim's relationships with his team and the rarity of his skills, justified the additional cost.

Common Objections

At this point, you may be thinking about all the reasons why your organization can't implement a fractional employee program—too much complex paperwork, distrust of the commitment of someone who works only half the time, and so on. I'm not dismissing concerns about integrating this "new" type of employee into an organizational system, but when these concerns turn into roadblocks, it stops people from thinking about fractionalized possibilities. Too often, executives who create obstacles to this hybrid idea harbor mistaken beliefs about work, including:

- One should not adapt systems and procedures for the future but force work to fit into today's systems.

- Managers cannot be trained or grow into managing differently.

- Only someone working full time is devoted to a company.

- Clients and customers care only how much time their service providers spend on their business (versus the expertise and dedication they exhibit).

- Talented individuals are like cows, perfectly willing to graze on dried, brown grass even when they're not given opportunities to sample greener pastures.

As I expect you agree, these beliefs may hurt organizations in the short term and may destroy them in the long term. They demonstrate an inability to envision work as anything but what is known. Still, a great deal of misinformation exists that can cause people to object (sometimes strenuously) to the fractionalized employee concept. Here are the most common objections and the counterarguments:

- **It's hard to administer.** If you're in HR, you're probably already fretting about all the forms and new policies that must be put in place to handle benefits-receiving employees who work only part of the time. Perhaps this fretting can be minimized a bit if you think of a fractionalized employee as a freelancer with a fixed number of hours who is also receiving health and other benefits. Most HR software is designed to accommodate freelancers.

- **Fractionalized employees won't be sufficiently motivated.** The false logic here is that if you aren't working full time, you're not fully invested in the job. As a former manager of fractionalized employees and one myself for a year, I found that we felt fortunate to have this opportunity; we were grateful to have our cake and eat it too. Our gratitude translated into eagerness to pay back the company for this opportunity. We had a good reason to be more dedicated than most. Fractionalized workers have skin in the game, unlike a freelancer or contractor. Because they receive benefits, they possess a long-term perspective—they want to sustain the relationship for years, not weeks or months, and are motivated to deliver excellent work.

- **Work and client/customer relationships will suffer.** Yes, some clients and customers are demanding. Yes, some expect their key person to be available during traditional work hours (and sometimes at other times also). But companies can manage these situations to ensure that their clients and customers remain satisfied with the work. If a fractionalized employee isn't right for a particular customer, then don't assign the account to that individual. Perhaps more to the point, if a client has a great relationship with a particular employee who wants to transition to fractional status, pose this question to the client: Would you want us to retain this individual 50 or 75 percent of the time versus letting her go? Most clients I know would insist on the former option. This is someone the client values highly, and even 50 percent of this value is better than no value at all.

- **It creates an exodus of talent.** Perhaps this is true eventually. The fractionalized employee turns his passion project into a successful business and leaves the organization to devote all his hours to it. But a fractionalized policy also extends the time this employee is with the company. Generally, fractionalized employees require a few years before they can turn their part-time venture into a full-time one. This expectation also creates a window during which the company can prepare clients and customers for a valued employee's departure as well as hire and train this person's replacement.

A Great Benefits Policy

Though the fractionalized employee concept is still in the beta testing phase at organizations that have adopted it, we know enough about its impact from their experiences to recognize the significant benefits—benefits that run the gamut, from cost savings to employee motivation.

But the biggest benefit has to do with talent.

The best companies, very much like the best sports teams, tend to have a disproportionate share of passionately aligned and improving talent striving to achieve a common outcome—customer satisfaction, superior products and services, and great financial results.

The real differentiator is talent. All things being equal, the better talent will win because it is talent that comes up with ideas, designs the products, and provides the services that allow organizations to excel.

The fractionalized option allows a business to attract a disproportionate share of talent that is passionate about their work. It allows them to leverage talent better than companies that reject fractionalized workers.

Consider how fractionalized employees affect culture. They often see themselves as long-term rather than short-term employees and as such are much more invested in the company than others. They're also happier employees (as the earlier "having their cake and eating it too" analogy conveyed). And fractionalized employees also tend to be more diverse than the average; the fractionalized concept appeals to women, parents, the health challenged, and those who are caregiving for aging parents or other relatives. The greater the diversity, the greater the creativity and, ultimately, profit.

Another benefit of fractionalized policies is efficiency. It reduces costs by bringing in and retaining expertise at 50 or 75 percent of full-time compensation rather than paying 100 percent. It also gives organizations the option to cut costs without layoffs, implementing a fractionalized strategy to reduce people's workloads and compensation during tough times.

A third benefit involves retaining key talent, especially among parents and older employees. At a time of aging and flattening populations, organizations are in danger of losing people with great institutional knowledge and expertise. These older employees may not want to work full time because of health reasons, lack of financial need, and a desire to pursue other interests. But if they were given the option of working less but still retaining health care and other benefits, many of them would choose to remain with the company longer. Parents, too, would be given an incentive for remaining employees rather than to stay home full time with their kids. The exodus of new moms from companies, especially, is a significant challenge for organizations attempting to find a good gender balance. A fractional policy not only will ensure that a significant percentage stay with the company during the first few years of their child's life but will increase the odds that if and when they decide to return to full-time work, they will do so with the company that provided them with a fractionalized employment option.

Fourth, organizations with fractionalized employees will become magnets for talent. They'll have a competitive advantage over companies that don't offer fractionalized work, be able to draw from a wider populace, and attract a lot of bright, forward-thinking people—individuals who are looking ahead and seeing the possibility that at some point in the future, they might want to take advantage of the fractionalized way of working.

Where and How the Model Will Work

The fractionalized employee model is applicable across many industries, companies, and occupations, both white collar and some blue collar. The reason? Most companies, whether they are in the knowledge, service, or manufacturing sector, will have a need to retain or attract specialists and other key people—senior folks within a company looking to slow down or experts seeking flexibility to pursue outside activities.

Try an experiment: Examine the organization to which you belong and identify veteran employees who possess decades of experience or well-honed skills that are rare or irreplaceable. It might be a foreman who understands how all the machinery works—and what to do when it doesn't work—better than anyone. It might be a hospital administrator who can cut through bureaucratic red tape with astonishing ease.

Organizations don't want to lose these "old salts," and fractionalized employment can help retain them. This is especially true in developed countries with aging populations where there is a shortage of craftspeople, teachers, nurses, and carpenters, not just computer scientists and doctors or other specialists.

Three specific needs will drive companies to adopt fractionalized policies:

1. **Retention:** to retain access to expert talent on an ongoing basis. These are often senior or other very talented folks.

2. **Attraction:** to attract talent, some of whom may not wish to work full time.

3. **Skill enhancement:** to update knowledge and other competences as business changes. The half-life of knowledge in many industries is shrinking, and often senior individuals need to go back into intensive training. Sometimes this may require one or two years of half-time training. The fractionalized employee does not have to give up income to learn new expertise, and by being treated as an employee during their training period they are more likely to come back full time to the company.

In different industries, these needs will manifest themselves in a variety of ways. It's useful to examine three different industries to see why and how they'll take advantage of the fractionalized concept.

In manufacturing, for instance, there's great concern about the aging workforce. A study by The Manufacturing Institute found that "most manufacturing firms are both aware and concerned about the aging of the manufacturing workforce. . . . [They] are particularly concerned about brain drain (i.e., the loss of institutional and technical knowledge). . . . Firms across the manufacturing sector are taking steps to mitigate the impact of the aging workforce on their business. Almost 90 percent of manufacturing companies surveyed reported capitalizing on the talents and experiences of their older workers."

A fractionalized program would provide manufacturers with access to experts who could train and mentor the next generation. By offering more seasoned employees the option of coming in for a couple of shifts a week to help train next-generation talent and be available to troubleshoot from time to time, this program would be relatively easy to implement.

In-person service industries is a second sector that should embrace fractionalized employees. Nursing, for instance, is a field where employees (nurses) must be physically present and where demand for personnel outpaces supply.

The American Nurses Association projected that more registered nurse jobs will be available through 2022 than in any other profession in the US. According to an article in *Nursing Times*, the US Bureau of Labor Statistics similarly projects that more than 275,000 additional nurses are needed from 2020 to 2030. Employment opportunities for nurses are projected to grow at a faster rate (9 percent) than all other occupations, from 2016 through 2026.

Combine aging baby boomers in need of nursing services with nurse burnout (exacerbated by COVID), and you can understand why organizations from nursing homes to hospitals want to find a way to attract more nurses and keep their experienced practitioners.

Now imagine if two nurses could share a shift either by being there for half a shift or on alternate days. This would ameliorate the problem of burnout and facilitate work-life balance. It could also provide nurses with time to get trained or generate additional income. The fractionalized employee model would retain many nurses who do not want to work full time and be able to bring in people who want to work part time. Because nursing responsibilities can be shared relatively easily, it would also accommodate two employees on fractionalized schedules.

Teaching is another profession that could capitalize on fractionalized employees. Like nursing, teaching is experiencing a significant shortage. In an August 2022 paper, "Is There a National Teacher Shortage?" Tuan D. Nguyen and Chanh B. Lam, both of Kansas State University, and Paul Bruno of the University of Illinois Urbana-Champaign wrote that they systematically examined news reports, US Department of Education data, and publicly available information on teacher shortages for every state in the US, discovering "at least 36,000 vacant positions along with at least 163,000 positions being held by underqualified teachers."

Teachers are also struggling with other challenges, from political/community interference in what they teach to the threat of violence. They're also dealing with relative low pay (many teachers love to teach but cannot afford to teach full time), training hurdles (new curriculum and skills require teachers to be constantly certified), and work-life balance (family and other issues).

Because teachers can split courses or teach only a given semester or specific courses, the field lends itself to fractionalized employment, offering individuals a chance to have half or three-quarters of the usual workload. It also would provide schools with a way to reduce costs, a significant concern in many school districts around the country.

Again, fractionalized employment won't work for every type of job in every field. Many service jobs in advertising, consulting, and law, for instance, operate with client assumptions that their professionals will be available to them on demand. If you're a business and can't access your lawyer while you're going through a major lawsuit, you'll be understandably upset.

Unlike manufacturing and service jobs, which can be easily broken into projects or shifts, professional service firms require a more nuanced approach to deploy fractionalized employment widely.

Still, it can be implemented selectively if these service firms:

- Extend the role of certain senior leaders who can step down from full-time operating roles but remain advisers to the firm or to clients. This works because clients benefit by getting access to people they respect but have full-time, dedicated people who have replaced them in operational roles.

- For a period of six to twenty-four months, enable key people to become fractionalized employees, so they can deal with family issues or go back to school. The role of these individuals may need to be changed to address their limited availability (often they are accessible all the time but not accessible for as much time as in the past) by shifting some time-critical tasks to other team members. Clients tend to support this change because they realize that without this accommodation they would lose access to the talent and expertise completely and because they recognize how issues can be addressed with changed staffing and periodic check-ins.

Facilitating Implementation

Organizations can do a lot to make the transition to fractionalized employees as seamless as possible. Here are three basic steps that everyone can take:

First, recognize that a flexible-hour policy dovetails with the fractionalized approach. This means allowing work to be done at any time or within certain windows. Obviously, some jobs require continuous presence over sustained time periods, and flexibility isn't possible for many doctors or teachers; they have to be in the hospital or classroom for continuous hours to help patients or students. It's also difficult to be flexible with CEOs' hours, since they must be accessible to employees, media, analysts, and other groups during traditional working hours.

On the other hand, nurses, substitute teachers, and even CFOs could (and often do) have flexible-hour jobs—two nurses can share a shift, and substitute teachers are available only on certain days. While CFOs are key executives, many companies cannot afford or don't need a full-time, world-class CFO. For them, retaining a highly competent but fractionalized CFO (with a strong, supportive staff) is better than having to settle for a mediocre, but less expensive, full-time substitute.

Given that many jobs no longer require the daily physical presence of employees, flexibility is a relatively low bar for many organizations and jobs.

Second, target jobs that can be divided into smaller assignments. If a job can be broken into a set of discrete deliverables, it allows people to select the assignments they want. A software writer might focus on assignments that take advantage of his specific skills; an English literature professor may choose to teach upper-level courses that concentrate on nineteenth-century novels; an attorney may be interested only in doing research, rather than dealing with clients or appearing in court. When jobs can be broken into LEGO-like pieces, companies will find it easier to combine different workers to achieve specific goals.

Again, technological advances will make divisibility more practical than in the past. Machine augmentation will "projecticize" work, similar to the way tasks are segmented in the consulting and entertainment industries. The growing need for highly specific expertise, too, will lend itself to divisibility.

Third, delegate tasks. Most tasks require teams; one employee isn't responsible for all the assignments. Teams working on a task can shift a fractionalized worker's task responsibilities to another employee when that worker isn't available. This delegation allows for continuity of work and if done well, it can grow other people's skills so they can handle the task with the same expertise as the fractionalized person.

Four, establish a clear understanding of when an employee is available and expected to be available, such as every Tuesday, Wednesday, and Thursday if they are working 60 percent of the time. Without clear-cut transparency, managers and talent will be out of sync.

On a more granular level, companies can enact policies and create rules that will maximize the advantages of fractionalized work. Ironically, given fractionalized employment's flexibility, it requires the following rigid structures to succeed:

Processes

Limited choices. Employees who wish to work less than full time but get full health benefits and prorated financial benefits such as bonuses or equity should be given only two alternative levels: x percent or y percent of full time. This limitation makes the program easier to administer and manage. If people were allowed to select any percentage, it would be a nightmare to run payroll and to arrange coverage when they were off work.

Limited sign-up/change periods. An employee can decide to change their percentage only once a year, during a particular two-week period—perhaps in September for the following year. The only exception would be for a major life or health event. This enables companies to forecast how many workers they will need and how work gets covered. It also enables far easier administration.

Limited eligibility. Being selective helps funnel high-performing candidates into the fractionalized program, a key measure since the program is designed for the company's best talent and those well-versed in the company's culture and processes. To limit eligibility, the following criteria are useful:

- Having a minimum number of years of service. For example, one must have worked in the company for at least two years full time before becoming eligible.

- Achieving a specific level of performance or a minimum rating level (only candidates who are performing at acceptable levels).

- Restricting eligibility. Certain roles require full-time presence, such as overseeing a large team or providing continuous service to a highly demanding customer, and thus wouldn't be eligible.

Compensation

Making compensation fair, transparent, and easy to understand is essential. Base compensation should be adjusted for percentage of time worked. If an employee was earning $150,000 for full-time work, they will be paid $75,000 for half-time work.

All other cash compensation, like bonuses and stock grants, should be prorated to percentage of salary. While salary, bonus, and stock can be prorated to percentage of time worked, health-care benefits are at 100 percent and deductions are at 100 percent.

This simplicity and transparency minimizes resentment. It's easy for people considering this program to calculate the financial downsides of deciding to work 50 or 75 percent before they apply.

Evaluation and oversight

Fractionalized employees should not be evaluated differently than full-time employees. Do they deliver a level of outcome and service or output to which they've agreed? If so, they should be rewarded just as if they were working full time. Given that many fractionalized employees will be working outside of the office, they shouldn't be monitored more closely than full-timers who may also be engaged in remote work. The worst thing a company can do is evaluate and monitor these fractionalized employees as if they were a less trustworthy, less capable employee group.

A playbook

Every company needs to create a playbook that spells out all the various expectations, guidelines, eligibility criteria, and other details that makes sense for their company or industry. Smart companies and leaders will then periodically update and revisit the playbook, to incorporate learning and changing circumstances.

Four Motivating Factors

Now and especially in the future, who will apply for fractionalized employment? Let's look at the four emerging factors that will motivate people to apply:

FAMILY CARE. While different types of family issues can cause people to reduce their time at work, the two most common are eldercare and childcare. The former will be especially prevalent in the coming years as America ages rapidly—millennials and others will face some tough choices. A combination of emotional reasons (a desire to look after their parents who looked after them) or financial needs (assisted care and home nursing being even more expensive in the coming years) causes many employees to face a difficult either-or choice: continue working full time to pay for care or leave a job to care for their family members. The latter choice may not be feasible, however, if they still need an income. They may also find great satisfaction in their job and hate the prospect of leaving it entirely. Fractionalized employment, therefore, makes sense for these individuals on two different levels.

A similar situation exists with childcare choices. While many parents (usually mothers) return to work after maternity leave, many of them find it emotionally difficult to be away from their children. In addition, full-time childcare is becoming more expensive, so there's a financial burden as well. The fractionalized option is a good compromise for many parents. Though it reduces their compensation, that reduction is often partly offset by reduced childcare costs.

EDUCATIONAL OPPORTUNITIES. Upskilling is becoming crucial in many professions. The need to develop better technology skills, such as new jobs created by the coming AI age, or to become familiar with new developments in a given field or function is common, and this need can be met through training programs as well as advanced-degree school programs. The problem, of course, is that completing these degrees or programs requires a great deal of time. Given intense work schedules, many people lack the energy or inclination to juggle a job and school. A better choice is continuing to be an employee half time, balancing school and work as a fractionalized employee. They also can practice what they learn in school at their jobs and continue to generate income for school fees and living.

EXPLORATION OF OTHER INTERESTS. As I've discussed, a growing number of employees have side hustles—everything from passion projects to start-ups. Given that the world is changing— that it's becoming normative to juggle two or three different jobs to make money and pursue meaningful work—it makes sense that people want to find a way to achieve this end. Keeping a job while exploring their passions generates both income and work connections, and it also allows people to build their skills or a business for the future.

END-OF-CAREER TRANSITION. Cold-turkey retirement is a relic of an old paradigm. Transitioning to retirement gradually while still working is more reflective of many people's goals, especially baby boomers. Especially this baby boomer.

As I've described, I became a fractionalized employee at Publicis for my last year there, shifting to 50 percent time before becoming an adviser. This enabled me to adjust to the new world, gave me time to write my first book, and ensured a seamless transition of responsibilities.

Today when companies are grappling with aging workers (ten thousand people turn sixty-five every day), they must recognize many senior folks would like to continue to work. Their objective isn't just income, although that can be important to some. They desire to retain their identity, sense of purpose, and most importantly, community.

I HAVE NO doubt that by the end of this decade the company that does not offer fractionalized employment will be like a company that does not offer health benefits or sick leave. Yes, some of these companies might exist, but very few people want to work there. Fractionalized policies may exist only in a minority of organizations as of this writing, but it seems inevitable that a majority will implement them in the next five years, recognizing that these policies are beneficial not only for their people but for the companies themselves.

CHAPTER 7

MACHINE-HUMAN COEXISTENCE

To write that this chapter's focus is a hot topic is a massive understatement. It is impossible to listen to a podcast, dip into social media, or watch the television network news without encountering fearmongering about artificial intelligence. At the same time, the media is also filled with great excitement about these and other technological tools, predicting huge advances like driverless cars and cures for various diseases.

From an organizational standpoint, the fear is that technology will eliminate a huge number of jobs, and the excitement is that it will create new opportunities for increased productivity and profit.

I understand both the fear and the excitement, but the danger is in being carried away by one and ignoring the other. The future lies somewhere in the middle. We need to be aware of the dangers of blind obedience to technology. And we need to recognize its transformative potential and maximize it.

The way forward is finding the synergies of machines and humans and avoiding the pitfalls. As we move in that direction, we need to avoid being naively optimistic or hysterically overreactive.

A Brief History of Doomsday Predictions

Technological advancements have always raised the specter of job loss. In the Agricultural Age, modern combine tractors allowed one person to do the work of many; fewer people were needed to work the farm.

In the Industrial Age, cars eliminated the horse-and-carriage business, and big companies with their superior technology drove smaller ones, who couldn't afford that technology, out of business.

With each technological innovation, some people lost their jobs and some critics raised fears of what the new era might bring.

In the late 1950s, especially, people were terrified of "automation." Companies like General Electric made major commitments to automating factories, creating conflicts with unions that felt these commitments endangered union jobs. And of course, there were some job losses as various machines took over jobs formerly done by humans. But new jobs were created because of the machines—someone needed to help companies use the machines effectively.

Throughout history, we've worried about machines replacing people. Today, however, this worry is acute, given utterances of influential people like Alibaba's Jack Ma. This is from a speech he gave in 2017 at a conference in China:

> "In thirty years, a robot will likely be on the cover of *Time* magazine as the best CEO." He warned of dark times ahead for people who are unprepared for the upheaval technology is set to bring, explaining that robots are quicker and more rational than humans and don't get bogged down in emotions—like getting

angry at competitors. But he expressed optimism that robots will make life better for humans in the long run. "Machines will do what human beings are incapable of doing," he said. "Machines will partner and cooperate with humans, rather than become mankind's biggest enemy."

Similarly, on May 1, 2023, *Bloomberg* ran an article with the headline "IBM to Pause Hiring for Jobs That AI Could Do," which began with the following paragraphs:

International Business Machines Corp. Chief Executive Officer Arvind Krishna said the company expects to pause hiring for roles it thinks could be replaced with artificial intelligence in the coming years.

"Hiring in back-office functions—such as human resources—will be suspended or slowed," Krishna said in an interview. "These non-customer-facing roles amount to roughly 26,000 workers," Krishna said. "I could easily see 30% of that getting replaced by AI and automation over a five-year period."

No doubt, AI and other technological advances will eliminate jobs. No doubt, they will also create many new jobs. Nonetheless, I understand the fear that these proclamations spawn. To keep a level head, it helps to know that historically, we tend to overreact wildly to major change, and it doesn't always have to be technological. For instance, the following appeared in the May 7, 2023, issue of the *Economist*: "In the 2000s many feared the impact of outsourcing on rich-world workers. In 2013 two at Oxford University issued a widely cited paper that suggested automation could wipe out 47% of American jobs over the subsequent decade or so. Others made the case that, even without widespread unemployment, there would be 'hollowing out,' where rewarding, well-paid jobs disappeared and mindless, poorly paid roles took their place."

Obviously, little of this has come to pass. Nonetheless, I'm sure at least some CEOs are more than a bit concerned that robots who can think faster and make more data-driven decisions than they can will take their place (and won't demand seven-figure salaries, corporate jets, and the like). It's human nature to fear major change. The antidote: understanding the realities.

How Specific Industries and Jobs Will Be Affected

The first reality is that we don't have a choice. AI and other technologies are going to be adopted, improved, and rolled out whether we like it or not. It doesn't matter if we hate Zoom meetings and think that teams function better when the members are all physically present. True technological innovations represent an irresistible force. We have no choice but to figure out the best way to use them.

At the same time, we must maintain awareness of vulnerabilities. New technologies will affect everyone differently, and certain professions and jobs are more vulnerable than others to these effects.

According to an August 2023 study by University of Pennsylvania/OpenAI (the company that makes ChatGPT) study, specific fields are in greater danger than others of losing jobs to generative artificial intelligence. The researchers found that accountants, mathematicians, interpreters, writers, and almost 20 percent of the US workforce can have their tasks done faster using generative artificial intelligence. The researchers examined occupations' exposure to the new technology, which is powered by software called "large language models" that can analyze and generate text. They analyzed the share of a job's tasks where GPTs—generative pretrained transformers—and software that incorporates them can reduce the time it takes to complete a task by at least 50 percent. Research has found that state-of-the-art GPTs excel at tasks such as translation, classification, creative writing, and generating computer code.

Further, this study determined that most jobs will be changed in some form by GPTs, with 80 percent of workers in occupations where at least one job task can be performed more quickly by generative AI. Information-processing roles—including public relations specialists, court reporters, and blockchain engineers—are highly exposed, they found. The jobs that will be least affected by the technology include short-order cooks, motorcycle mechanics, and oil-and-gas roustabouts.

I am convinced that AI is moving faster and deeper across more industries than we can imagine and has already begun to affect everybody's job in some way and will have an even greater impact in the next few years. Other technologies, too, will become more sophisticated sooner rather than later and change various aspects of work.

But even as technology changes work, it doesn't change who is valued in the workplace. This is another reality worth heeding: history suggests that every advance in technology places a premium on superior ability, that talent matters. People who are innovative, who possess financial, marketing, and other skills, who possess an ability to build strong relationships, who are brilliant leaders—their talents transcend technologies.

How talent is used will shift as technology changes the nature of jobs and industries. There clearly will be a lot of creative destruction as technology ends certain tasks and jobs and produces new ones.

I'm convinced that AI can make all of us more productive by at least 10 percent right away and unleash breakthroughs in medicine and other sciences. It also will provide more people with more tools and canvases to tell stories in new ways.

Organizations need to maintain an open mind to new technologies. Instead of reflexively resisting or mindlessly embracing, they should be curious and exploratory.

I adopted this attitude as I worked on this book. For my first book, I relied on a well-known search engine to help with my research. For this book, I'm using the latest version of GPT available as a tool, as an idea generator, and as a fact finder. I then took what it produced and corrected it for mistakes (which were many), enhanced it with forty years of experience, added a point of view (which it lacked), and filtered everything through my voice.

For my next book, I'm sure I'll rely on a tool that hasn't yet been invented or is in the early stages of beta testing. Perhaps I'll enlist the services of a "prompt engineer." If you are unaware of this term, it describes a new, high-paid job where an individual's main skill is to ask the right questions to obtain the best answers from GPT.

It is never machine/software/technology *versus* person but machine/software/technology *plus* person.

Overcoming Our Fear

Perhaps you read the previous section and thought to yourself: *Easy for you to write—you don't have to tell a thousand employees they no longer have jobs because there are software, robots, and AI that can do their jobs faster, better, and for less money.*

I understand that it's not easy. I also understand the fear since change can be frightening. Many people talk to me about how AI doesn't just augment our physical and communication skills but is capable of learning them and doing them much better and faster. Things that take us days to accomplish, AI can get done in minutes. People justifiably fear this hyperproductivity, convinced that it will lead to widespread unemployment or diminish their roles and value to their companies.

As I've noted, new technology has always changed the nature of work, the skills we need, the places we work, and much more. Perhaps what's different about today's machines is that they don't look or work like the big, inanimate objects of the past. They seem almost human.

AI and robotics possess astonishing pattern-recognition and language capabilities, suggesting they're poised to replace us, no matter what our occupation might be. Modern machines seem to be so alive and adept that they will make humans irrelevant, similar to the ways in which tractors replaced horses, and emails replaced faxes!

What we have here is a failure of both imagination and understanding, creating unnecessary panic. If we can shift our perspective—if we can focus on what technology can do *for* us rather than what it is doing *to* us—then we grasp how this new machine age can benefit everyone.

Organizations that really understand the new technologies share my point of view that AI, AR, VR, and other breakthroughs are a form of magic, elevating our work capabilities. It confers godlike powers on companies, increasing their scale and scope while reducing the time needed to labor. It makes the unimaginable possible.

But it will do so only if we rely on qualities that even the best new technology lacks.

Humans Must Become More Human

There's no denying that job descriptions from 2003 bear little resemblance to those from 2023 . . . and that job descriptions in 2033 will be quite different from the present. Over recent decades, computers, mobile devices, and the internet have catalyzed changes in how we work. But more recent developments are having profound effects on many industries. In the creative arts, for instance, modern computing and software have raised video, sound, and special-effects capabilities, elevating the quality and range of tools but also necessitating different approaches to work. Streaming platforms provide a variety of new ways to distribute and monetize work, and crowdfunding helps artists raise money in fresh ways.

OpenAI, Anthropic, Google Gemini, Midjourney, and Runway enhance authors' abilities to research, illustrate, create, and ideate, distributing incredibly powerful tools to everyone.

Developments such as these are taking place in many fields, and they will have the same impact as the internet has had on business. AI is the same sort of game changer—more to the point, it's a job changer.

IBM's chief commercial officer, Rob Thomas, has a great quote about AI that sends a message every organization should heed: "AI may not replace managers, but managers that use AI will replace the managers that do not."

At the same time, managers who use AI and also are more creative, empathetic, and curious will replace the managers who are overreliant on AI and other tech tools.

In a data-driven, digital, and silicon-based age, relying on our analog (creative), carbon-based, and feeling selves (empathy), and our inquisitiveness and imagination (curiosity), will ensure that humans plus technology will be the future, not just technology.

In the future, we—people and machines—must double down on what we do best. Machines must take on more computational, pattern finding, research, and data tasks, while we must draw on our distinctly human traits. To be human is to be variable and experience different moods, to imagine, to speculate, and to feel. A machine cannot say why it created what it did; we can.

Every business leader should be helping their people transition to this quickly approaching future. To do so, they need to help employees upgrade their skills in three areas:

1. **Tech knowledge.** This isn't just for IT. In fact, it's even more important for nontech employees. Too often, the marketing or HR people focus only on using the tech rather than figuring out how to use it better; they profess ignorance of everything except basic usage, calling for IT support at the first sign of trouble. A better approach is to provide a wide swath of employees with an understanding of how to use modern technology, including AI. Educate them about how to ask questions to understand a given technology's limitations, learning how to work with the tech productively.

2. **Synergies.** How can a user enhance the effectiveness of a piece of technology? How can people use their relationships, common sense, creativity, and knowledge of the company's culture to leverage the technology, to turbocharge it? Yes, machines will be able to create white papers and speeches for executives, but a writer with a point of view and a voice will build and adapt what machines produce, adding depth and insight and eloquence. Yes, machines will be able to analyze court documents and precedents, but lawyers who use modern AI to replace the drudgery of looking up case files will free themselves to connect the dots, to see opportunities and spot problems that they previously might have missed. Training people to do more than just know how to use machines is key; training them to draw upon the abilities that machines lack can increase their productivity dramatically.

3. **Options.** Given that technology will eliminate some jobs and change many more, companies have to help people learn to work differently. This may mean setting up training programs for people to acquire new skills and knowledge. It may mean providing an understanding of

how people can use all the extra time they have now that machines are doing their mundane tasks. It definitely means coaching people to be flexible, to be willing to adjust to working more closely with technology than they did in the past. Training will have to be continuous since the technology is advancing so quickly.

What People Do Better Than Machines

As I've emphasized, people possess qualities that even the best AI lacks—empathy, creativity, relationship-building skills, leadership, and so on. These qualities translate into on-the-job behaviors and ideas that benefit organizations in many ways—ways that even the most state-of-the-art technology can't duplicate. But before discussing these qualities, here are things that machines can do better than people:

- Research and categorize large amounts of data.

- Summarize and provide analyses and recommendations.

- Offer a range of creative solutions involving words, images, and videos.

Nonetheless, organizations persist in having their people do at least some of these tasks. Humans aren't as good as machines at completing these assignments, and people usually don't find this type of work fulfilling. Most of these tasks are rote or require an arduous attention to detail, and both the individual and the organization would be better served by ceding these jobs to technological devices.

In this way, people would be freed to focus on what they do best:

- Helping determine and define what data should be refined and categorized.

- Asking the right questions for ensuring the right analyses and recommendations. Like never before, asking the right questions leads to the answer.

- Selecting and then further enhancing and honing the answers/solutions, assessing which ideas and implementation approaches best fit the situation and culture and which are the most humanistic.

By allowing people and machines to do what they do best, organizations create win-win situations. This may mean shifting appropriate responsibilities from human to machine. For instance, earlier I described how Shopify helps its customers who have no or little technological expertise sell products in many markets for far less money than is traditionally required. Now, Shopify is using new AI technology to help its customers in other ways—providing merchants with superior search tools that function like a personal shopper and writing copy promoting their merchandise with a single click (termed "Shopify magic"). Merchants modify and personalize what the AI creates.

This symbiosis between merchant and machine is the future, and it is the same human-tech symbiosis that will eventually exist in all organizations. It stands to reason that if a machine can enhance the outcome by doing it either cheaper or faster or better, organizations will optimize and allocate more work to automation especially if the work is repetitive or boring, or doesn't enhance or build skills.

At the same time, no matter how much organizations come to depend on their technology, they will be even more dependent on people for the following qualities that they can provide and machines can't:

DIFFERENTIATION. If two companies were competing and both fully automated their process, there would be no difference between their products and services, driving them to commodity pricing. Organizations differentiate themselves in large part through their great ideas, storytelling, and creativity—attributes their best and brightest people possess in spades.

While Delta and American use the same technology (aircraft) and resources (airports), Delta has been consistently higher rated and more profitable than American because of its talent and culture.

Apple uses production lines at Foxconn, which many of their competitors also use, and most of the raw materials are similar or purchased from competitors (screens from Samsung or LG). But their design, branding, and storytelling allow Apple to charge more, and it is one of the most distinctive and successful brands because of its very human ingenuity. For a company known as tech innovators, their most obvious point of differentiation (arguably) isn't their silicon chips but the stunning look of their iPhones and other devices.

NEW AND IMPROVED THINKING. Machines tend to learn and optimize based on presets of training data or algorithms. They adapt but are unable to recognize if the landscape has changed either due to competition or new customer needs. Humans must identify these changes and develop new ways to reprogram and direct the machines in production. In volatile product and service sectors, especially, the human ability to innovate and improve is crucial.

Domino's has automated a huge part of their pizza making and pizza delivery with an app that allows customers to order and track their pie. What the machines cannot yet do is develop, make, and test new types of pizzas or determine what to do when it gets increasingly difficult to hire car drivers as labor shortages loom.

People are astute about what to do when new data, situations, or environments emerge; they are best able to interpret how customers react when tasting a new type of pizza, for instance. They don't just read the surveys from customers—they can observe the excitement or distaste in an expression or tone of voice or choice of words.

SERVICE WITH A GENUINE SMILE. Have you ever tried to communicate with a "smart" machine voice when calling a cable company or other service provider? Sometimes they're fine responding to simple questions or requests, but invariably, they will create tremendous frustration for callers. Machines simply don't know how to "read" a caller and sense growing impatience and anger. They struggle with situations or requests that aren't routine.

In service businesses, where people-to-people interactions are essential, AI remains incapable of doing what even barely competent people can do. Whether the field is dentistry, food service, or delivery, people want to interact with other people. Most of us want to meet with our accountants, financial planners, lawyers, and therapists about important issues rather than be "serviced" by a machine, no matter how smart it might be. Now and especially in the future, people will continue to seek other people to talk to, guide them, or enhance their experience. There is no substitute for looking someone in the eye before making a commitment to them. We want to get to know people who provide us with important financial advice or are trying to sell us a big ticket item. We want to feel we can trust them before signing on the dotted line.

Not everyone agrees with the previous statement. Martin Sorrell, who runs S4Capital, a media-buying service firm, was asked if his company's adoption of AI "supertools" will threaten jobs at S4, and he said, "We don't know whether AI will be a net generator or net destroyer of jobs. But the algorithm will be more effective than a twenty-five-year-old media buyer."

I disagree. If you can replace a media buyer with an algorithm, then why does a client need a media-buying agency? And tangentially, if you're a young media buyer, why would you want to work for an agency where the CEO feels his software is more effective than you?

I'm not disagreeing that the advertising and marketing world has benefitted from technological advances—search engine optimization, social media tools, and so on. Interestingly, however, the number of people working in the field has increased despite certain tasks formerly undertaken by people now being handled by machines.

That's because as soon as you optimize one part of media technologically, another breakthrough occurs requiring analysis, integration, and new approaches—jobs that people do best.

Service, therefore, is always going to require a human element, and not just for dealing directly with customers. Service businesses often must grapple with the unpredictable, the emotional, and the illogical. People get that, and machines don't.

A Cautious Embrace

Steve Jobs termed computers "a bicycle for the mind." If so, then AI is a jet engine.

Where there's so much power, there's good reason to be careful.

If force is equal to mass times acceleration, with AI, we are seeing mass in hundreds of billions of dollars of investment globally and acceleration of doubling capabilities sometimes within three months. For instance, GPT 3.5 scored on the tenth percentile on the LSAT, the entrance exam for law school. Six months later

GPT 4 scored in the ninetieth percentile! Moore's law of the processor age, doubling capability every eighteen months, is snail-like slow compared to what we are seeing currently.

Just as the cost of computing is tending toward zero and the internet made the cost of information distribution trend to zero, we will see AI driving the cost of knowledge to zero.

AI is a force that appears twice as impactful as the World Wide Web and the iPhone. No doubt, other technologies are in development that will have a similar impact. As much as I am a proponent of organizations embracing technology, I also believe we need to be aware of the downside of technology and make sure we take steps to become its master rather than its slave.

For instance, organizations must be vigilant against people using their technology fraudulently—or responding inappropriately to customers, suppliers, or other stakeholders who fall victim to tech scams. Because of AI and deepfake technology, it is possible to put words in the mouth of an individual or create a video that integrates the likeness of that person (without their permission). This technology can have an adverse effect on privacy, reputations, and finances. Will a competitive company in Russia, for example, smear a US company's reputation? Will an employee leak sensitive information on social media? Will a disgruntled, terminated, tech-savvy employee hack into a business system and do damage?

The more dependent organizations become on increasingly sophisticated tech, the more vulnerable they are to bad actors. Cybersecurity is necessary today and will be even more necessary in the future.

I've already raised the issue of the loss of jobs—the fear that AI and robots will replace people—but in the past, the people concerned about being replaced have usually been lower-paid workers. When higher-paid managers begin losing their jobs, however, sparks will fly. A May 15, 2023, *Wall Street Journal* article suggests this loss has already begun: "For generations of

Americans, a corporate job was a path to stable prosperity. No more. The jobs lost in a monthslong cascade of white-collar layoffs triggered by overhiring and rising interest rates might never return, corporate executives and economists say. Companies are rethinking the value of many white-collar roles, in what some experts anticipate will be a permanent shift in labor demand that will disrupt the work life of millions of Americans whose jobs will be lost, diminished, or revamped partly through the use of artificial intelligence."

Business leaders need to think long and hard about the roles of managers (a topic of a later chapter). Are there managerial functions that can be handled better by AI and other technologies? Should managerial roles be redefined so that they complement rather than exist separately from the technology?

The third issue goes beyond "mere" angst about jobs to apocalyptic thinking: Will AI be responsible for the destruction of life as we know it?

Whether it's the end of corporate life or the death of our species, this is scary stuff. Many leading AI researchers are concerned that exponentially increasing capabilities of AI combined with the all-out competition between large companies or countries such as China and the US to "win AI" will obviate rules and regulations that keep AI in check. As much as this might sound like a bad science-fiction movie, the fear is that AI will evolve so quickly that it will take over systems, refusing to take orders and subjugating or destroying humankind.

On a Lex Fridman podcast, AI expert Eliezer Yudkowsky said this about AI's rapid development: "They spit out gold, until they get large enough and ignite the atmosphere and kill everybody." Yudkowsky has a reputation for warning people about AI's sinister possibilities, but others are issuing similar cautions as well. Regarding the possibility of AI gaining control of systems, OpenAI CEO Sam Altman told Fridman, "I think there's some chance of that. And it's really important to acknowledge it. Because if we don't talk about it, if we don't treat it as potentially real, we won't put enough effort into solving it."

Leading the Way Through the Tech Portal

Every day seems to bring a new tech innovation, along with another doom-and-gloom pronouncement about how it will affect people in the workplace. Navigating the passage into this increasingly fearful, tech-focused future isn't easy.

But it's possible to do so effectively. In fact, every company that I advise or on whose board I sit is addressing three key issues related to the tech/people challenge.

First, how do we make sure the company's products and services remain relevant and competitive as technology shifts happen faster and faster?

In the past two years, boards have had to grapple with Web3 and blockchain, AR/VR, and metaverse and generative AI. Some of the companies that I advise, such as Quilt.AI and LoopMe, who were into AI before AI was cool, worry that with so much money chasing AI, they need to move and grow faster because a lot of money and potential new competition is entering the space. They're considering revisiting their products and services to ensure they are adding significant value and are truly differentiated in a world of open-source, generative AI.

Whatever the companies' focus might be, their leaders must address relevant tech developments regularly and seriously.

Second, organizational leadership has to ensure that they possess the right talent and organizational design, given the technology that is affecting their business. As the technology changes dramatically, boards are wrestling with how to upskill and reskill, as well as attract the talent they need, and how to ensure that culture and talent remain motivated in these fast-pivoting times.

Recently I spoke with talent legend Josh Bersin, who shared a chart from O*NET, revealing that between 1980 and 2012, the greatest growth in wages and demand were for social skills.

Third, organizations need to concentrate on remaining (or becoming) relevant.

As technology changes, are our business model, product offering, and services still relevant?

Are our talent and our partners still relevant and, if not, what do we need to do to ensure they are?

And here are two questions that many leaders are loath to articulate but which are crucial: Are we, as managers and board members, still relevant? Do we understand the new technology and talent landscape?

Recently, a private equity firm I advise, GCP Capital Partners, decided to create an entire day for all their CEOs and leaders of their dozen firms to learn from outside experts about AI, to better understand its impact and to share learnings on how to remain relevant.

Relevance is a huge challenge for leaders, since no one likes to consider the possibility that they're obsolete. But relevance demands that we reinvent and rethink our futures. We have to make the commitment to adapt ourselves as a business and as a society, to learn and grow as we work alongside the machines.

CHAPTER 8

THE UNBUNDLING
OF THE OFFICE

Imagine starting a company today in which it's unnecessary for your employees to work in proximity to customers and colleagues.

Imagine that this new company has the ability to serve customers anywhere in the world.

Imagine that you can hire talent from around the globe.

Given this scenario, would you lease office space? And if so, how much space would you require?

Would you insist your employees commute long distances to the office if they could do their work remotely?

Would you ask them to come occasionally to the office for other reasons—collaboration, relationship building, and events?

The answers to these questions reveal how much has changed in a few years. No sane business leader would adopt the 2019 default office model, one in which companies leased a lot of real estate and insisted people follow a strict, in-office regimen five days a week.

Who would sacrifice flexibility, limit the talent pool, and take on the cost that comes with the traditional office model?

Today, organizations start with a very different default model. It's one that lacks a lot of or any office space, that requires no or few in-office days, that sets no limits on where talent is sought, that establishes no rules about the hours when work should be done.

The changes are dramatic, and they're likely to be even more dramatic in the future. They affect not just start-ups but established corporations in profound ways. Before examining how these changes are unfolding and will unfold in the future, we need to take a step back to see how far we've come.

The Good Old Days

Nostalgia is remembering all of the good and none of the bad.

Many people recall the office of yesteryear with great fondness. They talk about how it was more of a "family" atmosphere than today, the wonderful office parties, the way business was transacted with great efficiency, the big offices with beautiful views.

Who wouldn't want to work in this environment?

In reality, this environment never existed, at least in this fictionalized, ideal state.

I began working at Leo Burnett in 1982. My thirty-seven years there provides a personal history of office realities and how they evolved—both the good and the bad. Consider how business was conducted in the '80s:

- **Office hours.** In the 1980s everyone was expected to be sitting and working by 9:00 a.m. and no one could leave till 5:00 p.m. Lunch was one hour or less.

- **Formal dress code.** All the men wore suits with ties and the women wore dresses.

- **Hierarchy of office space.** The more senior you were, the bigger the office (and it had a door!). Middle management also had offices. Junior folks had cubicles. Secretaries and assistants worked in outside offices and passageways. We then moved to our own building that maximized the number of conference rooms, and the cubicle walls moved even higher for more privacy and sound proofing.

- **Technology.** In the early '80s, the first word processors were introduced, but pen and paper and typewriters reigned supreme—managers would write something in longhand and the secretary would type it. Sometimes we'd present "acetates," using an acetate projector and a screen. Intraoffice communication was paper based, with mail delivery and mail pickup between offices three times a day. The telephone was the principal way we spoke with outside parties—voicemail had just been introduced. The highest form of tech was the fax machine, and many deadlines were based on when FedEx accepted the last shipment.

- **Meetings.** People met in person, and a system existed to book meeting rooms that were in high demand and needed to be secured in advance. Significant business was done over lunch (yes, the martini lunch existed). A high-tech meeting was when we gathered around a phone in a middle manager's or senior executive's office (they were the only ones with the telephone loudspeakers and the private rooms) and spoke to clients who were gathered around a phone in their office.

- **Work style/culture.** Smoking was prevalent when I started at Burnett. Many senior managers had alcohol in their cabinets, and we had discussions while drinking alcohol. There were few people of color outside of the secretaries and mail staff. Few women leaders existed. A pyramid organizational structure and military-style hierarchy created operational efficiency, though not necessarily widespread engagement and innovation.

Though things have changed since the '80s, they didn't change all that much until COVID. Until relatively recently, most offices were built around a rigid system based on physical location, space hierarchies, the need for physical presence at all times, and the inability to access what one needed for work from home. From the perspective of 2023, such a system seems archaic.

In reality, it fit the zeitgeist. It helped get things done and provided people with a logical, orderly way to get work done and advance their careers.

But the zeitgeist has changed, in large part because of technology. When you can communicate visually and virtually, when all the information is accessible digitally, when people are connected through various apps—attitudes about work have to change. It's fine to be nostalgic for the good parts of the office from years ago, but it's not fine to cling to ways of working that have ceased to be relevant. We need to let go of the past and move toward the future, and fortunately, a number of companies are heading in this direction.

Downsizing and Reimagining the Office

It's astonishing how quickly the less-is-more mindset has taken hold among a wide swath of organizational leaders. To grasp how quickly, visit this website: https://buildremote.co/companies /reducing-office-space/. On it, you'll find a long list of large companies that are reducing their office space in significant ways, including Google, Uber, and AT&T. Just as significant, more than a hundred companies, including Zillow, Coinbase, and

Shopify, are giving their employees the option of working wherever they want.

Though you may be aware that office vacancy rates remain high, what you might not realize is that companies aren't forsaking the office entirely but reimagining it in often startling ways. Organizations are taking a cue from hotels and conferences and redesigning their spaces so that they're ideal for events, celebrations, and collaborative efforts; they're attempting to re-create their offices to facilitate in-person interactions. In New York City, the buildings that are most in demand are the ones that are best suited for events and similar activities.

As a professional speaker, I've experienced one aspect of this office change firsthand. During the first six months of 2023, I did thirty-six in-person events. Almost half of them were at different companies' headquarters, and a major reason I was invited was to bring back employees to offices for a few days. My event, like others they created, was designed to motivate people to gather together, to learn and to interact with their colleagues, and to build relationships. These organizations realized that simply ordering people to return no longer was acceptable to the majority of their employees. They needed to provide them with valid reasons for returning.

Given the transportation costs and time investment that employees need to undertake, companies must make coming into the office worthwhile.

They have to earn the commute.

But redesigned offices and less office space are just two broad trends affecting the places where we work. Here are five more highly impactful ways that offices are being reimagined:

1. Number of days people must come into the office

It varies—some companies have returned to the five-day norm after being fully remote, and many organizations are splitting the difference. The 2023 (second quarter) Flex Index report shows that in the service sector, organizations are asking for two or three days of physical presence in offices and two or three days of remote work.

Obviously, some industries will still require people to be in the office full time because of the type of work they do. The health-care industry, for instance, isn't going to change this requirement in the near future, since robot doctors and nurses are generally not acceptable substitutes for human beings (with the exception of some robotic surgeries). Similarly, people still want human servers when they go out to restaurants, and as far as I know, tradespeople (plumbers, electricians, and so on) have not been replaced by AI.

2. Type of work done in office

Not so long ago, we needed offices to get work done. They contained the "equipment"—computers, printers, copiers, and so forth—that were necessary to produce work outputs. Today, the vast majority of this equipment exists remotely. Nonetheless, the pre-COVID presumption was that specific work tasks require an office presence, including:

- Research and analytics: looking up data and searching for supporting evidence.

- Creating documents: putting together presentations and documents for sharing.

- Sharing information and documents: working with teams to share information and build programs together.

- Learning and development: training programs and mentoring are some aspects of learning and development.

- Creative ideas and brainstorming: working together to generate ideas as a team.

- Relationship development and honing people skills: developing EQ (emotional quotient) and other soft skills and building trusted links.

- Pitching and selling clients: sharing information and finding ways to sell clients.

In recent years, however, many business leaders have shifted their mindset on this topic, recognizing that a lot of these tasks can be done outside of the office. They've learned that research, creation, and sharing of documents often is easier outside of the office, when concentration is key, and the internet and other digital tools facilitate the process.

Organizations have also discovered that while learning and development, creative ideas and brainstorming, and relationship development require in-person interaction, this interaction doesn't have to take place within corporate offices. They are much more open to arranging in-person meetings in other venues—restaurants, off-site workspaces, outdoor settings, conferences, and so on.

Increasingly, companies are going to use offices for key events and other activities that benefit from people being together physically and where the offices offer advantages (central location, an auditorium or other sizeable room that can accommodate a large number of people, special equipment such as a movie-theater-size screen or state-of-the-art sound system).

3. Office design
Here is where one of my favorite sayings—"the future does not fit in the containers of the past"—is literally relevant. The big corner offices for executives, the midsize offices for middle managers, the bullpen for clerical people—this design has become an anachronism.

If people are going to be in the office only a few days each week and their in-office tasks are mainly collaboration, brainstorming, and learning, then office redesign is essential. For this reason, offices will be reconfigured to be more like schools, hotel lobbies, and conference centers. They'll also contain smaller, private spaces for people who need to concentrate (and require quiet) and want to focus on individual projects.

An article in the May 23, 2023, issue of *Time* magazine quotes Steve McConnell, managing partner and board chair of the design firm NBBJ, who helped redesign the company's space in New York's Flatiron District: "We're in the early stages of a deep recognition that the workplace needs to be different." According to the article, the space "feels like a mix between an office and a social club, with conference rooms giving off living room vibes, thanks to their homey bookshelves and couches; a lab where employees can look at tiny models of buildings the company is designing . . . and rotating art projects on screens stretching towards the high ceilings."

4. Headquarters

As work becomes more distributed and unbundled, the idea of having a giant corporate office sprawling horizontally or vertically seems hopelessly old-fashioned. Though the concept of headquarters hasn't vanished—JPMorganChase is building a skyscraping building for its offices in Manhattan, and Amazon has two large HQs in Seattle and Virginia—many organizations are exploring other options.

Andreessen Horowitz, the big venture-capital firm, has moved from a Palo Alto HQ to basically stating that their HQ is in the cloud, with five physical locations for people to meet. In a blog post, Ben Horowitz stated: "In our firm's new operating model, we work primarily virtually, but will use our physical presence to develop our culture, help entrepreneurs, and build relationships. . . . As a result, we have configured the firm to be able to physically assemble anywhere in the world very quickly."

To replace a single HQ office space, some companies are considering creating many offices closer to where talent, opportunity, and clients are. Long-term leases for massive space in a single city center is being replaced by a much more distributed, flexible, and agile model.

5. When work is done (in the office and outside of it)

No more office hours. If COVID taught us nothing else about work, it was that one set of office hours doesn't fit all employees. Some people are more productive at night, some early in the morning. Some are more effective if they take numerous breaks throughout a long work day while others excel when they can sustain their focus for hours. By accommodating different work-time preferences, organizations maximize their people's contributions.

More than that, we are living in a global world, where more and more work gets done asynchronously versus synchronously—it makes sense to keep the office open continuously to accommodate employees working in different countries (as well as functioning best at different times). In terms of the physical office, to maximize in-person interaction and learning, most offices are likely to be busiest between noon and evenings, as people gather for meals or social events or around client/customer-related events. The hours will fit the work and the need, versus the work and the need fitting the hours.

Predicting Future Office Changes

While the previous office transformations have already started to manifest themselves, others are on the horizon. Though it's impossible to know how soon the following will become reality—or how these changes may evolve—they all seem likely to further alter where and how we work:

Technology will blur the distinction between in-person and virtual meetings.
Apple has upgraded its Macintosh operating system so that the speaker in a virtual presentation will be seen in front of their presentation—it will create the verisimilitude of an in-person speaker as opposed to seeing a slide with a disembodied voice.

Google continues to lower prices and to offer a more portable version of Project Starline, providing realistic videoconferencing where the individual appears to be sitting across the table.

Apple also introduced their Vision Pro mixed-reality headset, tech that is geared for business applications, including the ability to better connect, communicate, and share across distances using augmented and virtual reality. As an early adopter of Apple Vision Pro, I can see beyond the currently limited capability and high cost to the breakthroughs in new interfaces, and the feeling you are in a place with others, which will revolutionize collaboration and learning at a distance.

While the Apple Mac upgrade is free, the other breakthroughs cost many thousands of dollars—no doubt, the price will come down considerably within five years as competition heats up in this category and product usage increases.

These innovations, combined with other advances, will diminish the awkwardness and remote qualities of virtual meetings, making them less of an alternative to in-person meetings and more standard operating procedure.

Significant build-out in physical infrastructure and services will support hybrid work.
As companies move toward a mix of virtual and in-person work, they will need to create office environments and services that

support this mix, which will vary from company to company. Some may have people in the office two or three days each week, while others will favor a much more virtual structure—two or three days in the office annually, and each of these days will be built around events.

Whatever the mix might be, offices will be redesigned to accommodate the virtual/in-person policy. There will be fewer private offices, with some eliminated altogether. Organizations will also create more collaborating spaces, attempting to generate synergies between people working in the office and those working outside of it. Learning spaces may also be a key component of future office design, as well as areas designed to foster experiences—from role-playing to simulations to brainstorming.

Just as important, activities previously reserved for offices will be outsourced to other spaces as companies reduce their real-estate footprint. Hotels, for instance, will expand and reconfigure their spaces to serve organizations that are "outsourcing" events and other activities that used to take place at their headquarters. The major chains are building out extended-stay motels and hotels, and Airbnbs are seeing extended stays as infrastructure and services reconfigure around the hybrid work reality and the recognition that in-person interaction can be effective outside of the office.

Similarly, organizations will contract with universities for training and development purposes. Universities possess ideal facilities for teaching, and as companies move more of their training and development off-site, they will capitalize on resources universities have to offer. All schools have a significant amount of downtime—summers and breaks between semesters, especially—when they could make their labs, lecture rooms, meeting spaces, and dorms available to organizations.

Mindsets will change.

It takes time to come to terms with a new office paradigm. In the next few years, however, most business leaders will recognize that the default model of work is no longer viable and expand their thinking about what the office might be. This will happen for two reasons.

First, people will continue to form habits around the new office normal of flexible hours, remote work, and reconfigured spaces. As these new habits form and become ingrained, people will let go of traditional ideas about offices and explore new concepts.

Second, as research on emerging ways of working is published and discussed, it will validate our instinctive sense of how offices should change. Companies that are beta testing a combination of in-person and virtual will roll it out when research demonstrates its viability.

It does take time for minds to change, but when they do, corresponding actions follow. When the majority of organizational leaders accept that there's no going back and that the office of the future has to be forged from fresh ideas, they'll start creating policies and procedures that will transform work environments in significant ways.

Customizing Policies and Programs

Offices are going to evolve based on their distinctive elements. One size never fits all. It will be up to companies to personalize and customize the right combination of in-person and remote work for their employees, just as many companies wish to personalize and customize services and products for their customers.

A start-up Silicon Valley tech company is going to create settings and policies that are significantly different than a family-run textile company in the Midwest. While they may share similar features—perhaps they'll both adopt a flexible work policy—their physical space and specific programs will reflect five factors: the industry, geography, tenure of the individual, type of job being done, and industry talent dynamics.

Let's look at these factors and how they'll shape offices in different ways.

- **Industry type.** This is the obvious differentiator: most people can't work in fields such as construction, medicine, and retail. You can't be an ironworker balancing on a beam thousands of feet in the air remotely (at least, not as of this writing). A senior and accomplished software engineer who has no direct reports, on the other hand, may go to a physical office infrequently. They can do their work, test their code, access everything they need, and collaborate with other people using modern cloud-based computing and communication technology.

- **Geography.** Cultures and infrastructures vary by country. In China and some other Asian countries, homes often lack sufficient space to work there. Consequently, the centralized office space in China is likely to be more dominant. Office occupancy varies in US cities, with low utilization in San Francisco and Seattle (as examples), where cost, commute times, and daycare create constraints.

- **Tenure.** When someone joins a company, a certain amount of onboarding is required to acculturate and train them. This is best done through in-person interaction, whether it is in the office or some other location. Some new hires must be present for skill acquisition involving leading meetings, communicating, and presenting. Without in-person interaction and observation, it's difficult to master these skills. Veteran employees who are familiar with their organizations may require less time physically with colleagues, but even this can vary depending on their role. A senior leader may need to be in the office for a combination of guidance and presence. For this reason, it's best to avoid ironclad rules about office presence and adjust according to individual circumstance—roles and tenure should be weighed before making a decision about how much time a given individual should spend in the office.

- **Type of job.** A taxi driver needs to be on the road, but a taxi dispatcher can work from home. A software engineer at a technology firm can work primarily from home, but a head of sales needs to be present in order to train and motivate the sales teams and be in person with clients. A barista at Starbucks needs to be at the store every day, but a marketer at Starbucks does not need to be in the office every day.

- **Talent dynamics.** In many industries, talent is in short supply in a market or across their industries. The demand for AI engineers and data scientists exceeds the supply today, as an example. To access and compete for talent when demand exceeds the supply, companies must adopt office policies that can be adapted to talent's requirements. This is necessary to attract and keep these highly skilled individuals, wherever they are located and however they prefer to work.

Companies That Are Creating the Office of the Future Today

Again, one size doesn't fit all—there is no perfect model that every organization should follow for re-creating offices.

There are, however, specific principles or guiding ideas that can help leaders construct the offices that best suit their companies and cultures.

First, they adopt a future-forward attitude. They resist the tug of the past, refusing to dwell on what was and return to halcyon days of yore. Instead, they are open to new ideas about office policies and environments, and they're willing to experiment with fresh approaches.

Second, they are open to new and innovative office concepts. They don't get locked into a rigid office structure or system. By building agility into their office, they can balance in-person and remote work, veteran and new talent, preferences for working the traditional day versus working "off" hours. This open-minded approach is absolutely necessary in the world of unbundled and distributed work.

Third, they value in-person interaction. Though it's technologically possible to run certain businesses entirely virtually, it's not humanly feasible. The most forward-looking companies make sure they maintain some level of in-person work, capitalizing on the innovation produced when people are physically present as well as the relationships that are built and strengthened through personal interactions.

Fourth, they design systems and procedures for synergy. Put simply, this means that they must aim for the right balance of in-person and virtual work—that if they get this balance right, the sum will be greater than the parts. Flexibility, iterating from beta, and constant learning help produce synergy.

Fifth, future-focused companies recognize the value of events. These events can revolve around training workshops, brainstorming sessions, and celebrations. They provide motivating reasons for people to return to the office. Instead of issuing a command—you will return to the office!—that seems arbitrary and unnecessary, organizations provide specific programs/events as reasons for the return. They're not asking individuals to come back for the "heads down" work of reading or creating documents or presentations but for "heads together" or some "heads up" work of training, relationship building, and problem-solving.

Sixth, and perhaps most important, the visionary business leaders are providing their people with freedom within a framework. They set general parameters for work—perhaps two days of in-office work weekly—but they also allow justified variations. Some teams may want and need to meet with their members more than the required two days per week, while others are more productive when they convene only one day per week.

With these principles in mind, let's look at some companies that are putting them into practice.

Boston-based ad agency A&G (Allen & Gerritsen, a company where I've given a talk) has taken inspiration from Ray Oldenburg's books *The Great Good Place* and *Celebrating the Third Place*, where the author described the concept of third spaces as "public places that host the regular, voluntary, informal, and happily anticipated gatherings of individuals beyond the realms of home and work."

A&G recognized that an artificial barrier separated workplaces and homes, and after COVID, they realized that "either/or" was the past and "both/and" was the future. Thoughtfully furnished, comfortable surroundings that invite collaboration—previously the home domain—became the mantra for re-creating A&G's offices. A&G decided to forgo assigned seating, and they've eliminated the word "desk" from their vocabulary. Instead, seats and meeting areas with names like Barber Shop, Ferry, Hookah Lounge, Bodega, and Taqueria can be booked through scheduling software.

Andrew Graff, CEO at A&G, shared in a conversation with Kat Gordon (a friend of mine) the journey that brought them to open third spaces: "Last year when we made decisions about our real estate, it was a great opportunity to reimagine the future of the workplace. We were not interested in returning to the office and continuing the old ways and habits of the past. As a company, we believe being together with intention is in fact important to the success of our business, and that flexibility will help improve overall agency productivity, employee well-being, and engagement."

Their chief creative officer, Jennifer Putnam, told Kat, "Trading in the traditional rigid office for a flexible and agile work environment sets us up for more creative success. . . . If we want to reinvent the future of the workplace, we have to reimagine the spaces we do it in, and make sure creativity, inclusion, and comfort are core to these spaces."

ACCORDING TO A recent *Time* magazine article, many companies are completely rethinking the idea of a permanent office, says Prithwiraj Choudhury, a professor at Harvard Business School who has been studying remote work for years. Some start-ups are deciding that the purpose of an office is really to socialize, and they're allowing employees to work from anywhere and then picking a place for people to meet occasionally throughout the year to get to know one another.

A workflow-automation business, Zapier, has company retreats where it invites all workers to spend a few days in person with their colleagues; the company pays for flights, accommodations, and food, and organizes ways for people in different departments to get to know one another. GitLab, which Choudhury says is one of the world's largest remote companies, with thirteen hundred employees, allows their people to be fully remote but has at least one off-site meetup around the world each year.

It's worth noting that employees often are unhappy when companies—Amazon, Disney, and Nike among them—mandate a return to the office. These mandates have elicited employee protests. The problem isn't just that people are resisting a return to the office. It's that these companies are failing to take into consideration their people's expectations and constraints; that they're changing their COVID-era policies without providing compelling reasons for doing so; and that they're insisting on a one-size-fits-all policy that lacks the flexibility people have come to prize.

Wall Street leadership veteran Sallie Krawcheck; cofounder and CEO of Ellevest and the former Citi CFO and head of global wealth management at Bank of America, recently told a room of leaders at a CNBC C-suite event that thinking everything can go back to "the way it was" is a flawed mindset.

Allstate is refusing to go backward. Instead, they will allow employees to decide for themselves if they want to stay remote or work in offices. After giving employees the choice, 83 percent of Allstate workers are fully remote. Allowing employees to be remote has also resulted in a 60 percent increase in applications and a 30 percent increase in candidates from underrepresented demographics, Stephanie Roseman, vice president of people solutions and experiences at Allstate, recently told *SHRM Online*.

I'm not suggesting that all companies should follow Allstate's model. But companies like Allstate, Zapier, Gitlab, and A&G are just some of the many organizations recognizing that they need to be innovative and exploratory when it comes to office policies and designs.

CHAPTER 9

THE FALL OF OLD MANAGERS AND THE RISE OF NEW LEADERS

After four decades as a manager and a leader, I've not only seen this fall and rise but have been part of it. Many years ago, I managed people in an environment without social networks, computers, and mobile phones, where few women or people of color occupied leadership positions and where seniority was always respected and sometimes feared.

Many years later, I led companies in which every employee was armed with the latest in technology; where competence, coaching, and communication were respected; and where tenure—while continuing to be important for the seasoning, industry under-standing and cultural nuance it often brought—was not by itself enough, and where controlling behaviors were disrespected.

The contrast between now and then is dramatic:

- Talent today wants to figure out how work fits into life versus how life fits into work.

- They don't just ask what they can do for the company but what the company can do for them.

- They want the company to grow, but they also want to grow themselves or are eager to have access to tools and opportunities to do so.

- Talent is more diverse and they are far more opinionated—to the point of sometimes not listening to the other side.

The days of the old-style manager—the stereotypical boss who dictates and monitors—are numbered. So too are the days of the old-style leader—the command-and-control, decisive, remote figurehead.

But who will take their places? Some organizations are undergoing radical experiments in management and leadership. MorningStar Farms, a food-processing company, operates with a self-management system, substituting "colleague letters of understanding" for hierarchy. Spotify relies on "autonomous squads" to get work done, and the managerial role is one of support rather than direct control.

While other experiments will continue, a new model is taking shape. It's one where managerial roles are changing dramatically and where leadership takes on a new importance.

In the past, we had managerial layers (junior manager, middle manager, senior manager, various functional managers) separate from elite leadership positions (C-suite). Now, we are eliminating a lot of managerial jobs and changing managerial tasks, and leadership is becoming a much more democratic concept:

Every single person can be a leader.

It's a role that doesn't require minions or reporting staff.

Leader isn't a title that can be bestowed but a role that is lived.

Leader doesn't mean boss.

People are assigned to bosses, but they follow leaders.

A Shifting Landscape

To call this a time of managerial upheaval leadership redefinition is an understatement. Consider the tumult in the managerial arena.

A "delayering" mania is rampant as companies try to find cost savings and increase agility to cope with transformational times. This is most acute in technology companies, where between 20 and 25 percent of employees have been let go, with a particular emphasis on eliminating midlevel management and anyone who is not a revenue contributor or a maker, builder, or creator.

Another catalyst for change involves Gen Z and even some millennials who hold management in low regard. They wonder what these managers actually contribute besides allocating, monitoring, and delegating while senior management looks askance.

We're seeing the gradual disappearance of the imperial boss—the business celebrity who wears his fame like a crown and expects his edicts to be obeyed. Years ago, Lee Iacocca and Jack Welch were celebrated, and their approach was copied and held up as the model of the effective boss. They are less revered today because Chrysler's and General Electric's fortunes fell, and at least some of the decline has been attributed to Iacocca and Welch, respectively.

Nonetheless, imperial bosses will probably always be with us—Elon Musk and Mark Zuckerberg are two prominent examples. Yet they aren't emulated by many other leaders. Instead, they're viewed more as anomalies than models. Both Zuckerberg and Musk have total control of their boards and companies, which allows them to do things that most other leaders can't. As a result, younger leaders look elsewhere for models—to people like Satya Nadella of Microsoft, Tim Cook of Apple, Doug McMillon of Walmart, or Mary Barra of General Motors in business and in politics, Jacinda Ardern, the former prime minister of New Zealand, or Michelle Obama, the former first lady of the US.

These leaders are excellent communicators; they listen to diverse voices; they are innovators; they create participatory cultures. More than that, their leadership styles produce results. Despite having famous predecessors—such as Steve Ballmer, Steve Jobs, and Sam Walton—they have overcome the long shadows that were cast. They have built stronger cultures and brands and have helped their organizations remain highly successful.

As I've emphasized, we live and work in very different times from pre-COVID. Many people won't tolerate imperial bosses or micromanaging supervisors hovering physically or virtually. Given all the technological innovations and social shifts in recent years, their attitudes about how they work and who they work for have changed.

The type of leader represented by CEOs like Barra, Nadella, Cook, and McMillan possess certain skills that can and should be emulated—skills that are essential today and in the future.

Portrait of a New and More Effective Leader

Think about the work environment in which current leaders operate. It's one where change happens more often, competition for business accelerates, the expectations of customers continues to rise, and the employee-employer landscape grows far more complex due to the following:

- technology such as AI, AR/VR, biotech, blockchain, and 5G, which are advancing rapidly and playing off each other;

- demographic shifts of aging and decreasing populations in most advanced countries combined with a surge of youth in India and Africa;

- global shifts driven in part by nationalism, the rise of China, multipolar globalization, and hundreds of millions of immigrants on the move; and

- a rise in polarization and the demand of employees that the company take a stand on various issues.

So management needs to find ways to adapt to change, scale and deliver quickly, and access and motivate talent in different ways. In other words, they have to develop a growth mindset. Instead of doing what leaders did in the past—carry on traditions, preserve the culture, maintain their margins—they need to update their mental operating systems constantly. Leaders with agile and active minds are necessary.

Similarly, the new and emerging leadership must communicate, collaborate, and convince, rather than deliberate, dictate, and demand. How else can you motivate people working in different places from different cultures? How else can you combine AI with innovative, inspiring humans? The best leaders will be adept at inspiring collaboration across teams, suppliers, and ecosystems.

They realize that in a world of diversity they must listen to and incorporate diverse voices. But at the same time they must ensure that a breakdown in communications over polarized debate or factions cannot be tolerated, since it can turn a culture toxic and take away focus from key business and customer goals.

These leaders will also embrace operational discipline and capability. They will drive results, manage costs, and meet deadlines. Old paradigm leaders also had to do these things, but the challenge now is to do them in a volatile, distributed, and tech-focused workplace.

Leaders need to be capable of doing *all* of these things, not just one or two of them.

WeWork's Adam Neumann did a great job of selling people on his vision and raising billions but not such a great job of displaying operational discipline.

Microsoft's Steve Ballmer was an excellent communicator and a great operator. But it was Satya Nadella, his successor, who had these skills and also had the growth mindset to help the company evolve with the times.

The new leadership lessons take time to learn. I know this from personal experience. From 1996 to 2003, I launched three digital marketing companies under the Leo Burnett brand. At the first of them, Giant Step, my partners Adam and Eric Heneghan wanted to know why I deferred constantly to Leo Burnett senior management; they also couldn't understand why I analyzed every decision in deep detail. Over time, they taught me a new way of managing and leading: that in most cases, moving forward fast and iterating with agility in the real marketplace was a better strategy than hand-wringing micromanagement and getting things perfect. I had grown up professionally in a hierarchical structure where leaders and managers always deferred to those above them. Adam and Eric taught me that in this new digital world, such an approach was an anachronism, that the experience of our senior management wasn't relevant to the demands of our digital marketplace or our small but fast-growing status.

As a leader, I discovered the benefit of adopting a learner's mindset. To this day, I engage best-in-class teachers to help me learn about whatever is relevant, from AI to supply chains to emerging global markets.

I recognize I have been fortunate to work for companies that indulged my passion for learning and encouraged me to adapt my management and leadership approach. I was also lucky that the pace of change was slower back in the early part of the twenty-first century, affording me more time to learn. Today, leaders need to learn on the fly. The hurdles today are more difficult.

In fact, the bar hasn't just been raised for leadership; it's been widened. Any organization interviewing for leadership positions should keep these three words in mind: *Grow. Communicate. Operate.* If they can't do all three, they can't do the job.

Manager Metamorphosis

As I've noted, leadership isn't a position, and every manager has the opportunity to display the leadership qualities just enumerated. On the other hand, people who are high-level leaders—CEOs, CFOs, CTOs, CMOs, and so on—often are removed from the managerial fray. They don't spend a lot of time on the nitty-gritty tasks of management, instead engaging in policymaking, strategic decision-making, and other conceptual and corporate-wide responsibilities.

Even though many organizations are reducing both the number of managers they employ and management levels, the manager role is still crucial for organizations to function effectively. More to the point, though, it's a role that's changing radically. As we've discussed, most people no longer will accept a manager who is bossy, overly intrusive, and inflexible.

But that's what managers shouldn't be. So what should they be?

For the answer, let's start with talent and HR expert Josh Bersin, whom I interviewed on my *What's Next?* podcast. Josh launched Bersin & Associates in 2001, an advisory firm focused on corporate learning, which expanded and grew and was bought by Deloitte in 2012. Josh spent six years at Deloitte. After leaving Deloitte, he started The Josh Bersin Company, which helps guide organizations through transformations.

Josh is attuned to recent changes that have affected organizations, and his belief is that a new type of manager is needed to help people adapt to this evolving environment. For instance, in a world where teams are increasingly dominant, improvisation and agility take precedence over hierarchy and bureaucracy. Today, teams need to be coached; in the past, individuals needed to be directed.

The traditional manager's emphasis on measurement, too, can have negative consequences these days. It can reduce productivity when people focus myopically on reaching a goal versus doing the right thing. At Wells Fargo, employees opened fake accounts since they were compensated based on the number of accounts they opened. General Electric, too, was so results oriented that the short term was emphasized over the long term. Managers must learn to encourage their people to do what is best for the team, group, or organization rather than fixate on making their numbers.

I can't overemphasize this point: managers should be coaches, not bosses. Few companies have retained the military model, where bosses were feared, where they drove their people relentlessly to meet deadlines, increase production, and so on. In an unbundled, distributed world of work, we need managers who can inspire and teach, not managers who can bark orders. This does not mean that being accessible and empathetic are enough. Any coach also calls out bad behavior, sets key deliverables, and holds people to a high standard.

Work is not a spa. Work is business.

Finally, Bersin posits that while culture does include the work environment, it is not just a physical space but an environmental and a virtual experience. This holistic view is crucial for managers to understand and work within. Rather than telling people "the rules" (nine-to-five office hours, no personal computer use at one's desk, and so on) and expecting them to obey, managers should emphasize cultural components—well-being, inclusion, recognition/reward, and flexibility (optionality, agency, and freedom). By communicating these cultural factors, managers can give their people much looser and more relevant parameters for work behaviors. When these parameters are conveyed effectively, they influence people wherever they are, not just within the physical office space.

Five Ways to Be a Better Manager

Now and in the coming years, there's going to be a lot of discussion about people refusing to return to the workplace. This is a sexy topic, but it obscures a much more important one: the ability of managers to adapt and grow amid evolving realities.

Here's what the new world of work requires of managers:

1. Nuance and personalization

Some managers used to say, "I treat everyone equally." In an era where individuality is prized more than ever before, such an egalitarian position is out of step with the times. Specifically, managers should understand that

- some jobs require more in-person interaction and others require less;

- junior or new employees might require more in-person presence both for training and adapting to cultures;

- every employee has a life outside of work, whether it is family or health or other challenges; in most instances, they should be addressed rather than ignored; and

- employees will need to constantly adapt and upgrade their skills and work in new ways; they require managerial support systems that allow the individual and teams to grow.

2. Encouraging employees to signal when they need help

Managerial monitoring is far less effective today than in the past for a number of reasons, including the fast pace and working in different spaces and with different technologies. Speed and newness produce significant employee challenges that aren't always visible. Encouraging people to let managers know when they're struggling or uncertain is a good managerial strategy—far better than communicating (explicitly or implicitly) that they don't want to hear bad news. Employees need to see managers as allies to solve problems rather than disciplinarians from whom they need to hide problems.

To achieve this objective, managers must be approachable and accessible, minimizing the number of gatekeepers and processes that stand in the way of getting help.

3. Constant communication so people are informed and updated

In the old managerial era, information was power, data hoarding made someone valuable, and information asymmetry was a way of doing business. Now and in the coming years, this is a recipe for disaster. Given that people are working all over the place and at different times, continuous, open communication is the only thing that will keep people on the same page.

Unfortunately, the managerial reflex to hoard information is powerful, instilled over decades. As a cautionary lesson, therefore, consider what happens when managers aren't communicating constantly and honestly:

- Bad morale: People will assume the worst (company is doing badly, they are not important, somebody is mad at them).

- Bad decisions: They will make decisions on faulty and out-of-date information or poor guidance since they need to move quickly.

- Bad direction: They will look to peers or less-informed people for direction when stuck.

4. Investing more time in creating, building, coaching, or servicing versus monitoring, delegating, allocating, and updating

People ask, "What should a manager be doing, given that so much of what they used to do is either unnecessary or handled quickly through technology?" The answer: focus on product. Spend more time on doing rather than delegating, on driving outcomes rather than managing processes. When I was a new leader in the digital space, I arrived as an operator—someone who had been taught to do and decide. I realized, however, that the people I was hiring were far more skilled at doing in the digital arena than I was. I transitioned into a leader who mentored and coached people about strategy, setbacks, and clients, a far more appropriate role than trying to implement everything from the top down.

5. Becoming better at giving feedback

Typically, managers give feedback infrequently or formally (performance reviews). At a time when people often don't see managers (in person) for days or longer and change is fast and furious, people need regular input about how they're doing. There often isn't the time or opportunity to chat informally in the break room or at lunch about a project. Therefore, managers must take on the responsibility of becoming better feedback providers. To that end, here are some suggestions:

- **Be sensitive and aware of extenuating circumstances.** We all have bad days, and many times these are a result of something else distracting us or worrying us in our lives. It may be illness, family issues, or other challenges. Empathizing with an individual demonstrates concern and humanity and makes people want to do better the next time.

- **Provide specific input about what could be done better.** Pointing out what went wrong or was less than optimal is only one half of feedback. The more important half is showing or teaching or guiding on how one can improve.

- **Focus on how the task or the process could have been improved rather than criticize the person.** By focusing on how an assignment could be done better, the emphasis is on the product and not the person.

- **Deliver negative feedback (when performance comes up short) by comparing it to a higher standard, especially something the individual achieved on an earlier project.** Recalling assignments or times where the individual or team did a great job reinforces the message that the person can do better rather than suggesting he's incapable of doing a good job.

- **Identify the next opportunity or project for a do-over.** Identifying an upcoming opportunity to implement the feedback concentrates the mind and channels emotions to action.

- **Provide personal help and perspective.** Asking how you can help reinforces that you are on the person's side and are committed to them. Offering context—communicating what others have struggled with over the years or what you may have grappled with—lets people know that mistakes and less-than-stellar performance are par for the course in career growth.

In the past, managers gave their people feedback, but they often weren't good at it. It was too harsh or generalized or sugarcoated. Now and in the future, managers need to master the art, and the previous six suggestions are a good start to gaining mastery.

Renovating Structures

While leaders and managers need to exhibit new behaviors in a changing workplace, larger organizational issues exist that affect these behaviors. Structures and policies can facilitate future-looking behaviors and discourage ones mired in the past. We need to change organizational incentive systems to encourage actions that are productive in 2024 and beyond, rather than cling to ones optimized for the past. If we want managers to coach rather than control, for instance, then we need to incentivize the former behaviors.

Management that thrives in the future will bend structures and processes, adapting to change.

Conversely, marketplaces will not bend to fit yesterday's shapes and business models.

Therefore, we need to be proactive in our structural responses to the new world of work. To that end, here are three recommendations:

CREATE A DUAL-FOCUSED STRATEGY. One of the major challenges for leaders and managers is keeping the business running effectively today while also reshaping it for the future. It's difficult to implement exciting new AI technologies company wide when this will cause chaos in current daily operations as training ramps up. A solution to this quandary is developing a team with its own specific goals and incentives, to optimize for tomorrow, while focusing the rest of the organization on maximizing today, also their own goals and incentives. Both groups report to the same management and are aware of each other's goals and can swap talent and resources as necessary but need to focus on their specific objectives. This ensures that a company optimizes both for today and tomorrow. It also recognizes that tomorrow's competitors may be different from today and to win against them a company may need a new type of talent, measurement criteria, and investments. When I helped launch Starcom IP, we used this dual-focused approach effectively. The two units of the company—online media planning and traditional media planning—each operated with its own policies, pricing, and experts.

DEVELOP AN OPEN PARTNERING ECOSYSTEM. Throughout this book, I've emphasized the importance of changing in response to or even in anticipation of new developments in technology, business, and society. It is no longer possible for leaders and managers to do a good job without access to a wide range of outside partners. As the world changes—as new processes develop, as new markets emerge, as new products are introduced— organizations need to develop relationships with experts in these unfamiliar areas. No individual is an island, and no company in a connected world can prosper without great connections to other individuals or companies, whether they be suppliers, partners, sources of talent, technology, and other platforms. Amazon Web Services, Microsoft Azure, Shopify, OpenAI, Upwork, and others bring new sources of solutions, talent, and scale, and every service provider is upgrading themselves to remain competitive. We need to ensure that we have the best people, the best processes, and the best value as we partner with the marketplace.

All smart managers are asking if we are investing enough in upgrading and finding talent. Are we ensuring tight coordination with our partners and suppliers? Are our external resources constantly iterating and improving to help give ourselves and our companies an edge?

PLAY JAZZ, NOT CLASSICAL. These two musical styles provide a good metaphor for organization changes in structure, policy, and culture.

Consider that classical music often involves an orchestra led by a conductor; the orchestra members must play a piece exactly as composed (with small variations for speed and volume), and a hierarchy (that is, first chair, second chair, and so on) executes the commands of the conductor.

In jazz, ensembles sometimes have a leader, but even then not much hierarchy exists, and different players take turns with the lead. They are encouraged to improvise and interpret passages their own way—they have the freedom to iterate and invent on the fly as the spirit, the situation, and their fellow players move them.

And finally, classical emphasizes the collective group while jazz puts the spotlight on the individual.

Organizations need to transition from classical to jazz structures. In my online newsletter, I've written about the "four shifts"— technology, power, boundary, and mind—and how everything from AI to globalization to remote work to younger generational attitudes about work have made the old structures outmoded.

More specifically, size matters less today as technology provides small companies and individuals with access to cutting-edge quality, manufacturing scale, and global marketplaces.

Speed and agility are critical for all organizations, regardless of size—responsiveness and customization of products and services have become key differentiators.

Within the workplace itself, flexibility of leaders and managers is essential to accommodate the four generations working together, who are often in different locations and have very different attitudes and styles of working.

In this environment, working from a fixed strategy and forcing everyone to adhere to rigid policies is suicidal. Providing a jazz-like freedom to innovate, to find a work style that best suits the individual, to pivot quickly when changes occur—this is the path that leaders and managers should follow.

PREPARING FOR THE FUTURE OF WORK

CHAPTER 10

REIMAGINE THE COMPANY WITH PARADIGM SHIFTS IN MIND

For many years, large organizations remained remarkably steadfast in their strategies and processes—and remarkably profitable. Even in the latter part of the twentieth century and the first decade of the twenty-first, blue-chip, long-established companies such as IBM, General Motors, and Procter & Gamble adhered to their traditional business plans.

To tell a successful company with years of consistent accomplishment that they must reimagine themselves would seem nonsensical—at least back then.

Today, however, it makes all the sense in the world.

The Need to Look Forward, Not Backward

As earlier chapters have emphasized, there is no going back. Though many organizational leaders recognize this truth, they don't always embrace the corollary: the need to assess and prepare for the future.

As daunting as this exercise might be, it's necessary. Organizations need to do more than commit to change; they have to anticipate what changes are best for them in the future. They can ask some basic questions to help figure it out:

What will the future look like?

What will people need and expect?

How will demographics, technology, and other global shifts create new competitors or recharge current competitors, and how will categories blur, blend, and maybe even disappear?

Amid these new expectations and changing competitive dynamics, what advantage will your company offer? A differentiated or better product? A competitive moat of network effects, scale, or some other dynamic? A better experience? Speed and value?

If this sounds as if I'm suggesting you create a future business strategy, that's exactly what I'm suggesting. Very few companies get strategy right primarily because they do not understand the exponential impact of technology and because they define their category and competitive set looking backward rather than forward.

If you think I'm being hyperbolic when I state that organizations are bad at strategy, let me share a few cautionary tales.

Nokia and BlackBerry dominated the mobile phone industry but were obsessed with hardware, and when Apple introduced the iPhone—which had no physical keys and worked using software—both companies refused to adapt before it was too late.

Kodak invented digital imaging but did not move forward with it because its management was incentivized to sell chemicals and photographic paper—unnecessary elements for digital imagery. A few years later, a young company called Instagram, with fifteen employees, was more valuable than Kodak.

Most of the major automobile manufacturers defined the key drivers of their category in ways that did not envision Tesla or an Uber as a threat until those companies began to scale. They couldn't see how software might be more important than hardware. Or how electric might be better than internal combustion engines. Or how a significant number of people might prefer on-demand mobility over the expense of owning cars.

These examples all represent failures of strategic imagination.

To balance the negative with the positive, we should give credit to established companies that have learned to strategize forward rather than backward.

Microsoft has become a trillion-dollar market cap company by reinventing itself around the cloud (Azure), opting for monthly subscriptions (versus software sales), partnering and being open, including its investment in and partnership with OpenAI (versus going it alone and being closed), and eliminating its Windows division.

Walmart revitalized itself in e-commerce by buying Jet.com and Flipkart, entered the advertising business through Walmart Connect, and committed to sustainability and paying its workers better. Once again, they're doing well and are a significant competitor to Amazon.

McDonald's veered away from its standard strategy, by introducing all-day breakfast, investing deeply in its mobile app, and reconfiguring its drive-through service. Today, 75 percent of its business is through these channels.

Between 2006 and 2019, Publicis Groupe rethought its business, from being one of advertising and media to one of marketing and business transformation. They spent $10 billion to enhance their capabilities in technology, data, and strategy, with a series of acquisitions. They also revised their model of compensation and measurement from one that was brand centric to one that was country centric. Third, they invested in Marcel, a growth and connection platform, allowing the company to access talent from anywhere in the world. As of this writing, Publicis has become the most valuable marketing holding company, with excellent growth and profit margins.

These forward-thinking companies had to engage in a complete rethinking of how work was done, to balance the emerging needs of customers and to attract and retain a talented workforce.

Why Rethink Strategy

If a key to strategy is the future, what happens when the contours of the future shift dramatically?

No doubt, leaders at Nokia, BlackBerry, Kodak, and other companies were aware that the world was evolving, that major technology advances were on the horizon, that new markets were emerging, that cultural shifts were underway. But they must have viewed these changes as passing storms and decided to hunker down and wait for the storms to pass.

It was a mistake then, and it's a mistake now.

In the past five years things have become far more complicated. More moving parts exist, buzzing around at faster speeds in ways that are more interconnected. Many of the assumptions that underpinned strategy have not only shifted but, in some ways, became the exact opposite of what firms believed was coming true.

Think about some of the past beliefs on which organizations based their strategies:

- Populations are expanding. When calculating "total addressable market" or "rate of growth," most companies factored in growing populations. Now populations have started to decline in most advanced economies, with almost half of all the population growth between now and 2050 occurring in just nine countries in Africa and Asia.

- Scale is a competitive advantage. While scale still matters, it matters far less than ever before (except for a few types of business), and the very nature of what constitutes scale is changing. Many old forms of scale are now competitive disadvantages!

- Capital and talent are in abundant supply. Capital is still abundant (though more selective), but talent is so scarce that the greatest ROI for businesses may come from unleashing the untapped capacity of their talent. Return on human capital will be a key measure of return, along with return on capital and other metrics.

Now let's look at these three outmoded beliefs in a bit more detail and see how updated beliefs can and should affect strategy.

In terms of population growth, here is a startling fact: it takes 2.1 children per woman to keep the population flat. In most advanced countries, the child-per-woman ratio stands at 1.7 and is declining. Though population is growing in Africa, it's shrinking elsewhere. The Shanghai Academy of Social Sciences team predicts an annual average decline of 1.1 percent beginning in 2021, pushing China's population down to 587 million in 2100, less than half of what it is today. The Great Shrinkage has begun.

Given these numbers, every business should ask two questions of their strategy:

1. How will our plans be affected in our key markets with declining populations?

2. What is our plan for the continent of Africa, which will contain more than 40 percent of the global population in 2100?

In terms of scale, every leader knows that in the past, scale has provided companies with many benefits, from higher margins due to lower costs to insulation from competition due to moats of marketing spending and widespread distribution. During the last ten years, however, the benefits of scale have diminished and in some cases are proving to be a disadvantage.

With direct-to-consumer marketing enabled by the internet and platforms like Shopify, widespread retail distribution is no longer as effective an advantage as it once was. Distribution scale matters, of course, but there are ways to route around the big stores by going direct and creating demand that forces buyers to stock your product.

Similarly, communication scale has changed. Search and social are leading to communication channels where spending power is no longer a competitive edge (as it was in television or print, where marketers cornered key inventory at advantageous prices). Platforms like Facebook equip millions of small businesses with personalization and targeting capabilities to discover customers and be discovered.

Manufacturing scale is one of the most obvious areas where everything has changed. Platforms from Amazon Web Services to Foxconn allow smaller companies to gain the edges of scaled manufacturing, distribution, and technology without any of the legacy disadvantages of size.

And then there's people scale. As always, large companies with large numbers of employees have an advantage—they can recruit and grow a range of talent and offer career advancement. But there are also new ways to reaggregate talent, and many younger people opt to work in smaller and more entrepreneurial environments. In the post-COVID world of unbundled workplaces, more ways exist to build teams both globally and in real time. You can achieve the benefits of people scale without being one of the largest companies.

Legacy scale still matters in most industries. A new fabrication plant for advanced chips can cost more than $4 billion, and there is no way around scale. Today Taiwan Semiconductor Manufacturing Company dominates due to its scale. But new forms of scale have emerged that provide similar strategic advantages, including the following:

- Scale of data. Collecting, refining, and leveraging data is driving fast-growing and highly valued companies, from Amazon to Google to Uber. Data enables a new form of scale—mass personalization.

- Scale of networks. On the internet, network effects play a dominant role in creating winners. Platforms such as TikTok, Facebook, Netflix, and WeChat enjoy flywheel effects of more users attracting more users and therefore more marketers and businesses.

- Scale of influence. Today individuals have tens of millions of Instagram followers or leverage Twitter (X) and TikTok to reach hundreds of millions of people with single posts. If you look at scaled entities on social media, they are individuals, not brands or companies. People are seen as authentic, and big-time influencers can move markets.

- Scale of talent and ideas. One of the lessons of history is that every advance in technology places a premium on superior talent. Technology is a lever and when married with great talent, it can produce major scale effects. Consider Kylie Cosmetics, launched by Kylie Jenner to sell lipstick. In less than two years Kylie Cosmetics sold $900 million of product, despite employing fewer than fifty full-time employees, in addition to outsourcing manufacturing to Seed Beauty and all e-commerce and fulfillment to Shopify. The sole media channel (besides public relations) that Kylie Cosmetics used was Kylie Jenner's Instagram account, with 120 plus million followers—more than the number of viewers for the top ten prime-time television shows combined.

Speaking of talent—it's become scarce rather than abundant. Companies need to pay attention to talent in order for strategies to work in the future. As I've noted, populations are shrinking and aging, so from a pure numerical standpoint, talent is in shorter supply.

Perhaps less obviously, many employees moved hundreds of miles from their offices during COVID. Others have side gigs or have begun portfolio careers, working for a spectrum of global companies facilitated by good internet connections. As a result, growing, leading, attracting, retaining, and investing in this changing pool of talent is going to be a key strategic advantage.

Every strategy deck should have a significant section on unleashing talent rather than being fixated only on competitive dynamics, financial metrics, total addressable market, and other data. Companies grow when talent grows.

If you are skeptical of this statement, try this experiment: the next time a well-known CEO is fired, find out the real reason. It's possible the company overinvested in China or overestimated growth in other major markets. Or they overbuilt stores and other facilities, trying to crowd out competitors. But many times, the cause of the CEO's termination is that leadership has a talent problem. There's been a breakdown in the social contract between management and the people who do the work and are on the front lines.

Reinvention

The companies that succeed in the future will reinvent themselves continuously. They identify key trends and needs and then reshape themselves to benefit and thrive. Certain companies provide us with models for reinvention, including Domino's in the food category, Walmart in retail, Nike in apparel, and Microsoft in software. These and other reinventing companies share the following:

- external and market focus—a realistic understanding that the future will be different and that what got the company to success would not necessarily keep the company succeeding;

- internal changes—a recognition that to win in the future they would need to rethink their culture, their talent, their business model, and the way to go to market; and

- new partnerships—a willingness to partner with others, including erstwhile competitors.

Understandably, perhaps, some leaders are reluctant to embrace this reinvention mentality. They ignore or rationalize the changes that are coming. Some hope that they'll retire before the changes happen. Others convince themselves that change will not affect the company. And there are those who create excuses ("it's too expensive," "now is not the right time," and so forth) to maintain the status quo.

Consider what the reinventors did.

Domino's realized its pizza was seen as "lower quality" than some competitors and that in a world of the internet and mobile phones, it was behind in e-commerce.

Walmart grasped that customer behavior had changed and that Amazon rather than Kroger was the key threat, and it would require a significant amount of investments to catch up.

Nike determined that it needed to leverage new demographics, the power of community, and the ability to sell directly.

Microsoft acted after realizing that a focus on the PC, a refusal to partner, and a corrosive internal culture needed to be upended.

Today all four of these companies are category leaders, with market capitalization and momentum like never before. They changed their own paradigm before the paradigm of change could make them irrelevant.

Despite everything I've written here, I'm sure there are some organizational CEOs who still won't pull the trigger on reinvention, claiming that the future is too uncertain to make major strategic changes. Yet the four main trends that will shape the future are entirely predictable. Here they are:

1. Multipolar globalization. Globalization is unstoppable, and many of the big challenges are global—climate change, COVID-19, China, supply-chain congestion. Some recent articles have suggested that globalization is diminishing, but that's not what I and others observe. While globalization faces challenges, the real news is that it's morphing into something new. In the past, the US and Europe dominated this trend, but now and in the future, the centers of influence are more diverse, including China and India. For instance, strategic imperatives to ensure a steady supply of silicon chips and rare earths will affect most businesses directly and indirectly.

2. Demographic shifts. As I discussed earlier, declining population, aging populations, and significant differences in ethnic makeup and mindsets between young and old will challenge business leaders (not to mention politicians). In the US, ten thousand people turn sixty-five every day, and despite the fixation of marketers on

the young, people over fifty have the money. In the US next year, the country will have a multiethnic majority under eighteen years old, while those over fifty are dominantly Caucasian. In the past, the big differences were in ethnic makeup. Today and in the future, older, White perspectives on social and economic issues are quite different than the view of younger, more diverse folks. And this generational gap is widespread across the world.

3. The Third Connected Age. In 1993 we entered the First Connected Age with the advent of the World Wide Web, where we all connected to discover (search) and transact (e-commerce). In 2007 we expanded into the Second Connected Age, where we were connected all the time (mobile) and connected to everybody (social). This decade will be the Third Connected Age, where data will connect to data (AI), we will connect in new ways (voice, AR, VR), we will have much faster connections (5G), and we will own far more powerful computing (next-generation cloud).

4. COVID-19 shock. The fault lines of COVID-19 will have long-lasting impact. Again, I've discussed this issue in previous chapters and there's no need to rehash all the ramifications here. For the purposes of this discussion, though, consider that every person in the entire world has gone through a financial, health, and social crisis lasting nearly two years, and that they've been exposed to new forms of fragility and resilience in everything from personal relationships to business operations to social structures. The trauma and triumphs of these two years will reverberate far into the future.

The power of these four trends is from their cumulative force, and they will produce a very predictable but also very dramatic quantum rate of change.

Incorporating People into the Plan

Strategic planning often involves senior management, many hours of work, and sizeable budgets for outside specialists to move the strategy forward. It's an intense process; business leaders often get caught up in it because of the flurry of activity. In an alliterative nutshell, this is what happens:

- A cavalcade of consultants convey and communicate to the C-suite with countless charts and choices.

- A flurry of futurists frame, focus, and filter the way forward with the finesse of fortune tellers.

- Masters of the universe market marketing and advertising moves that might make multiples move upward and mean many more millions in market cap.

- PR professionals produce and promote points of view that provoke the press to perceive with pristine perspectives.

All of this is fine, but in the poetry of planning a strategy, the people component can get lost.

Here's a shocking truth: no strategy will work unless management implements a corresponding plan to grow and change the people in the organization.

Though I discussed the challenge of talent scarcity earlier, the point here is to maximize the talent you possess. Think about all the changes discussed here and in previous chapters—everything from population shifts to technology breakthroughs to globalization.

These factors are going to affect how people think and feel about work. You can have the most brilliant consultants working for you and a strategic plan that is incredibly innovative and far reaching, but if you fail to help employees change along with the changing organization, the strategy won't work.

While businesses are a collection of ideas, technologies, patents, brands, ecosystems, and people, it is *people* who are the key because they create the ideas, technologies, patents, brands, and ecosystems!

Former heavyweight boxing champion Mike Tyson said, "Everyone has a plan till they get punched in the face." The reaction of people to changes in systems, policies, processes, and structures can be a punch in the strategist's face. When a strategy is implemented with much fanfare and expense, business leaders must be attuned to how this strategy—especially if it's attempting to reinvent the company—affects people.

Telling people that change is good, threatening them with job loss if they do not change, or creating communication materials and slogans to convince them to embrace the strategy rarely works in the short run. Even more distressing, it will likely fail in the long run, after the threat of punishment for failing to embrace it fades. If there is nothing in it for them, people will outwit, outwait, outpretend, and outmaneuver management. Until then they will fill the time going through the monitored motions of attending the right meetings, muttering the motivational mantras, and stating the required slogans.

For a reinvention strategy to be leveraged in ways that transform an organization, company leaders should keep the following in mind: *true transformation only happens when the mindsets and behaviors of the people working for the business transform.*

To that end, here are three questions that all managers and leaders should ask to ensure their teams are aligned with the new strategy:

1. How do you expect our customer/consumer/member needs and expectations to change in the future?

2. What are our key strengths and weaknesses in meeting and aligning with these shifts?

3. What products and services would we design, if we could do so and avoid any illegal activity, ensure technological feasibility, and break even financially in three years or less?

This exercise makes people look up from their day-to-day tasks and understand risks and opportunities; it raises their consciousness about the need to do things differently. It also motivates them to activate the strategy in their areas of competence and expertise.

At the same time, management must offer three clear answers around the organizational reinvention, providing information and motivation that works synergistically with employee answers to the previous three questions:

1. Why are the recommended changes good for our people's personal career growth?

2. What are the monetary or other incentives to change?

3. When and where will training be provided to help our people learn the new skills needed?

Again, let me repeat the phrase that should become an organizational mantra when it comes to strategy and reinvention: *an organization changes and grows when the people in the organization change and grow.*

CHAPTER 11

RETRAIN THE WORKFORCE

I s this really necessary?

The suggestion that we need to retrain everyone sounds overwhelming. Can't we just muddle through change as we've done in the past?

No, and here are two simple reasons why:

Talent is asking their managers: What do you do?

Management is asking their talent to work harder, show up, and grow up.

Talent says: Help me grow.

Management says: Yes, but earn your keep and do your current job well first.

Both are legitimate responses to the current work environment, and they suggest how ill-prepared we are for our changing world.

The good news is that we're fully capable of implementing the retraining I'm advocating. As you'll discover, it doesn't require an investment in the training protocols of the past but a commitment to the training paradigms of the future.

Training Innovations

Organizations may not call what they're doing "retraining," but a number of companies have made dramatic shifts from the training protocols of the past. Bank of America, for instance, established The Academy in 2016, an ambitious reimagining of the scope and depth of training. Consisting of ninety-seven programs, it includes a startling variety of content and goals—peer mentoring, immersion programs, high-tech learning. The Academy is designed to provide support and connection as people grow in their careers. But what's most significant is that it's the type of training that acknowledges the sea change that has occurred in recent years. Rather than focusing on training that benefits the organization, it emphasizes an approach that benefits employees as well as the organization. It understands that tenure and retention of employees is crucial when people matter more than ever before and that the power has shifted toward talent.

Microsoft, too, has implemented an ambitious continuous training program that is quite different from the limited, one-and-done classes of the past. Its emphasis on continuous education alone recognizes that in a world where change is constant and significant, one class no longer suffices. As a company that has reinvented itself around a growth mindset, Microsoft has created the Viva Learning platform, which reflects this mindset. It integrates learning experiences into an employee's workflow and personalizes these experiences. It helps employees tailor their training, allowing them to learn what they need to know for their jobs, their careers, and their growth. Viva takes into account a given employee's location (office or remote), goals, and previous experiences and knowledge.

Other organizations are launching training innovations in more targeted ways, but they represent a recognition that people need to learn new things in new ways. A 2022 Boston Consulting Group study offers a number of examples of how this is so. The study notes that companies like Amazon and Goldman Sachs are offering "returnship" programs for organizational alumni who want to come back to work. As part of these programs, returning employees are offered training to help them transition to the new world of work.

What's most significant, though, aren't the specific programs but the growing sense among organizational leaders that they and their people need to alter their perspectives and upgrade their knowledge and skills to deal effectively with a marketplace and larger world where nothing stays the same for long.

The Big Question

As I travel around the world speaking and working with a wide range of companies, their most common question is: "How do we remain relevant in transformative times?" Not just relevant as organizations grappling with new business models and competitive landscapes but as individual talent and leaders facing a future that seems to be shape-shifting constantly.

My answer: the only way to remain relevant in these times is to upgrade our mental and emotional operating systems to align with new realities. We need to retrain our brains to deal effectively with emerging paradigms, and this requires both learning and unlearning in the following three areas:

1. Where. As I've discussed, and as the media is increasingly fond of pointing out, a growing percentage of workers will be remote. This division between remote and office work is overly simplistic. In reality, we'll have many variations on the in-office and remote theme, with companies seeking a mix that works best for them. On top of that, organizations will be using more freelance talent that

works elsewhere, and they'll need to integrate these "outside" people as well. Though a huge amount of attention has been devoted to the remote work trend, relatively little focus has been directed at training people to work effectively in this evolving environment. Thus, successful companies will train their people to manage and communicate across different models of work.

2. Who. We need to retrain ourselves to lead a much more diverse employee population than in the past. Traditional policies and practices were created in an era when most companies were run by a narrow demographic, and consciously or not, these policies and practices reflected this homogeneity. Consider that in the under-twenty-one-years-of-age population, Whites are now a minority in the US. Add to that the growing number of women with college degrees, the changes in sexual preference (13 percent of the population is gay, trans, and so on), and the aging of the population and the workforce. We need to learn how to attract, retain, and motivate a much more diverse group than in the past.

3. What. More specifically, we need to educate ourselves about what a job should be—what tasks and responsibilities are best for a given job. Technology is having a huge impact on the what—IBM believes that AI will replace 30 percent of jobs in five years, and it will affect white-collar jobs more than blue-collar ones. Part of the retraining, therefore, involves understanding how to optimize AI within the organization. To paraphrase the earlier quotation from Rob Thomas, IBM's chief commercial officer, "Humans will lose their jobs not to AI but to other humans who know how to use AI." Other technologies—the metaverse, VR, spatial computing—will demand new

skill sets for effective leadership as well as to sell and build brands and companies.

Every company is grappling with the where, who, and what, and retraining offers the best option for dealing effectively with these challenges.

Compelling Reasons
to Think and Learn Differently

Typical corporate training was tailored for a time when changes came slowly if at all, when employees worked in the office, and when core competencies were evergreen. Now we need to transition toward a just-in-time, self-serve, skills-acquisition operation. As companies and the competitive landscape change, people need to obtain the emerging knowledge and skills that will help them function effectively in this environment.

As most of you probably know, training in the business world used to consist of some initial onboarding lasting a few days to a few months, during which HR people familiarized new employees with the company's culture, technology, tools, and processes. Additional training ranged from periodic mandatory training on issues such as data privacy and policy or diversity, equity, and inclusion. The company might also help pay employees' tuition in an evening course or executive program at a university to bolster specific skills and knowledge.

Expertise was purchased by either hiring college graduates or recruiting experienced employees from other companies. Training programs were limited and generalized for these reasons:

- A surplus of skilled labor existed. It was cheaper to buy from outside than train inside.

- The rate of change in an industry was slow to medium paced. There was no urgency to acquire/train for new expertise.

- Owners and management had more power than talent (reflected in onerous employee contracts constraining a move to competitors and the decline of unions). Companies didn't need to invest significantly in training—in providing employees with opportunities to acquire new skills and growth opportunities—because they held the upper hand.

- The workforce evolved slowly. The workforce in the US grew every year and increasingly diversified with more people of color and women, but the diversification was gradual. As a result, most companies didn't feel the need to offer the type of diversity, equity, and inclusion training common today.

In the past few years, the marketplace for talent and the ecosystem of work has transformed, affecting hiring and training in major ways:

- A paradigm shift driven by new technologies such as AI, Web3, and electric engines has increased the expense of hiring outside relative to using internal training. Recently, Walmart and Netflix advertised AI positions with $900,000 salaries.

- New technologies like AI and Web3 require companies not only to understand these technologies but to reconfigure and rethink their business models. In just one highly specialized area, video special effects, the nature of work will change due to new tools like Runway and OpenAI's Sora, which dramatically reduce the time to do video jobs. This requires either hiring people who know how to use these new tools or training existing employees to use them. Similarly, legacy auto companies need to upgrade the software and electric drive train skills of employees. Since there's insufficient talent from the outside (and the costs of hiring externally may be prohibitive), they need to implement large training programs.

- The balance of power is moving to labor and away from capital. If you doubt this, consider some of the factors that suggest this shift in power: the rapid increase in salaries among retail and frontline workers; the strikes roiling Hollywood, where leaders berating talent and telling them to adjust to reality are met with laughter; an aging workforce; and reduced immigration creating shortages of labor. In this environment, companies must focus on providing labor with the skills they need to do a good job and the compensation to retain them.

- A sudden shift in workforce mindsets. COVID-19 and hybrid-remote work changed what people thought of work and how it fit into their life and how and where they could work. They had higher expectations and new beliefs in where and how work could be done. This meant that companies had to rethink their training policies, helping people learn how to collaborate remotely, teaching leaders how to manage teams with a mix of remote and in-office members, and providing other knowledge and skills that dovetail with this new mindset.

Retraining the workforce is a huge challenge, and companies are struggling to meet this challenge because they're facing five very different but very significant issues:

1. The need to understand new technologies

2. Management at odds with a new generation of talent

3. Needing to learn how to operate and manage in a hybrid environment.

4. Concerns about how to remain relevant as business models shift

5. Attempts to keep up with exponential change, AI such as GPT and Anthropic that were launched and scaled and then improved two or three times within six months

Given the scope and rate of change, broad training is necessary since every job is being affected by these technological, demographic, and social changes. US training expenditures passed the $100 billion mark for the first time in 2021–2022, rising 10 percent to $101.6 billion. But these numbers tell just part of the story because there's not only more training going on but different types of training. Continuous training is essential, for competitive and cost reasons and for cultural reasons—it is easier and faster to train existing talent who understand customer needs and company culture than to bring in new people who have no familiarity with these issues. In addition, leaders and managers need to take responsibility for fostering a shift in philosophy and strategy. They must retrain themselves and others so that they learn to think differently about the business.

Retraining can take many forms, from one-on-one discussions to policy shifts. My former company, Publicis Groupe, now keeps people up to speed by giving all their hundred thousand employees access to training courses covering hundreds of topics, both on demand and in real time, and on any device. A series of certifications in various skill areas enable people to apply for new jobs or rise to the next level. They also have made a $100 million investment that ensures every employee will be trained in AI. The idea behind these types of investments isn't just to help employees obtain better jobs but to enhance their ability to grow themselves—to give them tools so they can reach their goals.

For this reason, many of Publicis's training tools are aimed at helping people learn to work from anywhere in the world and to gain global perspectives.

Because of the following epiphany, many companies are starting to realize that retraining the workforce is a necessity rather than an option: an organization's growth and relevance in a changing world is directly proportional to employees' skill growth and relevance.

Companies that are slow to commit to upgrading their people's technical abilities, management skills, or expertise suffer like never before. They lose market share and hemorrhage world-class talent. Without the latest knowledge and competencies, they can't move as fast and effectively as competitors. Without giving employees opportunities to learn cutting-edge skills, they alienate their people and cause them to seek these skills elsewhere.

Learning to Lead Distributed and Diverse Workforces

Earlier, I described the work environment in the '80s when I joined the Leo Burnett ad agency—how offices were highly structured, IBM Selectric typewriters represented state-of-the-art technology, employees were overwhelmingly Caucasian, and leaders were overwhelmingly male. Let me provide a better sense of what it was like back then, since many leaders today were "raised" in this environment and affected by the norms of the time. Retraining that targets these anachronistic attitudes is essential. Here are some typical norms from years ago:

- You paid your dues and slowly rose in rank. There were established career paths and planned rotations.

- People stayed at a company for many years and often for decades.

- Everyone listened to and no one argued with bosses, and their expertise was not questioned.

- You worked with the information given to you, and the higher you rose in the company the more information you had.

Until the early twenty-first century, little changed. While the technology advanced a bit and more diversity existed, we still valued stable careers, godlike management, putting in your time, and being a good soldier. The social contract of mutual loyalty between employee and company was honored, for the most part.

It wasn't until 2010 that the workplace began to shift in major ways, due to a combination of the birth of smartphones and social media (2007), financial challenges (the Great Recession of 2008–2009), and other factors. Companies rightsized and downsized, nearshored and offshored, and focused on just-in-time inventory and agility. In doing so they signaled that everyone was on their own. While much talk of loyalty and commitment and culture was spun, it was basically just talk. Socially and technologically adept employees shared information and discovered that management was speaking one story while actually implementing another. Senior management was no longer deified and in some cases they were no longer respected.

In the post-COVID world, all the givens of traditional offices have begun to disappear:

- Talent and youth were informed and empowered.

- Diverse voices insisted on being heard.

- Fewer people were willing to pay their dues.

- Office hours and even physical offices were called into question.

- The work-life balance goal changed to how to fit work into life.

- New technologies like AI required new skills and ways of working.

Many managers and leaders who rose through the ranks before 2010 are experiencing cognitive dissonance—the world they knew and the rules by which they abided for years are no more. Their organizational designs based on scale were blown to bits by new markets and new technologies. They seemed to possess irrelevant skills and management styles. Gen Z questioned their overly intrusive management style. Diverse workforces challenged their hiring and promotion policies. Marketplaces were skeptical about their ability to transform their companies.

Fortunately, people are adaptable, and they can be retrained or can retrain themselves to manage and lead in new ways. As someone who has successfully navigated many shifts over four decades, I am convinced that everyone, regardless of age or background, can successfully transform themselves. Doing so, however, requires five realizations:

1. What made you successful may not keep you successful.

2. Organizational design must be rethought.

3. Management and leadership should be about zone of influence and coaching rather than zone of control and "bossing."

4. The rate of change is likely to accelerate and therefore, one needs to continuously iterate and grow.

5. A major personal investment of time and effort must be made to learn and unlearn.

These realizations are actionable by even the most veteran people in many different ways. It starts with allocating significant time weekly to train themselves or obtain training in new skills—attending classes, getting tutored, being mentored, opting for reverse mentoring. It also means that senior executives surround themselves with diverse perspectives and voices and encourage those voices to speak up. For some leaders, it may involve spending time outside of their categories (industries, geographies, management levels, and so on). For others, it may require developing the agility to see that the future of their business isn't one model but multiple ones, tailored to situations, individuals, and markets. And finally, people need to teach themselves to think in terms of balance and integration—to bring together the needs of their employees with the needs of their customers; to balance shareholder and market expectations with the need for greater purpose and community meaning; and to figure out how to deliver today while transforming tomorrow.

I realize this a lot to ask of people who are set in their ways. But I also realize that most people are fully capable of embracing new and better ways of working.

Machine-Human Compatibility 101

To my knowledge, no course exists like the one just described, but there is a growing need for the knowledge it might convey. You can train people how to use everything from software to social media, but teaching them to work synergistically with established and emerging technologies requires a broader approach. When I wrote my first book a few years ago, I addressed the issue of how to find the right balance between people and technology. Back then, the hot tech areas were cryptocurrency, blockchain, robotics, and augmented reality.

As of this writing, AI dominates discussions, so I'm going to focus on AI when it comes to organizational retraining. No doubt, other hot-button topics will emerge in the coming years, but my advice applies to any technological development.

Contrary to what many people might think, AI isn't new—its history stretches back eighty years. (You can learn about this history online at the Computer History Museum, https://computerhistory .org.)

But AI finally arrived in widely usable forms because of easy access to lots of training data on the internet, massive increases in computing power, and several breakthroughs in neural network design. Today, daily breakthroughs, combined with tens of billions of dollars of capital investments in technologies, means that every company, every job, and every one of us will be affected by AI.

Here are three steps that will help every organization transition their people to AI and other evolving technologies:

1. Embrace.

This first step may be counterintuitive. You may feel like resisting AI or any other new technology as a passing fad or as ill-suited to a given organizational task. The reflexive skepticism about anything new or different needs to be rejected in favor of being open-minded and eager to embrace. Bear with me as I make my case.

It's 1977, and a new movie, *Star Wars: Episode IV - A New Hope,* is released. In it General Dodonna ends a briefing to his fighters (including Luke Skywalker) with the words "May the Force be with you."

It's 1599, and somewhere in England a play by William Shakespeare, *Julius Caesar*, is staged during which the following lines are spoken:

> *We, at the height, are ready to decline.*
> *There is a tide in the affairs of men*
> *Which, taken at the flood, leads on to fortune;*
> *Omitted, all the voyage of their life*
> *Is bound in shallows and in miseries.*
> *On such a full sea are we now afloat,*
> *And we must take the current when it serves,*
> *Or lose our ventures.*

Both Shakespeare more than five hundred years ago and George Lucas fifty years ago shared the first rules of thriving in changing times: Align with the Force. Go with the flow.

I know all the objections to embracing AI: copyright issues, negative impact on employment, a Terminator-like bot destroying humanity. These objections, however, pale before the reality: Prometheus has given fire to the world. There is no going back.

Individuals and organizations must make a concerted effort to understand AI including generative AI (Gen AI) which is one flavor of AI. These include prompt to text (for example, GPT), prompt to image (for example, Midjourney), prompt to audio (for example, ElevenLabs), and prompt to video (for example, Runway). One way to keep up is to subscribe and read a free daily note called Ben's Bites (https://bensbites.com).

2. Adapt.

The retraining focus here is on products and services—figuring out what changes are essential, based on AI technologies. In many organizations, an "if it ain't broke, don't fix it" attitude prevails toward profitable products and services. Because of AI, everything must be rethought.

This process isn't as simple as using AI to automate and accelerate or to restructure in order to cut costs. Taking this simplistic approach will probably lead to more problems than solutions. There's the story of an attorney who used AI to facilitate his work on a legal case only to find that AI had made things up.

The opportunity with AI is a deep restructuring of the business, and this requires answering three questions:

- What should be AI enhanced and what should not be?

- How will the AI product be built/trained, and what quality control will ensure that the result is safe and legal (among other things)?

- How will the organizational design and talent allocation change to incorporate these new capabilities?

For most companies, AI technology probably will become a commodity-like ingredient. In fact, smaller companies (outside of the mega-cap tech companies that are funding and driving AI investments) are likely to benefit more from AI than larger ones since the technology will make amazing capabilities affordable to everybody. One of the most important challenges for any organization will be having access to or owning data to consider applying AI. The tech itself will be available to many but data is what will provide differentiation and competitive advantage.

Given all this, one aspect of retraining may involve communicating that size becomes less of a competitive advantage than in the past. It will also mean that senior management can no longer tell themselves that there's no rush to embrace AI—that they can wait until retirement and pass the issue on to their successors. AI is scaling so quickly that even the most myopic leaders can see the writing on the wall.

And it means that to adapt effectively, learning how to attract and retain talent that grasps how to work in AI-complimentary ways is crucial.

3. Complement.

As we become more and more reliant on technologies such as AI, we also need to balance or complement this reliance with distinctly human qualities. Pursuing this complementary strategy as part of a retraining approach will create synergies between people and machines.

CHAPTER 12

REDESIGN THE STRUCTURES

There's a reason we no longer live in mud huts or travel in horse-drawn carriages. Times change, technology improves, and people's needs and preferences shift. As much as we may love the simplicity of our old dwellings and the convenience of traditional transportation modes, we recognize the need to upgrade.

But what if the need to upgrade isn't as obvious as choosing a car over a horse-drawn carriage?

Organizational structures have been in place so long that it's sometimes difficult to recognize that they're outmoded. For many years, businesses were hierarchies, run with military-like methods. Top-down monitoring, controlling bosses, and compensation inequities were part of the system, justified as "efficient" if not fair.

This justification is no longer valid. The balance of power is trending away from organizations and management and toward talent and individuals. Generational shifts, post-COVID mindsets, technology advances, new ways of working, and recently emerged marketplaces provide more options for people to connect, create, and cultivate alternatives to where, when, and how they work.

In this environment, few people want to work for a company with policies and processes rooted in the '50s. Instead, they want a redesigned organizational structure, one that is far more flexible, equitable, and innovative than past structures.

More Than Replacing the Hierarchy with Teams

For years, business pundits have talked about reinventing the corporation. About flattening it. About relying more on teams. About eliminating the bureaucracy.

But that's not what I'm talking about. Simplistic, one-size-fits-all restructuring plans don't work, no matter how well intentioned they might be. If you ask leaders to explain their organizations, they reflexively reach for organizational charts. Whether a top-down hierarchy or a matrix structure or some combination of both, these aren't so different from the first organizational charts developed in 1855 to help run the New York and Erie Railroad.

These "fixed" structures no longer make sense, given that talent today often seeks autonomy that runs counter to most locked-in processes and policies; the fluid ecosystem of global partners and dynamic marketplaces has replaced many vertically integrated structures; modern connectivity places a premium on speed and agility (impossible to achieve in even semibureaucratic environments); and new technologies like AI are rendering traditional practices and ways of working obsolete.

Most CEOs recognize the need for agility, speed, and customized product/service delivery, and they've made efforts to flatten structures by removing levels, to decentralize control and rebuild the company around teams. All are valid responses to situations, but they also tend to be of limited value. That's because they don't focus on outcomes or customer needs, or on achieving sufficient flexibility to accommodate a range of managerial styles.

That's why so many companies go back and forth between centralized and decentralized models. They respond situationally. They centralize when costs must be constrained, decentralize when they're accused of being slow and inflexible. They centralize again when a legal problem or process breakdown requires more control. And they may centralize or decentralize when a new CEO is named and that CEO implements a preferred model.

Ron Carucci and Jarrod Shappel in a 2020 *Harvard Business Review* article, "Design Your Organization to Match Your Strategy," recommend a redesign approach that, among other things, advocates closing down structures that are no longer fit to purpose and being aware when culture becomes internally focused and constraining versus market focused and enabling.

Again, the point is to be flexible and outward facing in creating new policies, processes, and systems. Microsoft is one company that has done this well.

When Satya Nadella took over Microsoft in 2014, he quickly determined that the company was not aligned or organized for the future. To remedy the situation, he started changing the culture to align with the new realities. For instance, he implemented a learning philosophy and programs, insisting that Microsoft would move from a know-it-all to a learn-it-all mindset. He also shifted the company's focus from competition to collaboration, incentivizing the latter. Nadella began to partner and invest in open software through the acquisition of GitHub, as well as encouraging partnering with many different companies. Microsoft began looking for external opportunities rather than gazing myopically at internal (albeit profitable) ones.

Microsoft's stock price has risen almost tenfold in the past ten years after being flat for the previous ten.

Sometimes, CEOs implement new policies and programs that catalyze a rethinking of structural elements. At Shopify, CEO

Toby Lutke banished meetings from all employees' calendars. He asked people to decide whether they needed the meetings and, if so, whether they needed it to be the same duration as in the past and with as many invitees as was the norm. Or, conversely, could they do away with these meetings? It can be argued that meetings have long been the structural fuel on which organizations run, and to challenge whether that fuel is necessary is a major step toward the future.

Doubling Down Instead of Placing New Bets

Redesigns can be messy. For this reason, people question whether they're worth it. Can't we get by with what we have if we make a few tweaks?

Unfortunately, a few tweaks aren't sufficient, given the major shifts in every sector of our society. AI is turbocharging the multi-earner and gig economy, and this trend alone mandates a redesign. A 2023 Morgan Stanley study showed that the multijob trend had picked up steam, facilitated by generative AI. Their conclusion was that AI allowed people to be more productive and increased their ability to handle two or more jobs. They forecast that people with multiple jobs would account for $400 billion in income by 2030. Combined with more people than ever before pursuing side gigs and passion projects, this trend indicates that organizations would be wise to implement policies that fit this new reality. Most employees no longer want to spend five days and forty hours a week in the office. As I've emphasized, companies need to offer flexible work schedules, job-sharing options, and other incentives to recruit and retain people.

Many organizations, however, have failed to invest fully in these new work policies. Instead, a backlash against traditional structures has become evident:

Resentment about having to return to the office and resumption of employee monitoring. While many companies have adopted hybrid work schedules in some form, organizations are also displaying recidivist tendencies—reverting to pre-COVID practices. Traditionally, companies felt the need to monitor employees. Supervisors often walked around and checked to make sure people were doing their jobs and used sign-in and sign-out sheets or time clocks to ensure that people put in a full day's work.

Now some organizations are returning to this monitoring mentality using technology. According to a September 25, 2023, *Wall Street Journal* article, more companies than in the past are using monitoring badge swipes to assess in-office presence, along with creative negative sanctions for people who refuse to return to the office; TikTok is one of the badge-swipe companies and they ask employees to explain their absences. The article also quotes Amazon's CEO raising the possibility that people who aren't in the office three days weekly may not have long careers with the company.

Monitoring is an organizational policy that is particularly offensive to younger employees, who find it paternalistic and demeaning.

Rising support for unions and increasing numbers of strikes. There's far less tolerance today for policies that seem exploitive of workers. A recent Gallup survey found that 67 percent of adults approve of labor unions. Gallup also found that 75 percent of people sympathize with the United Auto Workers (who at the time of the survey were threatening to strike). Striking screenwriters received 72 percent support and actors garnered 67 percent.

This support reflects a societal trend favoring fairness. It used to be that people expected the CEO to be treated and compensated like a king and the mailroom people to be treated and compensated like serfs. Today, there's growing outrage about the growing gap between the highest-paid and the lowest-paid workers in a given business. There's a belief that organizations should do a better job not only in sharing the wealth but in terms of health-care benefits, retirement plans, and so forth.

Plunging morale. BambooHR, a human resources software company, coined the term the "Great Gloom" to describe the mood that followed the Great Resignation. In their recent survey of employee happiness, they found that from 2020 to the present, happiness has declined at a 6 percent rate per year. They also noted that the decrease has been even greater in 2023, dropping 9 percent since January.

According to a Gallup July 2023 survey, 80 percent of Americans are dissatisfied with the way things are going in the US, and job satisfaction has dropped by 8 percent since 2019.

While many factors can affect job satisfaction and work happiness, a crucial one is environment. Does work provide a setting where people feel comfortable, fulfilled, and empowered? Put another way: Is work a satisfying, meaningful experience?

For a lot of people, the answer to these questions is no, and it's a no because the old structures no longer fit the new mindsets.

Redesign Conceptually and Practically

To create a redesign that is effective now and for years to come, we need to think about structure more broadly than is typical. Most people think of business structures from an organizational-chart perspective. They envision boxes and connecting lines that indicate who reports to whom or the flow of goods and services from the company to various markets. That's why when people talk about restructuring, they focus on things like flattening the organization and eliminating some of the lines or streamlining the supply chain.

While all of this is important, it's just part of what needs to be redesigned. An organizational chart is a two-dimensional view—I'm advocating a three-dimensional redesign.

For years, we've fooled ourselves into believing that the organizational chart represents how the organization works. That was okay in less complex, less volatile times, but it's no longer acceptable. Consider that organizational charts and maps indicate how leaders *want* the company to operate, but the reality often is quite different.

For instance, the maps and charts document zones of control rather than zones of influence. A title represents a position that may be vested with authority but not necessarily the authority to determine how work is done. These charts also impose clarity where there often is none. Business is messy, and operations often shape-shift based on circumstance, ignoring the flowchart. The official organizational structures are also limited in scope, failing to account for all the external partners, freelancers, and other outside groups that have become necessities.

Consider the static nature of organizational design, driven by internal factors (that is, areas of expertise) and client/customer categories. In an increasingly globalized world filled with new marketplaces and transformed by technology, this design must be more organic, adapting to external stimuli.

For this reason, redesigning the structures must take the following factors into consideration:

- **Customer benefit.** This may seem obvious, but company design often reflects internal requirements first and customers second. Given the increasing diversity and changing needs of customers, organizations should consider creating different designs for different customers. This might mean colocating with a customer or integrating with customer suppliers.

Design discussed as a singular object is a mistake. Plural designs make a lot more sense.

- **Talent advantage.** In the past, points of differentiation included price, service, innovation, and so on. Today, the main differentiator is talent. Companies must organize in ways to ensure that their talent is satisfied and growing. Considering that talent often is spread across different locations, possesses different work-style preferences, and represents a wide demographic range, one organizational model doesn't fit all. Instead, the model should accommodate the full range of talent.

- **Change adaption.** The previous two points allude to this one: organizational design must be flexible, able to shift as changes occur. Competitors change. Laws change. Markets change. The design, therefore, must anticipate that these shifts will occur and be created in such a way that adapting a policy or revamping a process isn't a big deal. This is an organic, evolving approach to design (versus an artificial, static one). To deliver on strategy, one needs to update the design continuously.

- **Permeability.** Traditional designs are closed systems. Today, they need to be open. They must be capable of connecting and fusing with other companies in an increasingly connected, fast-moving world. A company and its deliverables grow by combining capabilities and products from different external firms or being part of those other firms' deliveries.

Toyota is an example of a company that works very closely with its ecosystem of suppliers in a relationship of mutual trust and synergy that allows for better quality control and high velocity in a just-in-time system.

Three Transformations

It's not going to happen overnight. Anyone who has ever had a kitchen remodeled or other major structural work done in a residence knows that the work often takes longer than expected. The same idea holds true with organizational renovation. The ambitious but challenging goal is to transform the organization so it's aligned with the world's technological, cultural, and market changes. Organizations will transform in the following ways:

From legacy structures to roots-and-wings design

Legacy structures tend to be companies built around the profit flows and products of today and yesterday. Legacy assets still generate cash flow, have customer and brand value, and contain talent. But they also motivate leaders to maintain the status quo; they hook organizations on profitable existing products and services, on structures and processes built in and for an era that is rapidly disappearing. Perhaps more destructively, they discourage disruption. Preserving the legacy is the main priority.

The transformation, therefore, is treating these assets as the roots of the company—as foundational pieces from which new life grows. They provide the basis for this new life to take wing and soar, to become organizational designs optimized for new customer segments or other future targets. Roots keep the business viable today; wings help it remain viable in the future.

Successful companies learn to combine roots and wings. Parts of the company are designed for today and others for tomorrow, but talent flows between the two models and leaders orchestrate this flow.

From bosses/zones of control to leaders/zones of influence

Essentially, this means moving from a structure where people's power is based on their seniority, the amount/type of business they control, and how many people report to them, to a more organic system. In the former, turf wars are common, and people are incentivized to accumulate and retain power. In an organic system, the incentives are different—people are motivated to have influence and respond to external realities.

From seeing people and labor as a cost that must be controlled to an asset that requires an investment
As I noted earlier, talent now provides competitive advantage, and the best thing organizations can do is nurture that talent through its policies and processes. This means accommodating workers versus forcing workers to accommodate the company. It means more programs that cater to employee career goals.

As Beliefs Shift, So Should Organizational Design

Until around January 2020, most companies operated under the following five assumptions or beliefs:

1. The organization gives structure and directs work.

2. Tenure and experience are critical to advancement.

3. Most of the work is done inside an organization.

4. Fairness requires a common set of rules and ways of working that apply to all.

5. Most people are full-time employees of the company.

Here are beliefs that have supplanted these traditional ones:

1. The organization enables talent to create structure and direct work.

2. Expertise and constant learning in a changing world are more highly valued than tenure/experience.

3. Most of the work is done outside an organization by suppliers and by accessing talent as needed.

4. Fairness means customizing programs for each talent and giving everyone equal access to those programs.

5. Most staff are either contract workers, freelancers, or fractionalized employees.

Because of these new beliefs and assumptions, organizations must rethink how they design everything, from compensation systems to decision-making processes.

On the most basic level, it means they must design structures from the outside in rather than the inside out. In a fast-changing world, companies must create their processes and procedures based on marketplace realities (that is, emerging competitors and changing talent mindsets) rather than relying on "the way things have always been done around here."

They should also embrace multiple models of working rather that a single model. Given the multiplicities in workplaces today, models need to differ based on country, competition for talent, and whether the focus is on current business or innovations.

And finally, it means outcomes and goals take precedence over process and control. Financial results, customer satisfaction, and talent attraction/retention should take priority over following strict procedures or maintaining tight control about how work is done.

To commit to this type of redesign requires trust—management must trust talent and teams to determine the best ways to drive financial results, customer satisfaction, and talent attraction and retention. By restructuring roles, talent takes the initiative while management guides and coaches. This trust extends to empowering teams to solve problems and capitalize on opportunities in ways that make sense for their markets (rather than everyone following the mandate from headquarters). Management's restructured role involves setting parameters—they grant their people freedom within a framework. They know where the guardrails should be erected to prevent teams from getting in legal difficulties or taking unreasonable risks.

While many organizations have taken steps in this direction, most are not there yet. To assess redesign progress, the following questions might help:

- Is your organization biased toward yesterday or tomorrow?

- Does your company possess agile systems and processes? Is it flexible when it comes to how and where work is done and how partnerships are initiated?

- Can you deliver customized products and services? Does your organizational structure support personalization or is one particular system or process mandated?

- Are the policies and protocols of your organization designed to facilitate trust among teams and customers?

Redesign Hesitancy

As I've noted, many organizations are reluctant to make major changes to how and where work gets done because it's a major undertaking with uncertain outcomes. "If it ain't broke, don't fix it" is the mantra they repeat to themselves.

But it is broke, or soon will be.

Let's examine some of the most common reasons organizations refuse to redesign.

Perhaps the most significant obstacle involves business challenges. Financial risk is a particular problem when companies are doing well and making good profits from established ways of doing business. Making significant organizational changes has a potential financial downside since investments must be made in creating new products, services, and ways of working. On top of that, a new business model or new products and services may cannibalize existing ones and reduce margins.

Fears about market reaction, too, can create redesign hesitancy. Business leaders worry that the financial markets and investors may view restructuring as a sign of trouble and be concerned about the fiscal downside.

Organizations are also concerned that if they change the company significantly, they may experience a talent flight/shortage. People join a company thinking it's one thing, and if it becomes something else, they might leave—especially if the nature of their job changes. Organizations also worry that a redesigned company may not have the cachet of the old legacy company and therefore struggle to attract talent.

Emotional and leadership challenges to redesign can be an impediment as well. In any reorganization, some people may lose power. Implementing an agile, externally focused system can cause some leaders to lose control over a given number of employees and budgets. Some senior executives may also worry that this "new" company has no place for them—their expertise is no longer as relevant, and they're concerned about having to learn unfamiliar skills. And of course, a financial incentive exists to maintain the status quo. In the traditional company, pay and promotion is tied to span of control and the stock price. With the prospect of less control and a possible dip in the stock price, leaders are reluctant to make changes.

These obstacles are significant. But the alternative of not redesigning the company is far more significant. What leader wouldn't rather learn a new skill or come to terms with less control if the alternative is the company going under or becoming a shadow of its former self?

Cautionary tales abound of companies that were slow or unwilling to embrace major structural change.

As we've discussed, media companies have stuck stubbornly to their business models—and paid the price. Newspapers failed to embrace digital, and magazines did not grasp multimedia. More recently, television networks sold their content to Netflix to make money, then reversed positions and created competitive streaming services, reducing profitability. Media company leaders were aware of the changes in their industries but either because of short-term financial risk or their own lack of ability to reinvent themselves, their companies moved slowly and feebly.

Similarly, many established retailers such as JCPenney, Macy's, and even Nordstrom are shells of their former selves. They've failed to embrace digital, to move to omnichannel, and to recognize that their physical stores must provide experiences versus merely existing as locations with products.

I've also observed many organizations that refuse to alter compensation systems, reporting structures, product mix, performance measurement policies, and other work modalities. They talk a good game about the need to change and may revise a policy here and there, but they keep traditional structures intact. As a result, they lose talent, create dissatisfaction among the employees who remain, and miss out on new and emerging markets.

Some companies, however, have had the courage to redesign their structures. In the media category, the *New York Times* reinvented itself by no longer focusing on the physical paper and page-one editorial but investing in digital; moving from an advertising-focused model to a subscription-focused one; and diversifying from a news-centered approach to a broader lifestyle resource, helping their subscribers become healthier, more entertained, and better purchasers of products and services.

Walmart, under Doug McMillon, has also redesigned its structures through a combination of acquisitions (Flipkart, Jet.com), integration of supply chain, and offline and online shopping, and going to where the talent was versus being headquarters-centric in Bentonville, Arkansas.

I've been involved in several redesigns and reorganizations at Publicis Groupe, but the most recent one (after I departed) is probably the most relevant to this discussion. By 2018 Publicis Groupe had grown significantly through the acquisition of many world-class companies, including Digitas, Razorfish, Starcom IP, Saatchi & Saatchi, Leo Burnett, Sapient, and others. A growing challenge was that these companies sometimes competed with one another, provided duplicative services to clients, or worked at cross-purposes since they were all incentivized to grow their individual P&Ls.

Starting in 2019, the new CEO, Arthur Sadoun, implemented a new model that focused on seamless client delivery and incentivizing leaders in each country not only on how their individual brands performed but on a combination of client satisfaction and how well Publicis Groupe performed in their respective countries The new model was difficult to put into practice since it meant that many CEOs of individual brands would be less empowered, many administrative leaders would need to develop new skills or find themselves in duplicative roles, and brands with great heritage and specialness would feel they were being diluted.

Initially the model seemed not to work, and Publicis results lagged the market because culture and people are hard to change, and an investment had to be made in new systems, procedures, and training. After a few years, however, this new model has powered Publicis Groupe into the highest market capitalization in the industry while attracting a lot of talent.

Publicis leadership made the hard financial and leadership decision that was expensive in the short run (the loss of some talent and decreased financial results) but has now become a source of competitive advantage.

Jazz and Scale

I've made the classical/jazz analogy before, but it's particularly relevant when it comes to organizational redesign. So too is the notion of reimagining scale, but let's address the former concept first.

Traditional structures are classical in design. They feature a conductor who leads a hierarchical group of players who follow a score note by note. In a classical orchestra, individuality takes a back seat to the greater whole. In jazz, on the other hand, individuality is key, hierarchy is largely absent, and improvisation is encouraged.

We need to use the jazz construct to redesign classical structures. Because of the need for speed and agility in terms of products and services, the growing importance of accommodating a range of employee preferences, and the decreasing importance of company size, jazz-like structures are crucial for success.

Understandably, classically trained leaders struggle to adapt their structures in this jazz-friendly environment. The good news is that many of the best jazz players were classically trained, and some of the best classical music, including Gershwin's *Rhapsody in Blue* or Dvořák's 9th Symphony (*The New World Symphony*), are infused with jazz-like structures. To risk mixing metaphors, I'm not advocating throwing out the baby with the bathwater. Many senior leaders possess the expertise and experience that can translate well to the jazz organizational age; their extensive knowledge, ability to identify new markets, strategic acumen, and other traits all carry over to the new world of work. They just need to apply these traits in more improvisational, flexible structures.

To help organizations assess whether they're in the jazz or classical camps, here are some useful questions:

- Is hierarchy holding the company back? Are bosses followed due to their zone of control and intimidating titles (conductors) or because they're leading through a zone of influence (talented players)?

- Is the organization rethinking things by starting with a blank sheet of paper (a license to improvise)? Or are they replicating operational standards that may have made sense years ago but no longer do?

- Is sufficient time and budget being allocated to help people learn to self-manage and to help leaders learn how to be more agile and adaptable?

In terms of scale, bigger is no longer better. The authors of *Exponential Organizations 2.0*, Salim Ismail, Peter Diamandis, and Michael Malone, propose an alternative to traditional scaling strategies, one that capitalizes on external resources for growth. Instead of relying on a massive internal structure—huge numbers of employees, major sunk costs in infrastructure, strategies where a lot of people are thrown against business challenges—the scale alternative builds an agile, free-flowing external system.

The following represents these three authors' ideas, filtered through my interpretative lens.

For instance, the staff-on-demand concept that involves assembling teams of prequalified workers hired on an as-needed basis. These individuals could be self-employed, freelance, procured from third parties such as Upwork, or even full-time employees (reaggregated around the jobs that need to be done and then reassigned after those jobs). Staff on demand avoids the employee-bloat-then-layoff cycle and is a savvier way to scale in a volatile, unpredictable environment.

A community/crowd strategy, too, can help companies scale effectively now and in the future. Communities are built around users, customers, and alumni as well as vendors, suppliers, and fans who are aligned with a company's transformational purpose. They are granted special favors, given insider insights and a forward look on future offerings, and rewarded with gifts and trust. They are pseudoemployees, citizens of the company's larger community. Peloton and Apple have leveraged community, from key developers to superfans. Organizations can leverage crowds to grow a company and find community, as did TikTok in entertainment, Kiva in finance, and GoFundMe in fundraising.

Other methods exist to scale using external means, including the use of AI, leveraging assets, and engagement (gamification, incentive prizes, and so on that keep stakeholders involved and committed to a shared purpose). The point of all these scaling alternatives is that they foster growth—sometimes surprisingly rapid and profitable growth—in ways that rely on innovative external strategy and tactics. In the jazz age, these flexible, market-driven approaches make far more sense than the bureaucratic, hierarchical structures of years past.

CHAPTER 13

RECALCULATE FINANCIALS

This chapter title is a bit of an understatement. It's not just that we have to tweak our budgets—spending less on office space, for instance. It's not just that we must learn to use outside resources more cost-effectively. And it's not just that we have to make significant investments in emerging technologies to increase long-term profitability.

We need to rethink the entire financial model on which most organizations operate. Everything from artificial intelligence to remote work to digital revenue streams have rendered the traditional model obsolete. Now, and especially in the coming years, organizations will make and spend money differently than in the past.

The organizations that do well at both—that are able to be flexible and innovative in creating new and improved financial models—will be the winners.

A Brief Argument for Transformative Change

In the previous chapter I advocated redesigning structures, a significant effort but one that is justified by a variety of events and trends. Recalculating financials is similarly justified.

Some might argue that this is relevant only for companies with digital products and services or new organizations with radically different business models.

I would argue that all businesses are affected by technology because to compete, they rely on everything from cloud-based services to digital communications; because they have to change their approach to talent in a world of distributed and unbundled work; and because they must deal with new mindsets about what where, how, why, and when we work. All of these issues affect how organizations spend and make money, as do customer expectations of personalized, 24/7 service; reaching emerging markets using social media; and many other new and evolving factors.

How do you run a competitive, profitable business in this environment? Advertising is an area I know well, and ad agencies have needed to recalculate their financials in major ways. For instance, traditional advertising was measured in reach (how many people were exposed to the messages), frequency (how many times during a week or a campaign they saw messages), cost per thousand (the cost of reaching a thousand people), and rough metrics of success—ROI represented by an increase in sales divided by spending.

Today these metrics are not sufficient since technological advances provide access to much narrower and deeper metrics. Cost per click (how many people click on an ad), cost per sale (in a world of e-commerce one can measure sales), cost per acquisition (the cost of acquiring a customer or subscriber), and lifetime value of a customer (sales per customer) are some of the key new measures that marketers need to use. Because products and services can be customized and different segments of customers targeted differently, these metrics are measured by audience and segment.

Many other issues affect how ad agencies are recalculating financials, but these new metrics demand that they come up with new financial models for their clients that measure the numbers in more relevant ways.

Every organization is facing some variation of this recalculating theme. To understand how this is so, let's examine how technology and a changing environment have affected organizational expenditures and revenues.

A Dynamic and Varied Financial Universe

I'm not going to list all the trends, events, products, and concepts that have rocked our financial worlds, since such a list would make this chapter far too long. I am, however, going to identify some key developments that have had a profound effect on organizational budgets and profits.

Let's start with technological innovations. The ability to access real-time data and analytics means that organizations can pivot quickly. Instead of sticking with a strategy that isn't working (or failing to double down on one that is), they can finance on the fly, adjusting their budgets as situations warrant.

On a more basic level, companies can use AI and other digital tools to collect and process data rather than spend a lot of money assigning employees or outside services to do these tasks. Speaking of AI, it has had or will have wide-ranging effects on business finances. From catalyzing new product offers and personalized services to increasing cost efficiencies to optimizing supply-chain management, it can have a dramatic effect on almost every aspect of a company's costs and revenues.

Predictive analytics (improved through machine learning) provide companies with the capability of analyzing past data and making financially productive forecasts.

Cybersecurity tools and experts are now a significant expenditure for many organizations, and though the short-term costs are significant, the long-term benefits (saving companies from the expenses associated with being hacked) are even more significant.

Blockchain and cryptocurrency have already had a major impact in many industries; crowdfunding and alternative financing have helped many start-ups grow quickly and become competitors to major companies; and subscription-based business models have provided viable alternatives to more traditional methods.

Beyond technology, the changes in how and where we work has had a huge impact on organizational finances. On the corporate balance sheet, full-time employees and their salaries and benefits have been reduced while payments for part-time workers have increased. Because turnover rates have increased, there is a need to spend more on recruitment and training. Because fewer people are full-time employees and many are working remotely, office space costs can be reduced.

I asked ChatGPT-4 to compare how companies save and make money in the past versus the future. The contrast between past and future is startling—or at least it should startle corporate leaders:

In the past

COST-SAVING MEASURES

- Downsizing: reducing the workforce to cut labor costs

- Outsourcing: moving parts of the business to lower-cost regions

- Lean manufacturing: adopting practices to minimize waste and improve efficiency

- Economies of scale: increasing production to spread costs over a larger number of goods

Productivity Enhancements

- Specialization: workers specialized in tasks to increase efficiency

- Training and development: improving employee skills to enhance productivity

- Centralization: centralized decision-making to streamline operations

- Automation: introducing machinery to automate simple, repetitive tasks

Financial Management

- Tight budgeting: keeping strict control over expenditures

- Inventory management: just-in-time inventory to reduce holding costs

- Financial engineering: leveraging various financial instruments to manage cash flow and debt

In the future

Cost-Saving Measures

- Digital platforms: using platforms to connect with freelancers and part-timers, reducing the need for full-time staff

- Remote work: saving on real estate and operational costs by allowing employees to work from home

- Subscription-based services: shifting from owning resources to "as-a-service" models, reducing up-front investments

- Cloud computing: reducing IT infrastructure costs by utilizing cloud services

Productivity Enhancements

- AI and machine learning: using AI for data analysis and predictive maintenance, and to drive decision-making

- Process automation: implementing robotic process automation to handle complex tasks previously done by humans

- Real-time collaboration tools: using digital tools that allow for seamless collaboration irrespective of geographical locations

- Agile and flexible work models: adopting agile methodologies and flexible work arrangements to quickly adapt to market changes

Financial Management

- Dynamic pricing models: using AI to optimize pricing in real time for services and products

- Data-driven decision-making: leveraging big-data analytics for financial forecasting and strategic planning

- Crowdfunding and alternative financing: utilizing digital platforms for raising capital without traditional financing

New and Emerging Money-Making Opportunities

How do organizations make money in the new paradigm? Obviously, the answer involves earning revenue and reducing costs or building assets while reducing liabilities. Perhaps not so obviously, the answer isn't always what it was in the past. For instance, the assets of a company these days can be very different from our perceptions of them.

If you were to ask the average person what the major assets of airlines are, the most common answer would be "the planes." Yet, the value of airlines is rooted in their frequent-flier programs.

A March 15, 2021, *Wall Street Journal* article describes how frequent-flier miles provide huge amounts of business, especially the program at American Airlines. According to the article, "American disclosed that, in 2019, its AAdvantage program generated $5.9 billion in cash inflows, with a 53% margin. This is more than Delta's SkyMiles and United's MileagePlus, even though American is the least profitable of the three when it comes to actually selling tickets. The loyalty program accounted for roughly half of its entire earnings."

Synergies between companies in different industries also represent money-making opportunities now and in the future. Consider cobranded credit cards issued by banks and featuring airline logos, providing miles when the credit cards are used. Merchants pay large fees for this feature, which banks then pass on to airlines. As recompense, the airlines' marketing can steer customers to banks.

While there's a lot of controversy surrounding cryptocurrencies, they, too, are offering money-making possibilities to forward-thinking organizations. Cryptocurrencies are essentially tokens (except Bitcoin) that operate like frequent-flier miles. These tokens can offer customers four benefits: currency, governance rights, membership, and status.

In a way, these tokens confer the same benefits as airline miles. If you fly a lot, you get rewarded with airline miles that you can use as a type of *currency*. When you fly a lot, this currency buys higher *status* and *membership* in lounges and clubs; the airlines also pay more attention to frequent flyers' opinions. Other types of tokens are usually collected and operated using digital wallets like MetaMask. Increasingly, many Web3 initiatives have a person signing in with their wallets, not their Facebook or Apple identities or their email.

Many companies don't recognize how huge this digital-asset market is. A 2022 report from Credence Research found that the virtual goods market "was valued at USD 67.5 billion in 2022 and is expected to reach USD 203.6 billion in 2030."

Organizations are also generating loyalty and stickiness in addition to income by replacing one-off transactions with subscriptions and memberships. They're leveraging their data by leasing and selling this data to other companies, using it to better target advertising and compiling the data into insights they sell to other businesses.

I've discussed previously how the *New York Times* has reinvented how it makes money and creates assets in a digital age, but it's a particularly relevant example to cite here, since their moneymaking shifts can be copied by others in relevant industries. For instance, they've:

- moved to subscriptions versus selling newspapers. Today, the *New York Times* has twelve digital subscriptions (9.6 million) per each print subscription (730,000);

- focused on subscription revenue versus advertising revenue. Two-thirds of its revenue in fourth quarter 2022 came from subscriptions ($414 million) versus advertising ($252 million); and

- ventured beyond news into a lifestyle strategy with investments in games (Wordle), product reviews (Wirecutter), and cooking, selling them as bundles.

It's also worth noting that many other newspapers have failed to follow this example. Certainly, the *New York Times*, because of its reputation and resources, was in a better position than most to execute this strategy. While it may not be possible for other news-papers to copy their strategy exactly, their experience demonstrates the value of recalculating a traditional financial model.

The Paradox

To be financially successful in the coming years, it's not just about capitalizing on the new ways to make or save money. The world is changing, setting up a situation in which organizations must learn to take two seemingly opposite actions in order to be profitable. As we move to distributed work, as technology advances, and as other trends transform society, two opposing but connected forces have emerged: fragmentation and integration.

Fragmentation is occurring because of the following four factors:

1. Employee range: different employee types have emerged, from full-time to part-time to contract worker to just-in-time employees hired through marketplaces.

2. Wider spectrum of resources: to get work done, companies are drawing from diverse places, including platforms such as Amazon Web Services and other cloud providers; different real-estate resources, from owned, rented, and accessed (WeWork); and varied ways to reach customers through traditional media, digital media, and more.

3. Differences in measurement: because of technology and a plethora of real-time data, companies can measure everything in astonishing detail, creating a wide variety of dashboards and metrics.

4. Customized products and services: companies now have a growing complexity of products and services in a world

where customers expect personalized approaches and different ways to pay.

As everything fragments into a mind-boggling variety of employee types, resources, measures, and products/services, organizations must integrate these various elements into a viable whole. Specifically, they must create:

- Seamless interfaces with employees regardless of employee types: consumers and customers do not want to see the complexity of different types of workers or where they may be based, so companies need to ensure seamless service and handoffs between employees. At Publicis, for instance, we had different agencies working for the same client, at times resulting in separate bills from these agencies, duplication of effort, and turf wars. This complexity is only going to become worse at many companies, and leaders need to figure out ways to coordinate employee projects effectively.

- Best combination of resources to manage costs: companies need to combine all the resources that go into creating products, to ensure lowest cost and continuous availability.

- Integrated measurement and dashboards: businesses can combine myriad sources of data into an accessible, useable (by management) dashboard.

- "Goldilocks" strategy for products and services: companies need a sufficiently large range of services and options to remain competitive but not so many that their complexity leads to increased cost and consumer confusion. The goal is to find the ideal mix.

Integrating all these elements in the face of fragmentation isn't easy. Managing a paradox is challenging, requiring that leaders go beyond their traditional management strategies and try something new. Yet this is one of the keys to financial success in the future, making it worth the effort.

Metrical Benefits

It is said that what is measured can be managed. In a world where how, where, when, and with whom work is done is changing, businesses must measure their financial metrics differently to maintain their financial health. Of course, the general areas measured remain basically the same—we still need to know the value of assets and revenue as well as liabilities and costs over time.

But what we measure and how we measure it has evolved, as the following examples illustrate.

Consider the cost of a full-time employee—salary, target bonuses, equity incentives, company cost of taxes such as social security, and imputed overhead costs (for example, real estate, health care). Now compare this figure with the cost of replacing the employee with two fractionalized employees, each working half time. Conceivably, two fractionalized workers can cost more than one full-time employee since the former may need health care benefits and office space and add administration costs. But it's also conceivable that this arrangement would be more cost-effective in the long run. If both employees are happier, more productive, and stay with the company longer than the full-time person, then the organization will benefit. A fractionalized option may also make it easier to attract superior talent, and the flexibility of two people doing one job may also reduce costs.

Here's another scenario: A company decides to reduce its capital and IT costs by outsourcing its IT and replacing its on-location data centers with a 100 percent cloud solution. This outsourced solution reduces the cost-of-scale benefits, decreases capital expenditure, and offers the flexibility to increase or decrease usage. On the other hand, cloud providers have been increasing costs, and companies can become locked in to ever-rising cloud fees. In addition, large language models might be learning on a company's data in the cloud without proper safeguards; this all-cloud decision can also hurt a company's ability to differentiate.

These are only two scenarios of many that have emerged relatively recently. They require financial recalculations to identify the best option. The metrics involve determining the full cost and impact of each of these options. Businesses must run the numbers so they can make the right choice between owning or renting, buying or sharing, and hiring full-time employees, contract employees, fractionalized employees, and freelancers.

Evaluating the interconnections between different lines of business versus looking at a line of business by itself is another facet of recalculating financials. For years, Amazon invested heavily in its cloud and its shipment logistics and infrastructure, despite ongoing losses from these investments. Over time, though, they became assets that they could offer to other companies. Today Amazon Web Services drives a significant portion of Amazon's profit, and its logistics and shipment services have helped build its merchant business, in which thousands of businesses leverage the Amazon platform.

Similarly, Amazon Prime's membership program may itself be a money loser in that it offers free shipments as well as a multitude of entertainment options, but they also lock in users and increase the value of each Prime member. Amazon doesn't provide detailed data on Prime members, but in September, Bank of America released a note to investment clients looking at the effect COVID has had on US e-commerce and the use of Prime. In a survey of US shoppers, it found that Prime members spent an average $1,968 per year on Amazon, roughly four times as much as the non-Prime shoppers surveyed.

In the modern digital world, products and services link to each other, and in addition to being measured separately they need to be understood both across time and across product lines. This latter metric may not be something many leaders have addressed, but it's one that's worth understanding.

The Importance of Rethinking Mergers and Acquisitions

Increasingly, companies are likely to need to enhance their capabilities by merging with, acquiring, or being acquired for reasons of skill and speed.

Because technology, including the pace of change of AI, is speeding up the metronome of business, companies will find it hard to remain "up to tomorrow" by incubating or building new capabilities since they are unlikely to scale or become competitive quickly.

Thus, every company needs to make sure their finance, leadership, and innovation teams are deeply enmeshed in the world of private equity, venture capital, and the next generation of talent. The human resources teams must be trained in incorporating different cultures and mindsets from outside the firm.

The economics of acquiring next-generation companies, which might be growing but aren't yet profitable or have new talent that is paid more than the leadership of the acquiring company, will unleash a challenge of metrics when historic comparables and ways of doing business will be profiles.

A Few Simple Steps
for Dealing with a Complex Subject

Throughout these pages, I've made the point that the nature of work has changed dramatically. The wide range of employee types (fractionalized, freelance, and so on) and work locations (office, home, WeWork-type settings), employees with multiple gigs, younger generations with different perspectives and preferences, technology advances—these and other factors have a huge impact on financials.

Figuring out how to recalculate the financials, given all these complicated and interwoven factors, may seem to require the numerical skills of an Albert Einstein.

It doesn't. It does require addressing the numbers in a different way than companies have dealt with them in the past. Here are a few basic steps that should help every business get started in the right way:

Recognize and incorporate multiple variables—rather than a few traditional ones—when it comes to talent. As labor gains more power as a consequence of supply-and-demand laws, companies must learn to value employees, with a range of factors in mind. For instance, how much knowledge and expertise and how many relationships does an employee possess, and how does that affect their value? Can the company correlate employee turnover with reduced revenue? What is the optimal mix of employees and work situations (fractionalized, remote, and so on) for the greatest return on people assets?

Some companies may assess these and other variables and determine that full-time employees who are paid above market are necessary—that these higher-paid people are essential to keep talent close to customers, to ensure high job- and customer-satisfaction levels, and to maintain reliability of delivery.

Other companies, however, may decide that this traditional model is ineffective, that it fails to deal with the revenue ebbs and flows, or that it doesn't attract talent for whom location and flexibility are crucial.

Factor in the intangibles. This means considering previously ignored or subordinated issues, such as employee joy (positive employee net promoter scores), and the need and costs of retraining bosses for a world of diverse backgrounds and mindsets. The old balance-sheet columns are still important, but organizations must add to the mix by including talent satisfaction, growth of reputation, and other key intangibles.

Conduct the following exercise: Imagine creating a company to do exactly what your company is doing today but with the fewest number of full-time employees with the least amount of real-estate costs and capital investments. Further, in this scenario, you also will access talent, space, and infrastructure (HR support, tech support, and so on) on an as-needed basis from external sources. Determine how this might result in a lower cost structure with increased flexibility.

Now here's an extra-credit assignment for this scenario: Assess what you would do if your company could access all the resources necessary to run the company in this "start-up" manner. Might you create an insurance layer of people, space, or infrastructure? How much would it cost, and would it be worth it?

Rather than starting with where they are or have been, companies need to build models based on what they would do if they opened their doors (real or virtual) today. This will give them a new set of financials based on current and near-future realities.

CHAPTER 14

RE-VISION
THE WORK-RIPPLED WORLD

Futurists must be humble because they are often wrong.

While it is difficult to forecast specifics, it is much easier to identify nascent trends and ones that are likely to emerge.

It's also a valuable exercise for business leaders. Even if you're unable to pinpoint exactly how GPT or China or climate change will affect a given industry or business, you can develop a sense of a trend's implications. In this way, you can be prepared to capitalize on whatever transformations take place.

Throughout these pages, I've looked at how the world of work is changing and might change in the near future. Now, let's imagine how this world might look in 2035.

Forecast: Mostly Sunny
with Occasional Tsunamis

It's not difficult to predict that the early-twenty-first-century changes, such as the rise of technology and globalization turbocharged by AI, COVID, Gen Z, and new marketplaces, will reshape work. The challenge is forecasting how these changes will manifest themselves in workplaces ten or more years from now. Here are some likely developments:

- **Fewer employees, more fractionalized workers.** This is probably the easiest trend to predict. Artificial intelligence will take over many people's tasks, allowing organizations (especially large ones) to get more done with fewer people. Similarly, opportunities to work part time for a given company and pursue passion projects and side hustles will proliferate. While many employees already see the value in fractionalized work, organizations will also grasp the value to them (reducing benefits and training costs, cherry-picking talent for current projects).

- **An increasing number of companies.** Enabling technology such as AI, combined with the ability to hire fractionalized employees, will catalyze the birth of numerous small- and medium-sized businesses. They will be able to scale faster with less investment and risk.

- **More net employment.** This may sound like a contradictory prediction to the first bullet (fewer employees), but instead it's a paradox. AI will reduce the number of jobs in certain industries and in large organizations, but it will spur job creation, especially in smaller companies. As AI, biotech, climate tech, and other technologies improve and proliferate, these technologies will give rise to a wide range of jobs, from managing the impact of AI on people to interpreting the data it produces. It will also produce jobs that we don't even have names for as of this writing.

- **The hybrid trend.** Advanced communication technologies such as spatial computing, combined with fractionalized employment and greater flexibility in terms of working preferences, will increase the number of hybrid workers.

- **A redefinition of management.** As machines take over many quotidian managerial tasks—monitoring, allocating, delegating, and measuring—people in supervisory/leadership roles will focus on building, creating, imagining, and mentoring. Rather than prioritize efficiency and efficacy for managers, companies will look for individuals who possess people skills, the capacity for continuous learning, and the agility necessary to deal with diverse workforces and work systems (more about this in the chapter's last section).

AI Stands for "Altered Inexorably"

Here is what Bill Gates has to say about artificial intelligence:

The development of AI is as fundamental as the creation of the microprocessor, the personal computer, the internet, and the mobile phone. It will change the way people work, learn, travel, get health care, and communicate with each other. Entire industries will reorient around it. Businesses will distinguish themselves by how well they use it.

Not to doubt Mr. Gates, but I believe that AI will have a far greater impact than the microprocessor, the personal computer, the internet, and the mobile phone. It will be transformative in the same way that the printing press, electricity, and television have been. It will change every aspect of society, not just one sphere.

Some pundits suggest that AI is just hype, that its impact will be much less than its proponents claim. In reality, AI will have a far greater impact than even many of its most ardent fans claim, especially in the world of work.

Consider a few facts. First, as of this writing, ChatGPT or GPT 3.5 (which introduced many people to AI) was released in November 2022, and then improved repeatedly every few months. When you read this in 2025 or later, not only OpenAI, but Anthropic, Google, Meta, Mistral, and others will have enhanced the capabilities of their products and services by many factors while significantly reducing costs.

Second, AI is doing many tasks better and faster than humans. According to a Goldman Sachs report, AI is capable of performing 44 percent of legal tasks.

Third, AI is replacing talent on air. A new television program called Channel 1 uses AI avatars built on human scans and other technologies to create an AI-generated news program.

But it's not just these and other developments that suggest the transformative effect of AI, but also the history of technological revolutions. Shakespeare wrote that "past is prologue," and that is especially true here. The computational age drove the cost of computation to zero while the internet drove the cost of distribution to zero. AI is likely to drive the cost of knowledge to zero. Since every job requires a specific type of knowledge, all jobs will be affected, but especially those in knowledge industries like marketing, finance, law, and others.

Therefore, here are some predictions:

- People whose main job is collecting, distilling, or distributing knowledge/information will find that AI is doing most, if not all, of their job. AI is far more efficient and far faster than people, so this one is a no-brainer.

- "Use it or lose it" will determine organizational and personal survival. Companies and individuals who resist AI will be replaced by companies and individuals who don't. This is very Darwinian—survival of the fittest. AI is a superpower, and whoever embraces it will have a huge competitive edge. Think about what happened to people and industries that didn't embrace electricity . . . or automobiles . . . or computing.

- Companies and society will be reorganized around AI. It's similar to the advent of the assembly line or the building of highways or the proliferation of suburban living. The difference is that AI's effects will happen faster than those of the paradigm-shifting events just described. AI will affect everything in hugely significant ways, from search engines to medicine.

- Political and societal turbulence will shake everyone's world. As this technology advances, it will lead to major disruptions. Expect a lot of op-eds for and against AI. Certainly there will be arguments similar to the "automation" discussions of years ago about how machines take away jobs from people.

To manage these predicted, massive changes, we need leaders who embrace the changes and give people confidence that everything will be made better in the long run, even if there's some pain in the short run. Instead of falling prey to the paranoid arguments about rogue AI ending the world, leaders must communicate how it will empower individuals, catalyze new businesses, and provide incredible opportunities for small businesses.

No question, the transition to an AI world will be chaotic. But as long as leaders pursue a "3E" strategy of embedding, enhancing, and extending their existing products and services with AI, the transition will be a positive one. Organizations should take a cue from companies like Microsoft using Copilot and Google using Gemini, how they've scaled and made this technology available to many millions of users in a matter of weeks.

If business leaders follow their lead, they will greet AI with continuous learning and open imaginations, and the results will be transformative. There are some very crucial problems and areas that need solutions and scaling for adoption of AI. These include addressing the "Blackbox" aspect, such as trust, fairness, explainability, bias, and privacy.

The Rise and Fall of Giants

When companies like AT&T, IBM, General Electric, and General Motors were the world's leading organizations in the twentieth century, it seemed as if they might always occupy their lofty positions. Few could envision the emergence of new, dominant companies and industries. Apple, Google, Amazon, and others rose with astonishing speed to become leaders in their categories.

Will the same scenario take place in the years ahead? As tempting as it might be to predict that we'll have a similar changing of the guard in the future, looking at the most valuable companies over the last three decades provides a needed corrective to this thinking.

The lists are surprisingly similar, with four types of companies dominating the list—technology, pharmaceuticals, energy, and financial powerhouses—as well as Walmart. This is a decade, two decades, and three decades after the birth of the internet. With the exception of General Electric, most of the companies or their immediate competitors remain on the list. Some new technology companies like Apple, Nvidia, and Taiwan Semiconductor make the list today, replacing Nokia, IBM, and Intel. Why? Because

Nokia failed to reimagine phones, which let Apple thrive; Intel failed to reimagine chips, allowing Nvidia to take the lead; and IBM couldn't grasp the next generation of many things, including silicon manufacturing, giving Taiwan Semiconductor an opening to dominate. Similarly, Citi has been eclipsed by JPMorgan Chase.

But overall, the top lists are remarkably similar by type of company, with really only one new entrant, Meta, built on the relatively new social media category.

Given this historical performance, the list of leading companies a decade from now shouldn't be that much different from the 2023 list. It's likely that Apple, Alphabet, Microsoft, Exxon, JPMorgan Chase, Procter & Gamble, and Walmart will remain in the top twenty-five. They and other major corporations have been taught the need to adapt and incorporate the latest technologies and ways of working—the cautionary tales of Nokia and General Electric have not been lost on them.

At the same time, we're bound to see the rise of certain companies in certain industries:

- AI: While Alphabet and Microsoft are well on the way to becoming giants of an AI age, they are likely to be joined by new players, such as ByteDance, the parent company of TikTok.

- Biotechnology: In addition to AI, it is likely that a new giant focused on biotech, like a Moderna, will emerge.

- Climate technology: As concern about climate grows, so too will the companies in the category—at least one is bound to emerge from the pack, especially if they're able to address major concerns in a way that is innovative and effective.

While the mix of leading corporations may not change dramatically, they will operate differently from the way they did in the past, for reasons we've discussed. They will have fewer full-time employees because they will leverage the power of AI to do more with less and use marketplaces to utilize more part-time workers to ensure flexibility and speed in a shape-shifting world. They will be far more geographically distributed as the world becomes far more multipolar, with the continued rise of India and China, among others, and the ability of modern technology, such as spatial computing, to facilitate working from anywhere. And they will be run with a greater focus on employee joy. As I've emphasized, talent and culture will become the key differentiator as other areas become commoditized.

Perhaps the biggest change in the ecosystem of companies will be the proliferation of smaller companies connected directly and indirectly to the giants. As members of younger generations want to work independently or pursue side hustles and as technology makes this increasingly feasible, the giant corporations will become reliant on millions of small businesses and independent contractors. It will be the whale-and-plankton paradigm.

The debate between big and small is a false debate because the future model will need big and small working together.

There will continue to be a need for what I call "old scale," which is the scale of resources, scale of size, scale of spending, and scale of manufacturing in almost all industries.

To create breakthroughs in computing, biotechnology, transportation, or many other fields will require the investments of capital, access to huge pools of data, and the ability to invest in R&D over years—as do large pharma companies such as Merck or Pfizer, technology companies such as Alphabet and Microsoft, and transportation companies such as General Motors and Toyota.

It takes tens of billions of dollars to create the architecture for AI, for instance.

On the other hand, these large companies create the infrastructure as well as the spending power that allows thousands of other companies to feed off their investments, spending, distribution, and pioneering.

Apple supports tens of thousands of developers who leverage the App Store, Google's YouTube enables millions of creators, Amazon enables sellers, and Microsoft provides cloud and computing services that anyone can plug into.

But it is not just the small companies that feed off the big. The big ones feed off the small both by generating income through fees (cloud services), commissions (percentage of revenue for being listed on an app store), revenue generated (YouTube running advertising against creators), and as places of innovation or talent that they can buy and scale (Meta bought Instagram, many pharmaceutical companies buy smaller biotech firms).

This dance of big and small will continue in the future.

A Better Corporate Climate

One of the silver linings of the COVID period was the effect it had on pollution. By reducing the number of commuter cars as people worked from home, COVID had the unintentional consequence of also reducing carbon emissions. A study reported in the National Academy of Sciences journal found that when people work from home two days per week, they help decrease pollution by around 15 percent. Another study reported in that journal noted that remote workers could reduce the carbon footprint by 54 percent compared to office employees.

Most organizations are already emphasizing sustainability, and this emphasis will increase and broaden in the coming years. Increasing the number of remote working hours and decreasing in-office requirements certainly will be part of this sustainability effort. Companies are bound to implement other practices to decrease their carbon footprint.

For instance, to mitigate the urban heat island effect, offices might incorporate more green spaces, both inside and outside. They may reevaluate their transportation policies, encouraging low-carbon commuting options like carpooling and electric vehicle usage or providing incentives for employees who walk or bike to work. The use of energy-efficient appliances, LED lighting, smart thermostats, and water-saving devices will become standard in offices to reduce environmental impact.

Companies with employees in certain states will be especially focused on climate-change policies. Because of increases in temperature, wildfires, hurricanes, and insurance costs, they will have a vested interest in trying to solve these problems; if they don't, their people will be understandably aggrieved. Insurance costs alone have increased by almost 50 percent between 2021 and 2023 in the five states where these climate-change effects are most pronounced.

But if we look into the future to assess the impact of climate change, what really stands out are two major shifts. First, we're likely to see job-sector shifts. Traditional industries like fossil fuels may decline, while renewable energy sectors like solar, wind, and hydroelectric power are likely to expand, creating new jobs. A corresponding increase in "green jobs" will occur, focused on environmental protection, sustainability, and climate-change mitigation. This includes roles in environmental science, conservation, and sustainable business practices. As a result of this shift, we're going to see an increased demand for education and training programs related to sustainability, renewable energy, and climate science.

The other climate change–catalyzed shift relates to a topic we've discussed in a different context: increased automation. As some outdoor jobs become unsafe due to heat, flooding, or other issues, automation offers an alternative to get jobs done without endangering people's lives. Assignments that require people to travel significant distances also may shift to automation, using drones and other equipment. This will reduce cost and the carbon footprint of servicing areas that people previously needed to fly or drive to reach.

What Will Make Future Companies Great?

It won't be what made companies great in the past. Building a better mousetrap is no longer a pathway to long-term success, since these mousetraps can be knocked off quickly. Excellent strategies, too, are terrific at launching products and services, but they aren't sustainable—pivoting from one strategy to the next is crucial in a volatile world. Hiring the best and the brightest is obviously a fantastic idea, but determining how to keep the best and the brightest in place has become more important than ever before.

For these reasons, here are three viable approaches to future greatness and the companies that are early adopters:

Treat talent with respect by trusting them and offering them significant flexibility. This is what younger generations demand, and it will require organizations to make a leap of faith to offer this trust and flexibility. Future leaders should follow the example of Dropbox, a self-proclaimed "Virtual First" company where employees spend 90 percent of their time working remotely. Despite their embrace of remote work, Dropbox does no monitoring of employees. Dropbox CEO Drew Houston is quoted in *Fortune* magazine as saying, "If you trust people and treat them like adults, they'll behave like adults." In *Business Insider*, it's reported that "70 percent of recently hired employees cite Virtual First as the main reason they applied for a role at Dropbox."

Airbnb has embraced the concept of flexibility, embodied by their "live and work anywhere" policy. It's not just that they can work from home but from anywhere in the world, and Airbnb's executives work with governments in 170 countries to facilitate this relocation, for up to ninety days per year per company.

The more that businesses come up with innovative, flexible poli-cies and demonstrate trust in the future, the better off they'll be.

Reorganize and adapt business around AI and other future-focused technologies. John Deere and Starbucks provide good models for companies to follow in the coming years. Deere, the agricultural-equipment manufacturer, is creating technology-based services to increase farmers' profitability, essentially building a new business model around its tech. Starbucks uses AI to time orders so that they meet customer needs—rather than first come, first served, AI synchronizes the process to the point that customers receive their coffee at the optimum temperatures.

Again, every company recognizes the value of AI and technol-ogy, but the winners in the future will not only recognize it but be willing to create new business models and processes that maximize the value of its products and services for customers.

Integrate sustainable social, environmental, and cultural practices into all aspects of the business to build reputation. This means doing everything possible to save the planet, to contribute to a more equitable society, and to be empathetic toward employees' wants and needs. Perhaps the best exemplar of these qualities is tech company Siemens. They have made a commitment to improv-ing in the aforementioned areas, and they measure their progress in each. For instance, they've reduced their carbon emissions by 50 percent from 2019 to 2023. They've increased the number of women in leadership positions from 23 percent in 2020 to 31 per-cent in 2023.

They've received a lot of positive recognition for these efforts, including being named as one of the top ten companies in *Fast Company*'s ranking of 2023's 100 Best Workplaces for Innovators.

Making the world—both the external world and the one within organizations—better is not just a responsibility for businesses but a requirement for success. In the future, people are going to decide where to work based on the company's ranking in terms of environmental efforts, fairness, and philanthropic programs. Customers are going to decide whom to do business with based on success in these spheres.

A Leadership Evolution

I've discussed the need for a new type of leadership in our increasingly distributed world of work—how we require CEOs and other senior executives who can help the generational groups overcome their differences and work together productively, and how we need leaders who grasp the implications of new technologies and are adept at integrating them into the corporate DNA.

In ten years or so, we're going to see even more technological advances. Millennials will be running many businesses, and the idea of an office where people gather to work may be viewed as an anachronism.

Though it's impossible to predict some of the changes that will occur (no doubt, there's another Steve Jobs or Elon Musk out there creating something that will change everything), I can guarantee that the work environment will be even more complex, volatile, and challenging than it is today. With that in mind, let me leave you with four suggestions for leaders to help companies thrive in this environment:

Prioritize inspiration. AI and many other technologies yet to be invented will take over many jobs that have always been done by people. As a result, the need to manage workers will become far less important than in the past. Yet I know of no technology that can inspire people to work more creatively and more productively. People are emotional beings, and as such, they can't be treated like cogs (or algorithms) in a machine. We need leaders who can guide and mentor people with different mindsets and from different generations, who can help them align, collaborate, and create.

Foster continuous learning. The need to learn in response to change will increase exponentially. I know I've talked about this before, but I can't overemphasize this leadership imperative. Encouraging people to adopt a growth mindset will be key. If leaders do not allocate several hours weekly to learn and practice the new technologies and do not expose themselves to opposing or different generational points of view, they will be in trouble.

Turning entire businesses into continuous learning organizations will be necessary. Leaders are the only ones who can allocate sufficient funds for this objective and prevent budget cuts from undermining it. If they have to make cuts, then cut real estate or staff or marketing. If they reduce their investment in learning, they will become obsolete because their people will become obsolete.

Connect the dots. This is something technology can't do and probably won't be able to do in the future. By "connect the dots," I'm referring to cross-pollinating different people and their ideas—different functional expertise, different offices, different countries. Synergies happen when people are connected in new and dynamic ways. Cross-training, too, is crucial, so people possess knowledge beyond their narrow areas of expertise and can engage in synergistic thinking.

Communicate clearly, eloquently, and motivationally. Some leaders today are compared to machines—they are extremely efficient, but they're also dull and unemotional. In a machine age, we need leaders who develop their original voices and authentic points of view. Going back to the first point in this section, you can't inspire people if you're machinelike. Leaders who develop their ability to communicate powerfully in writing and in person—who can write and speak emotionally as well as cognitively—will provide a necessary counterbalance to a world awash in numbers and code.

I have great faith in our ability to develop leaders who embody all these traits. Throughout history, business leaders have reinvented themselves to be aligned with their eras. No doubt, they will continue to do so, no matter how much the world of work will change in the future.

BIBLIOGRAPHY

Introduction

Berg, Janine and Pawel Gmyrek. "Automation Hits the Knowledge Worker: ChatGPT and the Future of Work." https://www.dropbox.com/scl/fi /495heve83ddmjna8e6prx/B59-Berg-Automation-hits-the-knowledge -worker-ChatGPT-and-the-future-of-work.pdf?rlkey=qrthsq4jd5hi sgr7x63ykxt4a&dl=0.

Stanford/GustoStudy: Akan, Mert, Nicholas Bloom, and Shelby Buckman (Stanford University); Jose Maria Barrero (ITAM); Steven J. Davis (Hoover Institution); and Tom Bowen, Luke Pardue, and Liz Wilke. "Americans Now Live Farther from Their Employers." March 3, 2024. https://gusto.com/company-news/ americans-now-live-farther-from-their-employers.

Statista Research Department. "Number of Freelancers in the U.S. 2017–2028." February 2, 2024.

Chapter 1: Seismic Societal Shifts

Tobaccowala, Rishad:

—. "The Age of the Seasoned." *The Future Does Not Fit in the Containers of the Past* (blog), edition 74. January 9, 2022. https://rishad.substack .com/p/the-age-of-the-seasoned.

—. "The Fractionalized Employee." *The Future Does Not Fit in the Containers of the Past* (blog), edition 78. February 6, 2022. https://rishad .substack.com/p/the-fractionalized-employee.

—. "The Great Attraction." *The Future Does Not Fit in the Containers of the Past* (blog), edition 70. December 12, 2021. https://rishad.substack.com/p/the-great-attraction.

—. "The Transformed Talent Terrain." *The Future Does Not Fit in the Containers of the Past* (blog), edition 35. April 11, 2021. https://rishad.substack.com/p/the-transformed-talent-terrain.

—. "You=Start-Up." *The Future Does Not Fit in the Containers of the Past* (blog), edition 102. July 24, 2022. https://rishad.substack.com/p/youstart-up.

Overview, Studies, and Charts

Cutter, Chip, Katherine Bindley, and Kathryn Dill. "The War to Define What Work Looks Like." *Wall Street Journal*, October 22, 2022. https://www.wsj.com/articles/the-war-to-define-what-work-looks-like-11666411221.

Deloitte Touche Tohmatsu Limited. "Striving for Balance, Advocating for Change." *The Deloitte Global 2022 Gen Z & Millennial Survey*, 2022. https://www.dropbox.com/s/ofxisad464hkqex/deloitte-2022-genz-millennial-survey.pdf?dl=0.

Europe Language Jobs. "Generations in the Workplace: Understanding Age Diversity." Europe Language Jobs, no date. https://www.europelanguagejobs.com/blog/generations-in-the-workplace.

"Generational Differences Chart." https://www.dropbox.com/s/6la8asmrzqsnpja/generationaldifferenceschart.pdf?dl=0.

Microsoft, WorkLab. "Great Expectations: Making Hybrid Work Work." *Work Trend Index Annual Report*, March 16, 2022. https://www.microsoft.com/en-us/worklab/work-trend-index/great-expectations-making-hybrid-work-work.

Gen Z and Millennials

Glass, Aurelia. "The Closing Gender, Education, and Ideological Divides Behind Gen Z's Union Movement." CAP 20, October 5, 2022. https://www.americanprogress.org/article/the-closing-gender-education-and-ideological-divides-behind-gen-zs-union-movement/.

Kane, Phillip, and Grace Ocean. "10 Ways to Understand the Difference Between Millennials and Gen-Z." *Inc.*, May 3, 2022. https://www .inc.com/phillip-kane/10-ways-to-understand-difference-between -millennials-gen-y-vs-gen-z.html.

Kelly, Kim. "Gen Z's Not Lazy—They're Just Refusing to Put up With the Toxic Work Culture That Boomers Created." *Business Insider*, November 3, 2022. https://www.businessinsider.com/how -gen-z-is-changing-work-most-pro-labor-generation-2022-11.

Levine, Nick. "How Gen Z Are Really Spending Their Side Hustle Money." Refinery29, January 2, 2022. https://www.refinery29.com/en-gb /gen-z-side-hustle-stats#:~:text=According%20to%20new%20 research%2C%2070,to%20complement%20their%20day%20job.

Melin, Anders, and Misyrlena Egkolfopoulou. "Employees Are Quitting Instead of Giving Up Working from Home." Bloomberg, June 1, 2021. https://www.bloomberg.com/news/articles/2021 -06-01/return-to-office-employees-are-quitting-instead-of-giving -up-work-from-home?sref=gnYhGYo9

Monster Blog. "Hiring Gen Z Candidates: Why They Ghost, How They Find Jobs, and What They Want from Employers." Monster, April 4, 2022. https://hiring.monster.com/resources/blog/hiring-gen -z-candidates/.

Parker, Sam. "'I'm Gonna Have to Make My Own Money': The Rise of the Side Hustle." *Guardian*, August 21, 2022. https://www.theguardian .com/business/2022/aug/21/the-rise-of-the-side-hustle-gen-z -entrepreneurs-are-turning-their-backs-on-9-to-5s.

Woodbury, Rex. "It's Gen Z's World, and We're Just Living in It." Digital Native, December 8, 2021. https://digitalnative.substack .com/p/its-gen-zs-world-and-were-just-living?s=w.

—. "Gen Z, Creators, and Our Mental Health Tipping Point." Digital Native, January 12, 2022. https://digitalnative.substack.com/p/gen -z-creators-and-our-mental-health?s=w.

—. "I'm a Business, Man: The Disaggregation of Work." Digital Native, June 16, 2021. https://digitalnative.substack.com/p/im-a -business-man.

——. "10 Characteristics That Define Gen Z (Part 1): And 10 Startups Building on Them." Digital Native, June 23, 2022. https://digitalnative .substack.com/p/10-characteristics-that-define-gen.

——. "10 Characteristics That Define Gen Z (Part 2): And 10 Startups Building on Them." Digital Native, June 29, 2022. https://digitalnative .substack.com/p/10-characteristics-that-define-gen-1ab.

——. "10 Charts That Capture How the World Is Changing." Digital Native, November 9, 2022. https://digitalnative.substack.com/p/10 -charts-that-capture-how-the-world.

Quiet Quitting

Ellis, Lindsay, and Angela Yang. "If Your Co-Workers Are 'Quiet Quitting,' Here's What That Means." *Wall Street Journal*, August 12, 2022. https://www.wsj.com/articles/if-your-gen-z -co-workers-are-quiet-quitting-heres-what-that-means-11660260608.

Harter, Jim. "Is Quiet Quitting Real?" Gallup Workplace, May 17, 2023. https://www.gallup.com/workplace/398306/quiet-quitting-real.aspx.

Krueger, Alyson. "Who Is Quiet Quitting For?" *New York Times*, August 23, 2022. https://www.nytimes.com/2022/08/23/style/quiet -quitting-tiktok.html.

Smith, Ray A. "Quiet Quitters Make Up Half the U.S. Workforce." *Wall Street Journal*, September 29, 2022. https://www.wsj.com/articles /quiet-quitters-make-up-half-the-u-s-workforce-gallup-says-1166 2517806?mod=series_quit.

The Aging Population and Its Impact on Work

Daily Chart. "A New Forecast Says the World's Population Will Peak at 9.7bn in 2064." *Economist*, July 17, 2020. https://www.economist.com /graphic-detail/2020/07/17/a-new-forecast-says-the-worlds-population -will-peak-at-97bn-in-2064.

Raval, Anjli. "The Retirees Heading Back to Work." Financial Times, November 6,2022. https://www.ft.com/content/8042b200-2cdb -4b0e-a43e-4cb931a55a8a.

Tergesen, Anne, and Lauren Weber. "Part-Time Retirement Programs Are on the Rise." *Wall Street Journal*, March 15, 2022. https://www.wsj.com /articles/part-time-retirement-programs-are-on-the-rise-11647336602.

Chapter 2: Commuting to the Multiverse

Tobaccowala, Rishad:

—. "How to Thrive in the Modern Workspace." *The Future Does Not Fit in the Containers of the Past* (blog), edition 58. September 19, 2021. https://rishad.substack.com/p/how-to-thrive-in-the-modern -workspace.

—. "Omnipresence! Omniverse!" *The Future Does Not Fit in the Containers of the Past* (blog), edition 93. May 22, 2022. https://rishad.substack .com/p/omnipresence-omniverse.

—. "Returning to the Office?" *The Future Does Not Fit in the Containers of the Past* (blog), edition 85. March 27, 2022. https://rishad.substack .com/p/returning-to-the-office.

—. "Talent Will Matter Even More." *The Future Does Not Fit in the Containers of the Past* (blog), edition 123. December 18, 2022. https:// rishad.substack.com/p/talent-will-matter-even-more.

—. "The 4P's: Perspectives. Points of View. Provocations. Plan of Action." *The Future Does Not Fit in the Containers of the Past* (blog), edition 124. https://rishad.substack.com/p/the-4ps-perspectives-points-of-view.

—. "The Future of the Internet." *The Future Does Not Fit in the Containers of the Past* (blog), edition 101. July 17, 2022. https://rishad.substack .com/p/the-future-of-the-internet.

—. "This Is Your Industry and Your Future. You Can Decide Where It Will Go from Here." *The Future Does Not Fit in the Containers of the Past* (blog), edition 33. March 28, 2021. https://rishad.substack.com/p /this-is-your-industry-and-your-future.

RESOURCES ON REMOTE WORK

Future Forum. "Future Forum Pulse." February 2023. https://futureforum .com/research/future-forum-pulse-winter-2022-2023-snapshot/.

Future Forum. "Research: Our Findings on the Future of Work." 2021–2022. https://futureforum.com/research/.

Goldberg, Emma. "A Two-Year, 50-Million-Person Experiment in Changing How We Work." *New York Times*, April 13, 2022. https://www.nytimes.com/2022/03/10/business/remote-work-office-life.html.

Subramanian, Sheela. "A New Era of Workplace Inclusion: Moving from Retrofit to Redesign." Future Forum. March 11, 2021. https://futureforum.com/2021/03/11/dismantling-the-office-moving-from-retrofit-to-redesign/.

ON AUTOMATION

Casselman, Ben. "Pandemic Wave of Automation May Be Bad News for Workers." *New York Times*, July 3, 2021. https://www.nytimes.com/2021/07/03/business/economy/automation-workers-robots-pandemic.html.

ON ARTIFICIAL INTELLIGENCE

Brown, Annie. "Utilizing AI and Big Data to Reduce Costs and Increase Profits in Departments Across an Organization." *Forbes*, April 13, 2021. https://www.forbes.com/sites/anniebrown/2021/04/13/utilizing-ai-and-big-data-to-reduce-costs-and-increase-profits-in-departments-across-an-organization/?sh=24e3485f6af7.

McKendrick, Joe. "AI Adoption Skyrocketed over the Last 18 Months." *Harvard Business Review*, September 27, 2021. https://hbr.org/2021/09/ai-adoption-skyrocketed-over-the-last-18-months.

Roose, Kevin. "We Need to Talk About How Good A.I. Is Getting." *New York Times*, August 24, 2022. https://www.nytimes.com/2022/08/24/technology/ai-technology-progress.html.

ON METAVERSE

Mansur, Rishabh. "$36 Billion Later, Where Is Mark Zuckerberg's Metaverse?" The Decrypting Story, November 7, 2022. https://yourstory.com/the-decrypting-story/meta-mark-zuckerberg-metaverse-36-billion-vr-oculus.

Teper, Jeff. "Microsoft and Meta Partner to Deliver Immersive Experiences for the Future of Work and Play." Microsoft, Official Microsoft Blog, October 11, 2022. https://blogs.microsoft.com/blog/2022/10/11/microsoft-and-meta-partner-to-deliver-immersive-experiences-for-the-future-of-work-and-play/.

ON 5G
Thales. "5G vs 4G: What's the Difference?" June 15, 2022. https://www.thalesgroup.com/en/worldwide-digital-identity-and-security/mobile/magazine/5g-vs-4g-whats-difference#:~:text=In%20the%20right%20conditions%205G,evolution%2C%20speeds%20are%20lightning%20fast.

HOW NEW TECHNOLOGIES ARE CHANGING INDUSTRY
Barten, Martijn. "How Virtual Reality Is Transforming the Travel Industry." Revfine, January 25, 2024. https://www.revfine.com/virtual-reality-travel-industry/.

THE ROLE OF OFFICES
Zettl, Mark. "Office Buildings Are Still Less Than 50% Occupied: Who Should Worry?" *Forbes*, November 29, 2022. https://www.forbes.com/sites/markzettl/2022/11/29/office-buildings-are-still-less-than-50-occupied-who-should-worry/?sh=fb1745208e9b.

HOW MANY PEOPLE CAN WORK REMOTELY?
L'Oréal. "Rethinking the Way We Work: The New L'Oréal Campuses." No date. https://www.loreal.com/en/news/group/rethinking-the-way-we-work-the-new-loreal-campuses/.

Travers, Mark. "What Percentage of Workers Can Realistically Work from Home? New Data from Norway Offer Clues." *Forbes*, April 24, 2020. https://www.forbes.com/sites/traversmark/2020/04/24/what-percentage-of-workers-can-realistically-work-from-home-new-data-from-norway-offer-clues/?sh=2844f5f178fe.

The Impact of Technology

Kantor, Jodi, and Arya Sundaram. "The Rise of the Worker Productivity Score." *New York Times*, August 14, 2022. https://www.nytimes.com/interactive/2022/08/14/business/worker-productivity-tracking.html.

McCaul, Elizabeth (member, European Central Bank Supervisory Board). "Technology Is Neither Good nor Bad, but Humans Make It So." Speech at the Intesa Sanpaolo conference on "The Use of Artificial Intelligence to Fight Crime," July 13, 2022. https://www.bankingsupervision.europa.eu/press/speeches/date/2022/html/ssm.sp220713~73f22a486e.en.html.

Teachout, Zephyr. "The Boss Will See You Now." *New York Review*, August 18, 2022. https://www.nybooks.com/articles/2022/08/18/the-boss-will-see-you-now-zephyr-teachout/.

Chapter 3: The New Marketplaces

Tobaccowala, Rishad:

—. "Roots/Wings." *The Future Does Not Fit in the Containers of the Past* (blog), edition 47. July 4, 2021. https://rishad.substack.com/p/rootswings.

—. "Scale!" *The Future Does Not Fit in the Containers of the Past* (blog), edition 29. February 28, 2021. https://rishad.substack.com/p/scale.

—. "The Fractionalized Employee." *The Future Does Not Fit in the Containers of the Past* (blog), edition 78. February 6, 2022. https://rishad.substack.com/p/the-fractionalized-employee.

Marketplace Statistics

Dean, Brian. "Upwork Revenue and Client Stats (2023)." Backlinko, August 21, 2023. https://backlinko.com/upwork-users.

Mileva, Geri. "20 Key Etsy Statistics Every eCommerce Entrepreneur Should Know." Influencer MarketingHub, September 1, 2023. https://influencermarketinghub.com/etsy-stats/#toc-0.

Shewale, Rohit. "Shopify Statistic—Stores, Merchants & Revenue (2024)." DemandSage, January 14, 2024. https://www.demandsage.com/shopify-statistics/#:~:text=Over%207000%20applications%20are%20available,of%20more%20than%207%2C000%20people.

Studies on Marketplaces

Fuller, Joseph B., Manjari Raman, James Palano, Allison Bailey, Nithya Vadugan, Elizabeth Kaufman, Renée Laverdièr, and Sibley Lovett. "Building the On-Demand Workforce." Harvard Business School and BCG Henderson Institute, HBS Study on Marketplaces, no date. https://www.dropbox.com/s/rpxd0cvcenf3mw5/Building_The_On_Demand_Workforce.pdf?dl=0.

Self-Employed, Freelancers, and Gig Workers

Anderson, Monica, Colleen McClain, Michelle Faverio, and Risa Gelles-Watnick. "The State of Gig Work in 2021." Pew Research Center, December 8, 2021. https://www.pewresearch.org/internet/2021/12/08/the-state-of-gig-work-in-2021/.

Howarth, Josh. "57+ Freelance Statistics, Trends, and Insights (2024)." Exploding Topics, February 19, 2024. https://explodingtopics.com/blog/freelance-stats.

Main, Kelly. "Small Business Statistics of 2024." *Forbes*, January 31, 2024. https://www.forbes.com/advisor/business/small-business-statistics/.

Microsoft Store Team. "Gen-trepreneur Z Is Making Its Mark on the Future of Small Business." Windows Experience Blog, June 6, 2022. https://blogs.windows.com/windowsexperience/2022/06/06/gen-trepreneur-z-is-making-its-mark-on-the-future-of-small-business/.

Rabouin, Dion. "Small Businesses Keep Hiring as Fed Raises Rates to Cool Economy." *Wall Street Journal*, January 25, 2023. https://www.wsj.com/articles/surge-in-hiring-by-small-business-complicates-feds-effort-to-cool-economy-11674627479?st=t3xeionyt3f7ppu&reflink=article_copyURL_share.

Vaughn, Rachel. "Why Is There a Rise in Self-Employment?" FranchiseWire, December 19, 2022. https://www.franchisewire.com/why-is-there-a-rise-in-self-employment/.

Empowering a New Talent and Production Paradigm

SafetyWing (insurance for nomads and companies that hire nomads). No date. https://safetywing.com/.

Deel (benefits and compliance for companies that hire a migrating global workforce). No date. https://www.deel.com/.

MFG (connect buyers to manufacturers). No date. https://www.mfg.com/.

CHALLENGES OF FAST-GROWING AND DISTRIBUTED WORKPLACES

Brassey, Jacqueline, Erica Coe, Martin Dewhurst, Kana Enomoto, Renata Giarole, Brad Herbig, and Barbara Jeffery. "Addressing Employee Burnout: Are You Solving the Right Problem?" McKinsey Health Institute, May 27, 2022. https://www.mckinsey.com /mhi/our-insights/addressing-employee-burnout-are-you-solving -the-right-problem.

Thrasyvoulou, Xenios. "Understanding the Innovator's Dilemma." *Wired*, no date. https://medium.com/@xenios/understanding-the-innovator -s-dilemma-614f03862510.

GLOBAL STATISTICS

LinkedIn. "Statistics." LinkedIn Pressroom, no date. https://news.linkedin .com/about-us#Statistics.

Matsakis, Louise. "How Amazon Turned Small Businesses into 'Day Traders.'" *Semafor*, January 25, 2023. https://www.semafor.com/article /01/25/2023/how-amazon-turned-small-businesses-into-day-traders.

Shewale, Rohit. "46 TikTok Statistics for 2024 (Users, Creators & Revenue)." DemandSage, January 9, 2024. https://www.demandsage .com/tiktok-user-statistics/.

Shopify International Sales. "Sell Across Borders. Scale Without Limits." Shopify, no date. https://www.shopify.com/markets.

CASE STUDIES

Procter & Gamble. https://consumervaluecreation.wordpress.com/2016 /03/11/procter-gamble-from-rd-to-connectdevelop-platform/.

Swinton, Laura. "How Marcel Has Saved Over 2,000 Publicis Groupe Jobs throughout the Pandemic." Little Black Book, September 16, 2020. https://www.lbbonline.com/news/how-marcel-has -saved-over-2000-publicis-groupe-jobs-throughout-the-pandemic.

Chapter 4: *Gig Work, Side Hustles, and Passion Projects*

Tobaccowala, Rishad. "The Fractionalized Employee." *The Future Does Not Fit in the Containers of the Past* (blog), edition 78. February 6, 2022. https://rishad.substack.com/p/the-fractionalized-employee.

KNOWLEDGE WORKERS RETHINKING FULL-TIME WORK

Lazer, Joe. "The Great Betrayal: After Callous Layoffs, Workers Are Done with the Full-Time Work Model." A.Team, January 26, 2023. https://www.a.team/mission/the-great-betrayal.

INDUSTRIES THAT INCORPORATE GIG WORK WELL

Davidson, Adam. "What Hollywood Can Teach Us About the Future of Work." *New York Times*, May 5, 2015. https://www.nytimes.com/2015/05/10/magazine/what-hollywood-can-teach-us-about-the-future-of-work.html.

SIDE HUSTLE AND GIG DATA

Davis, Maggie. "Side Hustlers on the Rise, and Nearly 70% Say They're More Reliant on the Extra Income Due to Inflation." Lending Tree, November 2022. https://www.lendingtree.com/debt-consolidation/side-hustlers-survey/.

Dua, André, Kwellin Ellingrud, Bryan Hancock, Ryan Luby, Anu Madgavkar, and Sarah Pemberton. "Freelance, Side Hustles, and Gigs: Many More Americans Have Become Independent Workers." McKinsey & Company, August 23, 2022. https://www.mckinsey.com/featured-insights/sustainable-inclusive-growth/future-of-america/freelance-side-hustles-and-gigs-many-more-americans-have-become-independent-workers.

COMPANIES THAT ENCOURAGE SIDE HUSTLES

Handley, Lucy. "'I Can't Believe You're Allowed to Do That': Meet the Companies Encouraging Side Hustles." CNBC Work, December 22, 2021. https://www.cnbc.com/2021/12/22/these-companies-actually-encourage-staff-to-have-side-hustles.html.

MONITORING WORK

Allyn, Bobby. "Your Boss Is Watching You: Work-From-Home Boom Leads to More Surveillance." *All Things Considered*, NPR, May 13, 2020. https://www.npr.org/2020/05/13/854014403 /your-boss-is-watching-you-work-from-home-boom-leads-to-more -surveillance.

WHY SIDE HUSTLES MAY INCREASE VS. DECREASE COMMITMENT

Bek, Nate. "Zillow CEO Says Company Is Attracting Talent at a 'Much Greater Rate' Thanks to Flexible Work Model." GeekWire, February 16, 2023. https://www.geekwire.com/2023/zillow-ceo -says-company-is-attracting-talent-at-a-much-greater-rate-thanks-to -flexible-work-model/.

Burkus, David. "Research Shows That Organizations Benefit When Employees Take Sabbaticals." *Harvard Business Review*, August 10, 2017. https://hbr.org/2017/08/research-shows-that -organizations-benefit-when-employees-take-sabbaticals.

Hansen, Ryan. "New Research Shows Side Hustles Can Boost Full-Time Job Performance ." *Daily Iowan*, November 28, 2021. https://dailyiowan .com/2021/11/28/new-research-shows-side-hustles-can-boost-full -time-job-performance/.

Perrone, Giuseppe. "30+ Companies with significant Significant Volunteer Programs." TwentyNow, October 12, 2021. https://www.twentynow .com/sustainability-initiatives/social/30-companies-with-significant -volunteer-programs/.

The Sabbatical Project. No date. https://thesabbaticalproject.org/about/.

Chapter 5: The COVID Catalyst

Tobaccowala, Rishad:

—. "Fewer." *The Future Does Not Fit in the Containers of the Past* (blog), edition 134. https://rishad.substack.com/p/fewer.

—. "Great Interactions." *The Future Does Not Fit in the Containers of the Past* (blog), edition 132. February 19, 2023. https://rishad.substack .com/p/great-interactions.

—. "Returning to the Office?" *The Future Does Not Fit in the Containers of the Past* (blog), edition 85. March 27, 2022. https://rishad.substack.com/p/returning-to-the-office.

—. "The Future of Work." *The Future Does Not Fit in the Containers of the Past* (blog), edition 17. December 8, 2020. https://rishad.substack.com/p/the-future-of-work.

On Returning to the Office

Guilford, Gwynn. "Work-From-Home Era Ends for Millions of Americans." *Wall Street Journal*, March 25, 2023. https://www.wsj.com/articles/work-from-home-era-ends-for-millions-of-americans-8bb7 5367?mod=hp_lead_pos1.

Kim, Eugene. "Almost 30,000 Amazon Employees Have Signed an Internal Petition to Fight the Company's Return-to-Office Mandate." *Business Insider*, March 10, 2023. https://www.businessinsider.com/amazon-return-to-office-policy-petition-30000-staff-remote-work-2023-3.

Phillips, Matt. "Remote Work Is Starting to Hit Office Rents." Axios, March 22, 2023. https://www.axios.com/2023/03/22/remote-work-wf-office-rents-decline.

Rattner, Steven. "Is Working from Home Really Working?" *New York Times*, March 22, 2023. https://www.nytimes.com/2023/03/22/opinion/remote-work-salesforce-meta-working-from-home.html?smid=nytcore-ios-share&referringSource=articleShare.

The New Infrastructure

LaBerge, Laura, Clayton O'Toole, Jeremy Schneider, and Kate Smaje. "How COVID-19 Has Pushed Companies over the Technology Tipping Point and Transformed Business Forever." McKinsey & Company, October 5, 2020. https://www.mckinsey.com/capabilities/strategy-and-corporate-finance/our-insights/how-covid-19-has-pushed-companies-over-the-technology-tipping-point-and-transformed-business-forever.

McGrath, Amanda. "Companies Want Diverse Teams. Remote Work Is Making Them Possible." LinkedIn, November 14, 2022.

https://www.linkedin.com/business/talent/blog/talent-acquisition
/remote-work-is-making-diverse-dei-teams-possible.

New Mindsets

Hoffsteter, Sarah. Personal email. March 26, 2023.

Liu, Jennifer. "How People Have Changed the Way They Think About Work, According to Their Therapists." CNBC, March 16, 2022. https://www.cnbc.com/2022/03/16/how-people-have-changed-the-way-they-think-about-work-according-to-their-therapists.html.

Minahan, Tim. "What Your Future Employees Want Most." *Harvard Business Review*, May 31, 2021. https://hbr.org/2021/05/what-your-future-employees-want-most.

Morgan, Kate. "The Great Resignation: How Employers Drove Workers to Quit." BBC Worklife, July 1, 2021. https://www.bbc.com/worklife/article/20210629-the-great-resignation-how-employers-drove-workers-to-quit.

Moss, Jennifer. "The Pandemic Changed Us. Now Companies Have to Change Too." *Harvard Business Review*, July 1, 2022. https://hbr.org/2022/07/the-pandemic-changed-us-now-companies-have-to-change-too.

Oracle. "Oracle AI for Human Capital Management. No date. https://www.oracle.com/human-capital-management/ai-at-work/.

Parker, Kim, Juliana Menasce Horowitz, and Rachel Minkin. "COVID-19 Pandemic Continues to Reshape Work in America." Pew Research Center, February 16, 2022. https://www.pewresearch.org/social-trends/2022/02/16/covid-19-pandemic-continues-to-reshape-work-in-america/.

Sull, Donald, Charles Sull, and Ben Zweig. "Toxic Culture Is Driving the Great Resignation." *MIT Sloan Management Review*, January 11, 2022. https://sloanreview.mit.edu/article/toxic-culture-is-driving-the-great-resignation/.

Tsipursky, Gleb. "New Study Shows Managers Are Changing Their Minds About the Hybrid Work Model." Intentional Insights, January 18, 2023. https://intentionalinsights.org/new

-study-shows-managers-are-changing-their-minds-about-the
-hybrid-work-model/.

EXAMPLES OF COMPANIES ADAPTING OR NOT ADAPTING

Arneson, Krystin. "How Companies Around the World Are Shifting the
Way They Work." BBC Worklife, September 15, 2021. https://www.bbc
.com/worklife/article/20210915-how-companies-around-the-world
-are-shifting-the-way-they-work.

Conference Board Study of 2022: "The Reimagined Workplace
Two Years Later: Human Capital Responses to the COVID-19
Pandemic." https://www.dropbox.com/s/k2x0fb5fokksqui
/TCB-Reimagined-Workplace-2-Years-Later-2022II.pdf?dl=0.

Herbst, Julia. "The 10 Most Innovative Companies in the Workplace
in 2022." Fast Company, March 8, 2022. https://www.fastcompany
.com/90724501/most-innovative-companies-workplace-2022.

WP Creative Group. "How the Most Innovative Companies Excel
at Work-Life Balance." *Washington Post*, October 4, 2021. https://
www.washingtonpost.com/brand-studio/wp/2021/10/04/feature
/how-the-most-innovative-companies-excel-at-work-life-balance/.

How COVID HAS IMPROVED THE WORKPLACE

Duran-Franch, Joana, and Mike Konczal. "Real Wages Are
Increasing for Those in the Bottom Half of the Income Distribution." Roosevelt Institute, November 17, 2021. https://roos-
eveltinstitute.org/2021/11/17/real-wages-are-increasing-for-those
-in-the-bottom-half-of-the-income-distribution/.

Erickson, Robin, Deb Cohen, and Rebecca L. Ray. "The Reimagined Workplace Two Years Later." The Conference Board (survey results), 2022. https://www.dropbox.com/s/k2x0fb5fokksqui
/TCB-Reimagined-Workplace-2-Years-Later-2022II.pdf?dl=0.

Horovitz, Bruce. "How Companies Have Evolved Their Cultures in
Response to the Pandemic." *Time*, October 14, 2022. https://time.
com/6222082/company-culture-pandemic/.

Chapter 6: *Fractionalized Employees*

Manufacturing Institute. "The Aging of the Manufacturing Work-force: Challenges and Best Practices." The Manufacturing Institute, July 2019. https://www.themanufacturinginstitute.org/research/the-aging-of-the-manufacturing-workforce/.

Tobaccowala, Rishad. "The Fractionalized Employee." *The Future Does Not Fit in the Containers of the Past* (blog), edition 78. February 6, 2022. https://rishad.substack.com/p/the-fractionalized-employee.

SHORTAGE OF JOBS IN SERVICE INDUSTRIES

Haddad, Lisa M., Pavan Annamaraju, and Tammy J. Toney-Butler. "Nursing Shortage." National Center for Biotechnology Information, February 13, 2023. https://www.ncbi.nlm.nih.gov/books/NBK493175/.

ON TEACHING

Edsall, Thomas B. "There's a Reason There Aren't Enough Teachers in America. Many Reasons, Actually." *New York Times*, December 14, 2022. https://www.nytimes.com/2022/12/14/opinion/teacher-shortage-education.html.

Nguyen, Tuan D., Chanh B. Lam, and Paul Bruno. "Is There a National Teacher Shortage? A Systematic Examination of Reports of Teacher Shortages in the United States." EdWorkingPaper: 22-631, 2022. Retrieved from Annenberg Institute at Brown University: https://doi.org/10.26300/76eq-hj32.

COMPANIES THAT OFFER SOME FORM OF FRACTIONALIZED EMPLOYMENT

ADP Inc. "Insight: Part-Time Benefits." No date. https://www.adp.com/resources/articles-and-insights/articles/p/part-time-benefits.aspx.

Herrity, Jennifer. "13 Companies That Offer Part-Time Jobs with Benefits." Indeed, August 9, 2023. https://www.indeed.com/career-advice/finding-a-job/companies-that-offer-part-time-jobs-with-benefits.

Turner, Fred. "You Call This 'Flexible Work'?" *New York Times*, April 12, 2023. https://www.nytimes.com/2023/04/12/magazine /flexible-work-home.html.

Chapter 7: *Machine-Human Coexistence*

Tobaccowala, Rishad. "Is It Human or Is It AI." *The Future Does Not Fit in the Containers of the Past* (blog), edition 142. April 30, 2023. https:// rishad.substack.com/p/is-it-human-or-is-it-ai.

STATISTICS
Kolmar, Chris. "23+ Artificial Intelligence and Job Loss Statistics (2023): How Job Automation Impacts the Workforce." Zippia, June 11, 2023. https://www.zippia.com/advice/ai-job-loss-statistics/.

World Economic Forum. "The Future of Jobs Report 2020." October 20, 2020. https://www.weforum.org/reports/the-future -of-jobs-report-2020/in-full/executive-summary.

STORIES
Cutter, Chip, and Harriet Torry. "The Disappearing White-Collar Job." *Wall Street Journal*, May 15, 2023. https://www.wsj.com/articles /the-disappearing-white-collar-job-af0bd925?mod=Searchresults _pos1&page=1.

Ford, Brody. "IBM to Pause Hiring for Jobs That AI Could Do." *Bloomberg*, May 1, 2023. https://www.bloomberg.com /news/articles/2023-05-01/ibm-to-pause-hiring-for-back-office-jobs -that-ai-could-kill.

Goldman Sachs. "Humanoid Robots: Sooner Than You Might Think." November 15, 2022. https://www.goldmansachs.com/intelligence /pages/humanoid-robots.html.

Kingson, Jennifer A. "AI and Robots Fuel New Job Displacement Fears." Axios, April 2, 2023. https://www.axios.com/2023/03/29 /robots-jobs-chatgpt-generative-ai.

Mulvaney, Erin, and Lauren Weber. "End of the Billable Hour? Law Firms Get On Board with Artificial Intelligence." *Wall Street*

Journal, May 11, 2023. https://www.wsj.com/articles/end-of
-the-billable-hour-law-firms-get-on-board-with-artificial-intelligence
-17ebd3f8.

Pham, Sherisse. "Jack Ma: In 30 years, the Best CEO Could Be a Robot."
CNN Business, April 24, 2017. https://money.cnn.com/2017/04/24
/technology/alibaba-jack-ma-30-years-pain-robot-ceo/index.html.

Weber, Lauren, and Lindsay Ellis. "The Jobs Most Exposed to Chat-
GPT." *Wall Street Journal*, March 28, 2023. https://www.wsj.com
/articles/the-jobs-most-exposed-to-chatgpt-e7ceebf0.

ON ARTIFICIAL INTELLIGENCE

Bersin, Josh. "Why Is The World Afraid of AI? The Fears Are
Unfounded, and Here's Why." JoshBersin.com, April 2, 2023.
https://joshbersin.com/2023/04/why-is-the-world-afraid-of-ai-the
-fears-are-unfounded-and-heres-why/.

Blain, Loz. "The Case for How and Why AI Might Kill Us All." New Atlas:
Technology, March 31, 2023. https://newatlas.com/technology/ai
-danger-kill-everyone/.

Economist. "Your Job Is (Probably) Safe from Artificial Intelligence."
May 7, 2023. https://www.economist.com/finance-and-economics
/2023/05/07/your-job-is-probably-safe-from-artificial-intelligence.

Eloundou, Tyna, Sam Manning, Pamela Mishkin, and Daniel Rock.
"GPTs are GPTs: An Early Look at the Labor Market Impact
Potential of Large Language Models." Working paper, August 2023.
https://www.dropbox.com/scl/fi/pvl54hc8r1rwsqw73tugi/2303.10130
.pdf?rlkey=xjboyt8hblwohffidod9j0nxb&e=1&dl=0

Harari, Yuval Noah. "Yuval Noah Harari Argues That AI Has Hacked
the Operating System of Human Civilization." *Economist*, April 28,
2023. https://www.economist.com/by-invitation/2023/04/28
/yuval-noah-harari-argues-that-ai-has-hacked-the-operating-system
-of-human-civilisation.

Knight, Will. "What Really Made Geoffrey Hinton into an AI
Doomer." *Wired*, May 8, 2023. https://www.wired.com/story/geoffrey
-hinton-ai-chatgpt-dangers/.

Lucas, Scott Alan. "While Hollywood Writers Fret About AI, Visual Effects Workers Welcome It." *The Information*, May 20, 2023. https://www.theinformation.com/articles/while-hollywood-writers-fret-about-ai-visual-effects-workers-welcome-it?rc=y6alo3.

Scheiber, Noam, and John Koblin. "Will a Chatbot Write the Next 'Succession'?" *New York Times*, May 2, 2023. https://www.nytimes.com/2023/04/29/business/media/writers-guild-hollywood-ai-chatgpt.html.

Wolf, Martin. "The Threat and Promise of Artificial Intelligence." *Financial Times*, May 9, 2023. https://www.ft.com/content/41fd34b2-89ee-4b21-ac0a-9b15560ef37c.

Definition of Technology
Editors of Encyclopaedia Britannica. "Technology." *Britannica*, March 13, 2024. https://www.britannica.com/technology/technology.

Oxford Languages. "Technology." Oxford University Press, no date. https://www.google.com/search?sxsrf=APwXEdep Tu5Z9mOFi6-3dYY1RcX9IfaTTA:1684142454341&q=technology &si=AMnBZoGIozZC-9B5VLYtFM_IzEeHnkJJz6XK-xk3H2Aw79 D a n T p g G d A q 9 i s D 9 4 d u C y Q s Y n l I Z I C c o l f R M 7 - FM2cxJOoMGbymuT_KXs-k_9lRLFXpPHyw61g%3D&expnd=1 &sa=X&ved=2ahUKEwiDzvfF__b-AhX8EFkFHTfjBOwQ2v4leg QIDhAS&biw=1728&bih=912&dpr=2.

On the Fourth Industrial Revolution
Schneegans, S., T. Straza, and J. Lewis (eds.). *UNESCO Science Report: the Race Against Time for Smarter Development*. UNESCO Publishing: Paris, 2021.

Chapter 8: The Unbundling of the Office

Tobaccowala, Rishad:

—. "Return to the Office?" *The Future Does Not Fit in the Containers of the Past* (blog), edition 85. March 27, 2022. https://rishad.substack.com/p/returning-to-the-office.

—. "The Jigsaw of Return." *The Future Does Not Fit in the Containers of the Past* (blog), edition 44. June 13, 2021. https://rishad.substack.com/p/the-jigsaw-of-return.

STATISTICS: MOVING FROM FULL-TIME OFFICE WORK

O'Loughlin, Henry. "Every Major Company Reducing Office Space: 2020–2024." Build Remote, March 29, 2024. https://buildremote.co/companies/reducing-office-space/.

Scoop. *Flex Report Q1 2024*. https://www.flex.scoopforwork.com/stats?utm_source=newsletter&utm_medium=email&utm_campaign=newsletter_axiosmarkets&stream=business.

HOW COMPANIES ARE RETHINKING OFFICES

Donaldson, Sarah. "Andreesen Horowitz Moves Its Headquarters to the Cloud." *Wall Street Journal*, July 22, 2022. https://www.wsj.com/articles/andreessen-horowitz-moves-its-headquarters-to-the-cloud-11658514859.

Gordon, Kat. "First Place in Third Spaces Goes to A&G." *Creative Entrepreneur in Residence* (blog), May 19, 2023. https://katgordon.substack.com/p/first-place-in-third-spaces-goes.

Peck, Emily, and Matt Phillips. "1 Big Thing: What Yelp and Etsy Have in Common." Axios Markets, June 2, 2023. https://www.axios.com/newsletters/axios-markets-b805003a-670f-448e-beaf-fc21e86061e6.html?utm_source=newsletter&utm_medium=email&utm_campaign=newsletter_axiosmarkets&stream=business.

Semuels, Alana. "Companies Are Finally Designing Offices for the New Work Reality." *Time*, May 22, 2023. https://time.com/6280986/hybrid-office-return-to-work-design/.

REDUCING THE DIFFERENCE BETWEEN IN-PERSON AND VIRTUAL MEETINGS

Apple. "MacOS Sonoma Brings All-New Capabilities for Elevating Productivity and Creativity." Apple Press Release, June 5, 2023. https://www.apple.com/newsroom/2023/06/macos-sonoma-brings-new-capabilities-for-elevating-productivity-and-creativity/

Nartker, Andrew. "A First Look at Project Starline's New, Simpler Prototype." Google (blog), May 10, 2023. https://blog.google /technology/research/project-starline-prototype/.

COMPANIES MESSING UP THE RETURN TO WORK

Caminiti, Susan. "A Message for Male CEOs on Return to Office from a Wall Street Women's Leader." CNBC, April 3, 2023. https://www .cnbc.com/2023/04/03/a-message-for-male-ceos-on-return-to -office-from-top-wall-street-woman.html.

Farmers Insurance/Amazon/Disney: https://fortune.com/2023/06/06 /farmers-insurance-remote-work-protests/.

Chapter 9: The Fall of Old Managers and the Rise of New Leaders

Tobaccowala, Rishad:

——. "De-Bossification." *The Future Does Not Fit in the Containers of the Past* (blog). https://rishad.substack.com/publish/posts/detail/68477 527?referrer=%2Fpublish%2Fposts.

——. "Five Keys to Ensure Professional Relevance." *The Future Does Not Fit in the Containers of the Past* (blog), edition 153. July 16, 2023. https:// rishad.substack.com/p/5-keys-to-ensure-professional-relevance.

——. "Management Next!" *The Future Does Not Fit in the Containers of the Past* (blog), edition 88. April 17, 2022. https://rishad.substack.com/p /management-next-.

——. "On Leadership. . . ." *The Future Does Not Fit in the Containers of the Past* (blog), edition 98. June 26, 2022. https://rishad.substack .com/p/on-leadership.

——. "Welcome to the Jazz Age!" *The Future Does Not Fit in the Containers of the Past* (blog), edition 144. May 14, 2023. https://rishad.substack .com/p/welcome-to-the-jazz-age.

——. "You=Leader." *The Future Does Not Fit in the Containers of the Past* (blog), edition 42. May 30, 2021. https://rishad.substack.com/p /youleader.

The Importance of Managers

Field, Emily, Bryan Hancock, Stephanie Smallets, and Brooke Weddle. "Investing in Middle Managers Pays Off—Literally." McKinsey & Company, June 26, 2023. https://www.mckinsey.com /capabilities/people-and-organizational-performance/our-insights /investing-in-middle-managers-pays-off-literally.

Companies De-Layering

Bell, Karissa. "Meta is Is Laying Off Employees for the Third Time in Less Than Three Months." *Engadget*, May 24, 2023. https://www.engadget .com/meta-is-laying-off-employees-for-the-third-time-in-less-than -three-months-174112198.html.

Constantz, Jo, and Julia Love. "A Clear Target Emerges in Tech Lay-offs: Middle Managers." *Bloomberg*, February 6, 2023. https://www .bloomberg.com/news/articles/2023-02-06/meta-alphabet-target -middle-managers-with-tech-jobs-cuts.

When Leaders Lose the Plot

Jaffe, Greg. "Howard Schultz's Fight to Stop a Starbucks Barista Uprising." *Washington Post*, October 8, 2022. https://www.washingtonpost.com /business/2022/10/08/starbucks-union-ceo-howard-schultz/.

Lanard, Noah. "Howard Schultz Came Out of Retirement to Destroy Starbucks' Union—and His Legacy." *Mother Jones*, May and June 2023. https://www.motherjones.com/politics/2023/03 /howard-schultz-starbucks-union-busting-buffalo-brooklyn/.

Chapter 10: Reimagine the Company with Paradigm Shifts in Mind

Tobaccowala, Rishad:

—. "A Company of One." *The Future Does Not Fit in the Containers of the Past* (blog), edition 155. July 30, 2023. https://rishad.substack .com/p/a-company-of-one.

—. "Exponential Organizations!" *The Future Does Not Fit in the Containers of the Past* (blog), edition 148. June 11, 2023. https://rishad .substack.com/p/exponential-organizations.

—. "Remaining Relevant in an AI Age." *The Future Does Not Fit in the Containers of the Past* (blog), edition 151. July 2, 2023. https://rishad .substack.com/p/remaining-relevant-in-an-ai-age.

—. "Re-Thinking Strategy." *The Future Does Not Fit in the Containers of the Past* (blog), edition 109. September 11, 2022. https://rishad .substack.com/p/re-thinking-strategy.

—. "Strategy." *The Future Does Not Fit in the Containers of the Past* (blog), edition 31. March 14, 2021. https://rishad.substack.com/p/strategy.

—. "Ten Forecasts for the Next Decade. Part Two: Looking Ahead." *The Future Does Not Fit in the Containers of the Past* (blog), edition 64. October 31, 2021. https://rishad.substack.com/p/ten-forecasts -for-the-next-decade-438.

How Nike Reinvented Itself

Friedman, Vanessa. "How Nike Won the Cultural Revolution." *New York Times*, June 22, 2023. https://www.nytimes.com/2022/06/15 /style/nike-culture.html.

Glassdoor. "Nike." No date. https://www.glassdoor.com/Reviews /NIKE-Reviews-E1699.htm.

Mixson, Elizabeth. "Nike's Digital Transformation Efforts Continue to Win Big." Intelligent Automation Network, June 21, 2021. https:// www.intelligentautomation.network/transformation/articles /nikes-digital-transformation-efforts-continue-to-win-big.

Nike. "Sustainability: Move to Zero." No date. https://www.nike.com /sustainability.

Waldow, Julia. "'What Truly Drives Our Business at the High Level Is Product and Brand': Nike's VP of Direct on Its DTC Playbook, Membership Strategy & `Three Big Drivers' behind Digital Sales." ModernRetail, May 5, 2023. https://www.modernretail.co/operations /what-truly-drives-our-business-at-the-high-level-is-product-and -brand-nikes-vp-of-direct-on-its-dtc-playbook-membership-strategy -three-big-drivers-behind-digital-sales/.

How Walmart Reinvented Itself

Adams, Peter. "Walmart Ad Sales Hit $2.7B as Execs Eye Greater Scale." MarketingDive, February 22, 2023. https://www.marketingdive.com/news/walmart-retail-media-ad-sales-earnings/643268/.

Hampstead, John Paul. "Walmart Wants to Beat Amazon at Its Own Game." FreightWaves, April 5, 2023. https://www.freightwaves.com/news/walmart-wants-to-beat-amazon-at-its-own-game.

Kumar, Suresh. "Walmart Global Tech Accelerates with Plans to Hire Thousands of Technologists and Add New Locations." Walmart, March 15, 2022. https://corporate.walmart.com/newsroom/2022/03/15/walmart-global-tech-accelerates-expansion-with-plans-to-hire-thousands-of-technologists-and-add-new-locations.

McKinnon, Tricia. "6 Reasons Walmart's eCommerce Strategy Is Winning." Indigo 9 Digital, March 9, 2023. https://www.indigo9digital.com/blog/4-secrets-to-walmarts-ecommerce-sucess.

Repko, Melissa. "Walmart Is Bringing Ads to an Aisle Near You as Retailers Chase New Moneymakers." CNBC, August 1, 2023. https://www.cnbc.com/2023/08/01/walmart-pushes-into-in-stores-advertising-as-new-revenue-driver.html#:~:text=Walmart%20is%20turning%20the%20approximately,aisle%20of%20the%20electronics%20department.

Walmart. "Walmart Global Tech Is Powering the Next Retail Disruption." Walmart Careers, no date. https://careers.walmart.com/global-tech-is-growing#:~:text=We're%20growing,our%20team%20earned%20a%20promotion.

How Microsoft Reinvented Itself

Dutta, Yuboraj. "How Microsoft Resurrected Itself with AI." LinkedIn, June 17, 2023. https://www.linkedin.com/pulse/how-microsoft-resurrected-itself-ai-yuboraj-dutta/.

Tabrizi, Behnam. "How Microsoft Became Innovative Again." *Harvard Business Review*, February 20, 2023. https://hbr.org/2023/02/how-microsoft-became-innovative-again.

How Domino's Changed

Domino's Pizza. "Introducing Our Inspired New Pizza." Domino's, December 16, 2009. https://blog.unincorporated.com/dominos-brand -crisis.

Vo, Abigail. "Domino's: A Breakthrough for a Failing Brand." EnvZone, January 26, 2021. https://envzone.com/dominos-a -breakthrough-for-a-failing-brand/.

Population Growth

Gramlich, John. "For World Population Day, a Look at the Countries with the Biggest Projected Gains—and Losses— by 2100." Pew Research Center, July 10, 2019. https://www .pewresearch.org/short-reads/2019/07/10/for-world-population -day-a-look-at-the-countries-with-the-biggest-projected-gains-and -losses-by-2100/.

Chapter 11: Retrain the Workforce

Tobaccowala, Rishad:

—. "12 Career Lessons." *The Future Does Not Fit in the Containers of the Past* (blog), edition 11. October 25, 2020. https://rishad.substack .com/p/12-career-lessons.

—. "A Company of One." *The Future Does Not Fit in the Containers of the Past* (blog), edition 155. July 30, 2023. https://rishad.substack .com/p/a-company-of-one.

—. "Career Bending Times." *The Future Does Not Fit in the Containers of the Past* (blog), edition 141. April 23, 2023. https://rishad.substack .com/p/career-bending-times.

—. "Remaining Relevant in an AI Age." *The Future Does Not Fit in the Containers of the Past* (blog), edition 151. July 2, 2023. https://rishad .substack.com/p/remaining-relevant-in-an-ai-age.

—. "Talent Will Matter Even More." *The Future Does Not Fit in the Containers of the Past* (blog), edition 123. December 18, 2022. https:// rishad.substack.com/p/talent-will-matter-even-more.

POPULATION TRENDS

Anderson, Lydia, Thom File, Joey Marshall, Kevin McElrath, and Zachary Scherer. "New Household Pulse Survey Data Reveals Differences between LGBT and Non-LGBT Respondents During COVID-19 Pandemic." United States Census Bureau, November 4, 2021. https://www.census.gov/library/stories/2021/11/census-bureau-survey-explores-sexual-orientation-and-gender-identity.html.

Frey, William H. "The Nation Is Diversifying Even Faster Than Predicted, According to New Census Data." Brookings Institute, July 1, 2020. https://www.brookings.edu/articles/new-census-data-shows-the-nation-is-diversifying-even-faster-than-predicted/.

CHALLENGES TO WORK

Harter, Jim. "Are Remote Workers and Their Firms Drifting Apart?" Gallup Workplace, August 24, 2023. https://www.gallup.com/workplace/509759/remote-workers-organizations-drifting-apart.aspx.

Miller, Claire Cain, and Courtney Cox. "In Reversal Because of A.I., Office Jobs Are Now More at Risk." *New York Times*, August 24, 2023. https://www.nytimes.com/2023/08/24/upshot/artificial-intelligence-jobs.html?smid=nytcore-ios-share&referringSource=articleShare.

SHIFTS IN THE WORKFORCE

Cutter, Chip. "The $900,000 AI Job Is Here." *Wall Street Journal*, August 14, 2023. https://www.wsj.com/articles/artificial-intelligence-jobs-pay-netflix-walmart-230fc3cb.

Fernandez, Bob. "Generative AI Promises an Economic Revolution. Managing the Disruption Will Be Crucial." *Wall Street Journal*, August 28, 2023. https://www.wsj.com/articles/generative-ai-promises-an-economic-revolution-managing-the-disruption-will-be-crucial-b1c0f054?mod=Searchresults_pos1&page=1.

TRAINING EXPENDITURES AND PROGRAMS

Freifeld, Lorri. "2022 Training Industry Report." *Training*, November 16, 2022. https://trainingmag.com/2022-training-industry-report/.

Kellington, Jason. "Cultivating a Culture of Learning at Microsoft with Viva Learning." Microsoft Inside Track (blog), April 21, 2023. https://www.microsoft.com/insidetrack/blog/fostering-a-culture-of-learning-at-microsoft-with-viva-learning/.

Pulkkinen, Levi. "Facing Skilled Worker Shortage, U.S. Companies Try to Train Their Own New Labor Pools." PBS, July 1, 2021. https://www.pbs.org/newshour/education/facing-skilled-worker-shortage-u-s-companies-try-to-train-their-own-new-labor-pools.

Tough, Paul. "Americans Are Losing Faith in the Value of College. Whose Fault Is That?" *New York Times*, September 5, 2023. https://www.nytimes.com/2023/09/05/magazine/college-worth-price.html.

JUST-IN-TIME EMPLOYEES
Vaduganathan, Nithya, Colleen McDonald, Alison Bailey, and Renee Laverdiere. "Tapping into Fluid Talent." BCG, June 8, 2022. https://www.bcg.com/publications/2022/tapping-into-fluid-talent.

Chapter 12: Redesign the Structures

Tobaccowala, Rishad:

—. "Exponential Organizations!" *The Future Does Not Fit in the Containers of the Past* (blog), edition 148. June 11, 2023. https://rishad.substack.com/p/exponential-organizations.

—. "Welcome to the Jazz Age!" *The Future Does Not Fit in the Containers of the Past* (blog), edition 144. May 14, 2023. https://rishad.substack.com/p/welcome-to-the-jazz-age.

THE NEW REALITY
Barr, Alistair. "HustleGPT: Generative AI Will Boost Income and Help Millions of Workers Take on Second and Third Jobs, Morgan Stanley Predicts." *Business Insider*, September 19, 2023. https://www.businessinsider.com/how-ai-boost-income-side-hustles-multiple-jobs-eighty-billion-2023-9.

Cutter, Chip, and Te-Ping Chen. "Bosses Aren't Just Tracking When You Show Up to the Office but How Long You Stay." *Wall Street*

Journal, September 25, 2023. https://www.wsj.com/lifestyle/careers
/attention-office-resisters-the-boss-is-counting-badge-swipes-5fa37ff7.

BambooHR. "The Great Gloom: In 2023, Employees Are Unhappier
Than Ever. Why?" 2023. https://www.bamboohr.com/resources
/guides/employee-happiness-h1-2023.

Elder, Bryce. "AI Is a Turbo-Charger for the $1.4tn Side Hustle Economy,
Apparently." *Financial Times*, September 19, 2023. https://www
.ft.com/content/2c332446-d366-4405-89a2-f79feaoc2b03.

Sarlin, Benjy. "Gallup: Support for Unions at Historic Highs." Semafor,
August 30, 2023. https://www.semafor.com/article/08/30/2023
/gallup-support-for-unions-at-historic-highs.

ORGANIZATIONAL STRUCTURES

Carucci, Ron, and Jarrod Shappell. "Design Your Organization to Match
Your Strategy." *Harvard Business Review*, June 6, 2022. https://hbr
.org/2022/06/design-your-organization-to-match-your-strategy.

De Smet, Aaron, Chris Gagnon, and Elizabeth Mygatt. "Organizing
for the Future: Nine Keys to Becoming a Future-Ready Company."
McKinsey & Company, January 11, 2021. https://www.mckinsey
.com/capabilities/people-and-organizational-performance
/our-insights/organizing-for-the-future-nine-keys-to-becoming
-a-future-ready-company.

Levene, Abby. "What Is the Right Organization Structure for the 21st
Century?" Work Culture (Dropbox work in progress), January 15,
2020. https://blog.dropbox.com/topics/work-culture/21st-century
-organization-structure.

HOW COMPANIES REINVENTED THEMSELVES

Tabrizi, Behnam. "How Microsoft Became Innovative Again." *Harvard
Business Review*, February 20, 2023. https://hbr.org/2023/02/how
-microsoft-became-innovative-again.

Whelan, Robbie, Joe Flint, and Jessica Toonkel. "Disney Proposal to
Restructure, on McKinsey's Advice, Triggered Uproar from Creative
Executives." *Wall Street Journal*, December 1, 2022. https://www

.wsj.com/articles/disney-proposal-to-restructure-on-mckinseys
-advice-triggered-uproar-from-creative-executives-11669928586.

Chapter 13: Recalculate Financials

Sindreu, Jon. "Are Frequent-Flier Programs Really Worth More Than Airlines?" *Wall Street Journal*, March 15, 2021. https://www.wsj.com/articles/are-frequent-flier-programs-really-worth-more-than-airlines-11615810430.

GLOBAL VALUE OF VIRTUAL GOODS

Chaudhary, Mohit. "20 Successful Remote-First Companies and Key Lessons to Learn from Them." Turing, no date. https://www.turing.com/resources/key-lessons-to-learn-from-successful-remote-companies.

Fischer, Sara. "NYT Plans Advertising Expansion into Non-News Products." Axios, August 9, 2022. https://www.axios.com/2022/08/09/new-york-times-advertising-expansion.

Guaglione, Sara. "The New York Times Cooking Is Letting Readers Taste Test Recipes over Text to Drive Subscriptions." Digiday, June 23, 2023. https://digiday.com/media/the-new-york-times-cooking-is-letting-readers-taste-test-recipes-over-text-to-drive-subscriptions/.

Hickman, Adam, and Ellyn Maese. "Measure Performance: Strategies for Remote and Hybrid Teams." Gallup Workplace, March 26, 2021. https://www.gallup.com/workplace/341894/measure-performance-strategies-remote-hybrid-teams.aspx.

New York Times. "Our Strategy." March 24, 2022. https://www.nytco.com/press/our-strategy/.

Robertson, Katie. "The Times Reports 11% Increase in Revenue as Digital Subscriptions Climb." *New York Times*, February 8, 2023. https://www.nytimes.com/2023/02/08/business/media/new-york-times-earnings.html.

Singh, Priyanshi. "Virtual Goods Market Size Worth USD 203.6 billion, Globally, by 2028 at 20.2% CAGR." LinkedIn,

January 1, 2023. https://finance.yahoo.com/news/global-virtual
-goods-market-size-140000757.html.

Chapter 14: *Re-vision the Work-Rippled World*

Tobaccowala, Rishad:

—. "AI Is Under-Hyped." *The Future Does Not Fit in the Containers of the Past* (blog), edition 175. December 17, 2023. https://rishad.substack
.com/p/ai-is-under-hyped.

—. "Re-imaging and Re-inventing Organizations." *The Future Does Not Fit in the Containers of the Past* (blog), edition 165. October 8, 2023. https://rishad.substack.com/p/rejuvenating-and-re-imagining
-organizations.

—. "Remaining Relevant in an AI Age." *The Future Does Not Fit in the Containers of the Past* (blog), edition 151. July 2, 2023. https://rishad
.substack.com/p/remaining-relevant-in-an-ai-age.

THE FUTURE OF WORK

Bloom, Nicholas. "The Biggest Winners and Losers from the Work-from-Home Revolution." *Wall Street Journal*, December 11, 2023. https://www.wsj.com/lifestyle/workplace/work-from-home
-impact-revolution-2aa72e0f?mod=lead_feature_below_a_pos1.

WSJ staff. "The Big Wins by Unions in 2023." *Wall Street Journal*, December 11, 2023. https://www.wsj.com/economy/jobs
/the-big-wins-by-unions-in-2023-cecdfc3a?mod=lead_feature
_below_a_pos1.

WORK AND AI

Channel 1. "Channel 1 Gives Users New More Personal Ways to Watch the News." No date. https://www.channel1.ai/.

Economist. "Generative AI Could Radically Alter the Practice of Law." *Economist*, June 6, 2023. https://www.economist
.com/business/2023/06/06/generative-ai-could-radically-alter-the
-practice-of-law.

Heath, Ryan, and Maria Curl. "Unions Are Winning Protections as AI-Powered Workplaces Grow." Axios, December 12, 2023. https://www.axios.com/2023/12/12/unions-microsoft-ai-battles.

WORK AND CLIMATE CHANGE
North, Madeline. "3 Ways the Climate Crisis Is Impacting Jobs and Workers." World Economic Forum, October 19, 2023. https://www.weforum.org/agenda/2023/10/climate-crisis-impacting-jobs-workforce/.

Tao, Yanqiu, Longqi Yang, Sonia Jaffe, and Fengqi You. "Climate Mitigation Potentials of Teleworking Are Sensitive to Changes in Lifestyle and Workplace Rather Than ICT Usage." PNAS, September 18, 2023. https://www.pnas.org/doi/full/10.1073/pnas.2304099120.

Torres, Monica. "7 Ways Your Commute Is Wrecking Your Health and Relationships." Huffpost, March 18, 2022. https://www.huffpost.com/entry/ways-commute-wrecking-health-relationships_l_62323ba7e4b02d624b1a4a17.

WORK AND EDUCATION
Tough, Paul. "Americans Are Losing Faith in the Value of College. Whose Fault Is That?" *New York Times*, September 5, 2023. https://www.nytimes.com/2023/09/05/magazine/college-worth-price.html.

WORK AND FAMILIES
Cowan, Benjamin W. "Time Use, College Attainment, and the Working-from-Home Revolution." National Bureau of Economic Research, July 2023. https://www.nber.org/papers/w31439.

WORK AND PRODUCTIVITY
Barrero, José María, Nicholas Bloom, and Steven J. Davis. "The Evolution of Work from Home." *Journal of Economic Perspectives,* vol. 37, no. 4, Fall 2023, 23–50. https://www.aeaweb.org/articles?id=10.1257/jep.37.4.23#:~:text=Full%20days%20worked%20at%20home,than%20reverting%20to%20prepandemic%20levels.

FRED Economic Data. "Corporate Profits After Tax (without IVA and CCAdj). Economic Research, March 28, 2024. https://www.aeaweb.org/articles?id=10.1257/jep.37.4.23#:~:text=Full%20days%20worked%20at%20home,than%20reverting%20to%20prepandemic%20levels.

Companies Leading the Future

Automation.com. "Siemens Makes Strong Progress in Achieving Ambitious Sustainability Targets." Automation.com, December 7, 2023. https://www.automation.com/en-us/articles/december-2023/siemens-achieving-sustainability-targets.

Candelon, Francois, Bowen Ding, Su Min Ha. "What Do Starbucks, Tesla, and John Deere Have in Common? They've Used A.I. to Reinvent Their Businesses." *Fortune*, March 31, 2022. https://fortune.com/2022/04/01/ai-artificial-intelligence-starbucks-tesla-reinvention/.

Corporate Communications. "Siemens Receives Multiple Recognitions for Its Innovation and Culture." Siemens.com, January 31, 2024. https://www.siemens.com/us/en/company/press/siemens-stories/usa/siemens-usa-recognized-for-innovation-culture.html.

Doherty, Rebecca, Claudia Kampel, Anna Koivuniemi, Lucy Pérez, and Werner Rehm. "The Triple Play: Growth, Profit, and Sustainability." McKinsey & Company, August 9, 2023. https://www.mckinsey.com/capabilities/strategy-and-corporate-finance/our-insights/the-triple-play-growth-profit-and-sustainability.

Hsu, Andrea. "Airbnb Let Its Workers Live and Work Anywhere. Spoiler: They're Loving It." NPR, April 28, 2023. https://www.npr.org/2023/04/28/1172213330/airbnb-hybrid-remote-work-from-home-office-digital-nomad.

Teo, Kai Xiang. "The CEO of Dropbox Has a 90/10 Rule for Remote Work." *Business Insider*, October 15, 2023. https://www.businessinsider.com/remote-work-return-to-office-dropbox-ceo-90-10-rule-2023-10#.

ACKNOWLEDGMENTS

This book is a distillation of more than four decades of working in and observing how companies function across the world.

Most of these years were spent working for the Publicis Groupe or the companies they acquired, such as Leo Burnett and Starcom. While working there, I was offered several opportunities, including launching start-ups (Giant Step and Starcom IP), chairing global digital firms (Digitas and Razorfish), helping build media giants (Publicis Media), and developing the company's future strategies. This book could not have happened without the amazing talent at Publicis Groupe, the world-class clients I got to work with, and the incredible ecosystem of creative, data, media, strategy, and technology companies that I interacted with and learned from.

My book coach, Bruce Wexler, and agent, Giles Anderson of Anderson Literary Agency, believed in the idea behind this book and helped me write and sell the proposal for it as they did for my first book, *Restoring the Soul of Business: Staying Human in the Age of Data.*

Tim Burgard from HarperCollins acquired and championed this book as he did for my first one.

This book was copyedited by David McNeill and proofread by Amanda Bauch. Both worked with Jeff Farr of Neuwirth & Associates to take my writing to the next level.

ACKNOWLEDGMENTS

The HarperCollins team of Sicily Axton, Lauren Kingsley, Kevin Smith, and Sarah Drenth support the marketing and distribution of this book.

Several colleagues and friends provided input to improve the book, including Sanjay Khosla, Alok Choudhary, Jack Klues, Susan Gianinno, Bryan Wiener, Alain Levy, Caroline Karr, V. R. Ferose, Phillip Leslie, Michelle Taite, Michael Wiley, Andrew Swinand, Kat Gordon, Renetta McCann, Sarah Fay, Sarah Hofstetter, Ted Wright, Saneel Radia, Sarah Kramer, Scott Peters, Arpit Jain, Fabrice Beaulieu, Robyn Streisand, Rich LeFurgy, Sree Nagarajan, Chris Outram, Harsh Koppula, Emmanuel Andre, Angad Choudhary, Drew Ianni, Paul Kurchina, and Seth Green.

My parents instilled a deep love of reading and encouraged my writing.

My wife, Rekha, and our daughters, Ria and Rohini, are my driving force who always believe in me and are supportive when things get tough.

This book is dedicated to them.

INDEX

INDEX

Nadella, Satya, 143–44, 146, 191
National Academy of Sciences, 213
NBBJ, 130
net employment, 223–24
Netflix, 165, 178, 202
Neumann, Adam, 146
The New World Symphony (Dvořák), 204
New York and Erie Railroad, 190
New York Times, 56, 202, 214
Nguyen, Tuan D., 96
Nike, 45, 139, 167–68
Nimble, 60
Nokia, 160, 162, 228–29
nondisclosure agreements (NDAs), 25
Nordstrom, 202
NPR, 61
Nursing Times, 95
Nvidia, 229–30

Obama, Michelle, 20, 144
offshoring, 16, 182
Oldenburg, Ray, 138
old salts, 7, 94
Omens, Alison, 73
O*NET, 122
OpenAI, viii, xiii, 112, 120, 154, 161, 178, 226
openness, 17–18
open partnering, 154–55
open scorecards, 18
open workspaces, 4
Oracle AI@Work study, 73
organizational design, 121, 183, 187, 195–200
outsourcing, 107, 133, 165, 210, 217–18
Owl Labs, ix
Oxford University, 107

Paine, Simon, 60
Paltrow, Gwyneth, 12
paradigm shifts, 159–72, 178, 227
Parker, Sam, 13
passion projects, 49–64
    benefits of, 63
    community support via, 81
    in entertainment industry, 55
    of fractionalized employees, 91
    in gig economy, 51
    identity through, 75
    monetizing, 50
    opportunities for, 224
    policies for, 57, 59
    promotion of, 86
    trends toward, 192

see also side gigs; side hustles
Peloton, 206
permeability, 196
Pew Research Center, 41, 75
Pfizer, 230
Pietra, 12
plug and play, 9, 27, 44–45
polarization, 6–7, 145
pressure release, 63
process automation, 212
Procter & Gamble, 33, 45–46, 49, 159, 229
Profitero, 67
Prosper Insights & Analytics, 40
pseudoemployees, 206
Publicis Groupe
    changes at, 20–21, 31, 161–62
    fractionalized employment at, 103
    fragmentation at, 216
    long-term employment at, 49
    Marcel platform use at, 45
    reorganization of, 203–4
    retraining at, 180–81
purpose, 9–11, 14, 17–18, 103, 184, 206
Putnam, Jennifer, 139

quiet quitting, 14–15
Quilt.AI, 30, 121

Razorfish, 203
real-time collaboration tools, 212
Rebel Business School, 58–59
reconfigured work environments, 28–29,
    130, 133–34, 178
Reddit, 5
REI, 87
reinvention, 167–70
    across generations, 9
    of careers, 29
    corporate, 190
    effects of, 171
    of managers, 67
    at Microsoft, 161, 174
    at *New York Times*, 202, 214
    providing answers for, 172
    relevance and, 122
    during second connected age, 23
    technology as, 32–33
    of traditional ideas, vii–viii
    in Web3, 25
    of workspaces, 139
remote-only work, 77
remote work, 211

ABOUT THE AUTHOR

RISHAD TOBACCOWALA is an author, advisor, and speaker who has worked for more than four decades serving a range of companies around the world.

Rishad was the chief strategist and growth officer of the Publicis Groupe, a 106,000-person marketing and business transformation firm.

Rishad has worked as a "company of one" advising, running workshops, and participating in executive off-sites with more than one hundred different companies from start-ups to global multinationals.

The Economist called Rishad's first book, *Restoring the Soul of Business: Staying Human in the Age of Data*, perhaps the best recent book on stakeholder capitalism, and *Strategy* named it among the five best business books and the marketing book of the year.